John Singer Sargent

John Singer Sargent

Patricia Hills

with essays by

Linda Ayres

Annette Blaugrund

Albert Boime

William H. Gerdts

Patricia Hills

Stanley Olson

Gary A. Reynolds

Whitney Museum of American Art, New York

in association with

Harry N. Abrams, Inc., Publishers, New York

Dates of the exhibition:

Whitney Museum of American Art, New York
October 7, 1986–January 4, 1987

The Art Institute of Chicago
February 7–April 19, 1987

This exhibition is sponsored by Merrill Lynch & Co., Inc.
Planning for this exhibition and catalogue was partially funded
by a grant from the National Endowment for the Humanities, a Federal Agency.

Library of Congress Cataloging-in-Publication Data

Hills, Patricia.
   John Singer Sargent.

   Bibliography: p.
   Includes index.
   1. Sargent, John Singer, 1856–1925—Exhibitions.
I. Ayres, Linda, 1947–   .   II. Whitney Museum of Art.
III. Title.
N6537.S32A4 1986   759.13   86-9136
ISBN 0-87427-049-9 (Whitney: pbk.)
ISBN 0-8109-1506-5 (Abrams)

Exhibition Assistant: Liese Hilgeman

This publication was organized at the
Whitney Museum of American Art by
Doris Palca, Head, Publications and Sales;
Sheila Schwartz, Editor;
Deborah Lyons, Associate Editor;
and Emily Russell, Secretary/Assistant.

Designed by Homans Design, Inc.
Typeset in Monophoto Van Dijck
Printed in Great Britain by
Balding + Mansell Limited

© 1986 Whitney Museum of American Art
945 Madison Avenue
New York, New York 10021

Cover:
Mrs. Carl Meyer and Her Children, 1896 (detail)
Oil on canvas, 79 × 53 inches (200.7 × 134.6 cm)
Private collection

Frontispiece:
Self-Portrait, 1886
Oil on canvas, 14 × 10 (35.6 × 25.4)
Aberdeen Art Gallery and Museums, Scotland

Whitney Museum of American Art
Trustees and Officers

List of Lenders

Aberdeen Art Gallery and Museums, Scotland

Andover, Massachusetts, Addison Gallery of
   American Art, Phillips Academy

Mr. and Mrs. Isaac Arnold, Jr.

Atlanta, The High Museum of Art

The Baltimore Museum of Art

Boston, Isabella Stewart Gardner Museum

Boston, Museum of Fine Arts

The Brooklyn Museum, New York

Buffalo, New York, Albright-Knox Art Gallery

Cambridge, England, Fitzwilliam Museum

Cambridge, Massachusetts, Harvard University
   Art Museums, Fogg Art Museum

Chicago, The Art Institute of Chicago

Chicago, Terra Museum of American Art

Cincinnati Art Museum

Colorado Springs Fine Arts Center

Dallas Museum of Fine Arts

Des Moines Art Center

Edinburgh, The National Galleries of Scotland

Mr. and Mrs. Jean-Marie Eveillard

Mr. and Mrs. Marshall Field

Flint Institute of Arts, Michigan

Florence, Galleria degli Uffizi

Rita and Daniel Fraad

Jo Ann and Julian Ganz, Jr.

Mrs. John William Griffith

Greensburg, Pennsylvania, Westmoreland
   Museum of Art

Dr. and Mrs. William Hayden

Houston, Museum of Fine Arts

Mr. Henry R. Kravis

Lincoln, Nebraska, Nebraska Art Association,
   Nelle Cochrane Woods Collection at the
   Sheldon Memorial Art Gallery,
   University of Nebraska

London, British Museum

London, Imperial War Museum

London, National Portrait Gallery

London, Royal Academy of Arts

London, The Tate Gallery

London, Victoria and Albert Museum

Los Angeles, The Armand Hammer Collection

Los Angeles County Museum of Art

Lugano, Switzerland,
   Thyssen-Bornemisza Collection

Manchester City Art Galleries, England

Dr. and Mrs. John J. McDonough

The Minneapolis Institute of Arts

The Newark Museum, New Jersey

New Haven, Yale University Art Gallery

New York, The Forbes Magazine Collection

New York, The Harvard Club of New York City

New York, The Metropolitan Museum of Art

Northampton, Massachusetts, Smith College
   Museum of Art

The Ormond Family

Oxford, England, Ashmolean Museum

Philadelphia, John G. Johnson Collection at the
   Philadelphia Museum of Art

Philadelphia Museum of Art

Philadelphia, Pennsylvania Academy of the
   Fine Arts

Pittsburgh, Museum of Art, Carnegie Institute

Providence, Museum of Art, Rhode Island
   School of Design

Mr. and Mrs. William F. Reighley

Richmond, Virginia Museum of Fine Arts

Rochester, New York, Memorial Art Gallery
   of the University of Rochester

Mr. and Mrs. Steven J. Ross

San Francisco, Bohemian Club

San Francisco, The Fine Arts Museums of
   San Francisco

San Marino, California, Henry E. Huntington
   Library and Art Gallery

Sheffield City Art Galleries, England

Mr. and Mrs. Peter Jay Solomon

Mr. and Mrs. Richard M. Thune

Tuscaloosa, Alabama, The Warner Collection
   of Gulf States Paper Corporation

Versailles, Musée National du
   Château de Versailles

Washington, D.C., Corcoran Gallery of Art

Washington, D.C., Hirshhorn Museum and
   Sculpture Garden, Smithsonian Institution

Washington, D.C., National Gallery of Art

Mrs. John Hay Whitney

Williamstown, Massachusetts, Sterling and
   Francine Clark Art Institute

Erving and Joyce Wolf

Worcester Art Museum, Massachusetts

15 Anonymous Lenders

Contents

Foreword   *Tom Armstrong*   8

Acknowledgments   *Patricia Hills*   10

On the Question of Sargent's Nationality   *Stanley Olson*   13

The Formation of a Style and Sensibility   *Patricia Hills*   27

Sargent in Venice   *Linda Ayres*   49

Sargent in Paris and London:
A Portrait of the Artist as Dorian Gray   *Albert Boime*   75

The Arch-Apostle of the Dab-and-Spot School:
John Singer Sargent as an Impressionist   *William H. Gerdts*   111

Sargent's Late Portraits   *Gary A. Reynolds*   147

"Painted Diaries": Sargent's Late Subject Pictures   *Patricia Hills*   181

"Sunshine Captured": The Development and
Dispersement of Sargent's Watercolors   *Annette Blaugrund*   209

A Portfolio of Drawings   *Patricia Hills*   251

Chronology   *Stanley Olson*   276

Selected Bibliography   284

Works in the Exhibition   286

Index   292

Foreword

Although the Whitney Museum of American Art collects only works of the twentieth century, with emphasis on the accomplishments of living artists, the exhibition program presents the entire scope of American art. "John Singer Sargent" features the work of an artist outside of our collecting interests but of primary concern because he is a major contributor to the history of American art whose images are a chronicle of his times. But perhaps more important is the recognition of Sargent's highly expressive manner and his treatment of subject matter and narrative content, all of which are of great interest to contemporary artists.

In approaching this project, Dr. Patricia Hills, Associate Professor of Art History at Boston University, was anxious to reveal new aspects of Sargent's life and art by presenting them from a variety of viewpoints. She invited a group of scholars to join in the investigation and in this publication. They provide us with a range of insights about a complicated, brilliant, and ambitious man who felt a need to be both apart from and embraced by the social milieu in which he played such a substantial role.

In organizing this exhibition, we were greatly assisted by our liaison with The Art Institute of Chicago. James Wood, Director, and Milo M. Naeve, The Field-McCormick Curator of American Arts, secured cooperation from major institutions, and the exhibition has been enhanced immeasurably through their help. We are equally indebted to all the owners of the pictures, who have graciously shared their objects for our increased understanding and pleasure.

I am pleased to have this opportunity to express our appreciation to Merrill Lynch which, with trust and perception, has funded this major exhibition with the largest grant ever received for a single exhibition in the history of the Whitney Museum. We and the public are grateful for this endorsement of American art and scholarship and we hope that Merrill Lynch shares the pride we feel in both the exhibition and this publication.

Tom Armstrong
Director

Merrill Lynch is proud to join with the Whitney Museum in presenting "John Singer Sargent," the largest retrospective of the artist's work in over sixty years. We are happy that our grant will make it possible for the public to see and enjoy the works of the most respected American painter on the international scene in the late nineteenth and early twentieth centuries.

The grant for the "John Singer Sargent" exhibition is part of Merrill Lynch's ongoing cultural support program that in 1985 earned our firm, for the second year, a national "Business In The Arts" award.

William A. Schreyer
Chairman and Chief Executive Officer
Merrill Lynch & Co., Inc.

Acknowledgments

John Singer Sargent undoubtedly holds the record as the most prolific nineteenth-century American painter — over eight hundred portraits, including portrait drawings, and at least eighteen hundred subject pictures, including watercolors. Add to these figures the hundreds of drawings from his childhood sketchbooks and the later mural studies and we have an artist who quantitatively surpassed any of his American contemporaries. In terms of quality, moreover, few in his generation could approach him. It has, therefore, been a pleasurable but not easy assignment to select a representative sampling from the treasure house of his oeuvre — to bring together a range of subjects, the early and late styles, and both familiar paintings and little-known works.

Without the generous help of a number of people I would have had difficulty bringing the project to completion. I want first to thank Margaret L. Kaplan of Harry N. Abrams, Inc., who initially suggested I write a book on Sargent during a lunch with Jeanne Hamilton and myself in 1978. I developed that suggestion into a proposal for a comprehensive retrospective of the artist's work. Tom Armstrong and Jennifer Russell at the Whitney Museum responded to the proposal with enthusiasm. The following year, 1979–80, the National Endowment for the Humanities awarded the Whitney Museum a planning grant for the exhibition that enabled me to travel throughout the United States and abroad. At that time Professors Albert Boime, William H. Gerdts, Martin Green, and H. Barbara Weinberg served as consultants. During 1984–85, Boston University provided me with financial support during my sabbatical leave, making it possible for me to proceed full-time on the project.

When the exhibition was still in the planning stages, Milo M. Naeve, The Field-McCormick Curator of American Arts at The Art Institute of Chicago, suggested that it travel to Chicago. His tactful diplomacy facilitated the agreement between the two museums. I have also greatly benefited from his advice at every stage of the selection process.

I want to thank those colleagues who collaborated with me by submitting a varied group of essays to the book: Linda Ayres, Annette Blaugrund, Albert Boime, William H. Gerdts, Stanley Olson, and Gary A. Reynolds. I spent many hours discussing with each of them problems of connoisseurship and the historical matrix of art and patronage at the end of the nineteenth century. To Stanley Olson I owe a special debt for sharing with all of us detailed information garnered in six years of indefatigable research on Sargent. He obligingly allowed us to publish an abbreviated version of his chronology on Sargent, from which all of the authors benefited.

My gratitude extends to other colleagues and scholars who have been involved with Sargent research for many years. Richard Ormond, Warren Adelson, Odile Duff, and Donna Seldin, who are preparing the catalogue raisonné of Sargent's work under the sponsorship of the Coe Kerr Gallery, Inc., reviewed my many lists of potential works for the exhibition. With Odile Duff I spent many enjoyable hours in Boston, Cleveland, and New York, examining paintings inch by inch in order to understand better the unique problems of Sargent's style. H. Barbara Weinberg and Trevor J. Fairbrother also graciously made available their unpublished research.

The collectors cited in the List of Lenders have provided me with the opportunity to view their Sargent paintings. Others have shared ideas and research, facilitated the loans of works, assisted in the acquisition of photographs, or were otherwise especially helpful: Herbert S. Adler, Joan Barnes, Shirley Boulay, David S. Brooke, Doreen Bolger Burke, Jay E. Cantor, Teresa Cederholm, Ann Compton, David Daniels, Hope Davis, James T. Demetrion, Cynthia English, Jane Farrington, Stuart P. Feld, Linda Ferber, Madeline Fidell-Beaufort, Richard S. Field, Lawrence A. Fleischman, Rita and Daniel Fraad, Peter Fusco, Glenda S. Galt, Jo Ann and Julian Ganz, Jr., Deborah Gardner, Inez Garson, Abigail Booth Gerdts, Frank H. Goodyear, Jr., Karen Haas, David Hall, Jane Hankins, John Hayes, Charles Hilburn, Fred Hill, Brad Hills, John K. Howat, Pam Hubbard, Tom Hudspeth, Rose and Lawrence Hughes, Jeanette Hughson, Malcolm Johnson, Patricia Johnston, Donald D. Keyes, Cecily Langdale, James Lomax, Meredith Long, Hugh Macandrew, Jonathan Mason, Richard Manoogian, James Maroney, Edward Mayo, Garnett McCoy, Anne Meservey, Elizabeth Milroy, Sally Meyer, George W. Neubert, Edward J. Nygren, Martha Oaks, Emily Ormond, Flavia and John Ormond, Ann Percy, Michael Quick, Peter B. Rathbone, William Rathbone, Sue Reed, John Rewald, Joseph Rishel, Phyllis Rosenzweig, Bertha Saunders, Mac Schweitzer, David E. Scrase, Darrel Sewell, Nancy Rivard Shaw, Meredith Shelley, Rosamond Sherwood, Brian Shrum, Marc Simpson, David Sokol, Natalie Spassky, Miriam Stewart, Susan E. Strickler, Nicki Thiras, Richard M. Thune, Michael Tooby, Daniel Tompkins, Robert R. Wark, Elizabeth and Jack Warner, Angela Weight, Ann Whyte, John Wilmerding, Hellmut Wohl, Alison Yates, Christopher R. Young, Denny Young, Laura Yudow, Kai Kin Yung, and Judith Zilczer.

Finally, I want to express my most heartfelt appreciation to two individuals: Liese Hilgeman joined me on the project almost two years ago as a curatorial assistant and has seen the exhibition and catalogue through every stage of development. Her critical acuity, steadfastness, and sense of humor were indispensable. Kevin Whitfield, my husband, lived with the project for eight years — teaching me computer skills, lending a helping hand in the tight spots, and sharing in my ongoing dialogue and fascination with nineteenth-century life and culture.

P.H.

On the Question of Sargent's Nationality

STANLEY OLSON

The magnificent simplicity of the first entry in Sargent's history — born in Florence to American parents — is also the start of an equally magnificent deceit. Of course the facts are solid enough, but they conceal more than they reveal. America had every right to claim him, but his knowledge of the country was at best slim: his first acquaintance came when he was twenty, and by the end of his life he had spent only about eight years on his "native" soil. And though he was never tempted to release his American passport, such documentation was singularly untelling.

Romantic mythology, well-stoked by Henry James, has been generous to Sargent, eager to misread all the superficial features of a graceful expatriate life spent roaming through European capitals. That his parents left Philadelphia to travel abroad sixteen months before his birth seemed enough to supply him with a silver spoon. But underneath this alluring surface, strange forces were at work. His parents had never intended to stay abroad, yet they never quite managed the return crossing. This oversight was craftily engineered by his mother, Mary Newbold Singer Sargent (1826–1906), and was the playful trick of an audacious untruth. At home she said she was ill, which was pretty bold considering her lack of worrisome symptoms and the fact that she was married to a doctor. She also said she could only recover abroad, yet once abroad, she showed every indication of being really very healthy. She climbed mountains, never missed a sight, managed long walks during the stopovers at every spa to and from Paris. When her claim on infirmity wore a little thin and her husband started to look up the homeward-bound steamers, she resorted to a slightly more obvious form of incapacitation: pregnancy. Between 1856 and 1870 she gave birth five times, at neatly spaced intervals which assured her extensions of her lease on European life. While her husband looked at the Atlantic as the great obstacle separating him from home, she saw it as a useful ally. She could never be expected to endanger herself or her infant by braving the sea. So, as the family increased, all hope of return was slowly but surely extinguished. Mrs. Sargent was a deft tactician. But at no time in her campaign was she trying to deny she was an American; her only purpose was not to *live* in America.

Photograph of Sargent at Fladbury, 1888–89
Collection of the Ormond Family

13

Photograph of Sargent with his sister Emily,
c. 1867
Collection of the Ormond Family

Mrs. Sargent would have never got away with her self-centered strategy were it not for the accommodating character of her husband, Dr. FitzWilliam Sargent (1820–1889). The natural Sargent modesty had refined itself over the generations to such a degree as to make Dr. Sargent a near introvert. "I am not, and never was, much given to talking," he confessed to his father in 1865.[1] He was no match for his wife. Yet he was a man of considerable, though quiet attainments. Before leaving Philadelphia he had managed a career which adequately expressed his unthreatening sort of ambition, one that relied on care rather than speed. He had a small private practice; he wrote and edited textbooks, among them the standard manual of minor surgical techniques which saved many lives when it was consulted on the field of battle in the Civil War, and which he had illustrated himself;[2] he had started to make investigations into disorders of the eye, and had risen to the post of attending surgeon at the Wills Hospital. Once abroad, however, all these activities stopped. After the birth of his daughter Emily (1857–1936), he officially resigned from the Wills Hospital and after the birth of his youngest daughter, Violet (1870–1955), he sent his microscope and medical books to his nephew. During the years of his reluctant exile, Dr. Sargent seemed to take to resignation the way his wife took to victory. It was as if his active life ended the moment his wife's began when they docked at Liverpool.

By the ironic workings of justice Mrs. Sargent's grand excuse became a sad truth. In time, she and her husband found themselves rotating in a merciless orbit, passing through illness and death and back again. They had good reasons for searching out spas. Their children succumbed to the usual childhood disorders with painful repetition. Emily Sargent, who was born in Rome a year after her brother, was the first to help her mother forget the counterfeit maladies. When she was three she was dropped by her nurse,[3] and her parents braced themselves for her death. But she survived, and local doctors prescribed complete immobility to aid recovery: she was strapped to her bed at night; strapped to a sprung platform to reduce the sharp jolts when traveling; only occasionally was she allowed to sit in a chair. When she was five, London doctors ordered her immediate release, allowing her to resume her childhood, in the unfortunate knowledge that what had been thought a remedy had deformed her for life. Throughout her long ordeal, her only companion was her brother. The Sargents' third child, Mary Winthrop (born in Nice in 1860), enjoyed no better passage; she held on to life fiercely but lost the battle before she was five. Her brother watched her turn into a "withered flower,"[4] stage a brave rally, and then decline once more. "Poor little Minnie," Sargent wrote to a friend when he was nine, "is getting thinner every day. She does not care for anything any more. Emily and I bought her some beautiful Easter eggs but she would not look at them. She never talks nor smiles now."[5] Two days later she died. And the fourth Sargent child, a second son, brought no glimmer of happiness; the day he was born his parents knew he would not survive: "We think for his own sake," Dr. Sargent wrote to his father in 1867, "the sooner he goes to heaven the better."[6] The baby lived for less than two and a half years. (The last child was more fortunate; Violet, born in Florence in 1870, lived to the ripe age of eighty-five.)

The strained fiction which had sent the Sargents abroad kept them abroad. They conducted an energetic nomadic existence, settling nowhere for more than a few months at a time, because they needed to be nowhere specific. They never indulged in long-term plans. Their requirements were of the broadest measure. The enemy, Mrs. Sargent declared, was climate because cold meant the unwelcome return of her bronchitis and heat meant cholera or malaria, and thus they moved up into the mountains during the summer and south to warmth in the winter, imposing an artificial sense of the temperate on their relentless routine. They inhabited a world cluttered with crates, boxes, luggage, rooms fragranced with camphor and peppercorns, shifting from boarding houses to furnished apartments. They developed a pattern of life which thrived because they perversely reckoned it was temporary. Dr. Sargent needed to believe they could return home at any moment; Mrs. Sargent had to keep alive the myth that she was ill, and both of them knew settling down would expose the fraud, the corruption of honesty that controlled their lives.

Mrs. Sargent achieved her triumph because she held the family ledgers; she funded the family purse; she financed their perpetual wanderings. And here she showed the extreme subtlety of her campaigning: "Mary's income," Dr. Sargent explained to his brother in 1869, "is only such as enables us to live on with a constant effort to spend as little as possible consistently with the requirements of rather delicate health in all of us, which makes it necessary to resort to places of residence which are more expensive than we should think of going to if we were well enough to avoid them."[7] For Mrs. Sargent, money equaled the purchase of health and the freedom to stay away from America. She negotiated the accounts for her own purposes, making it impossible for them to settle down. The Sargents did have the means to be independent, but they never considered themselves rich and never lived in a style consistent with wealth. Of course they did live the purposeless shifting expatriate life glorified by Hawthorne and James, but the Sargents' peripatetic indulgence removed them from the ambitious cultural refinement which inspired great literature.

The components of the deceit were moving into place. The dense atmosphere of death which threw the survivors so close together — suffocatingly close — was scarcely relieved at any of the stops on their ever extending itinerary. Everywhere they went they were surrounded by illness, by people waiting to die or struggling to recover. They moved through the least stimulating towns in Europe, because they were on the prowl for an agreeable climate.

Sargent's education was at the mercy of his parents' idea of stability and their idea of stability was more attached to physical than intellectual well-being. As "home" was intensely mobile, national frontiers meant nothing to him. He did not know the impediment of "foreign" languages. His parents spoke English, the servants spoke Italian, French, German, or Spanish. For a few months in Nice he

Dr. FitzWilliam Sargent, 1886
Oil on canvas, 14½ × 13½ (36.8 × 34.3)
Sargent-Murray-Gilman-Hough House
Association, Gloucester, Massachusetts

Mrs. FitzWilliam Sargent (Mary Newbold Singer), 1887
Oil on canvas, 16¾ × 13¾ (42.5 × 34.9)
Sargent-Murray-Gilman-Hough House
Association, Gloucester, Massachusetts

was taught by an Englishman, another time in Florence by a Frenchman who had a small school for the sons of Italian aristocrats, and in Rome by a German. Everywhere he went he moved in a fake population: the expatriate mind was admirably vague about the local inhabitants, knowledge of whom was gained via temporary servants, who naturally fleeced them at every turn. Dr. Sargent honestly believed Italians only fell back on the truth when lying was of no use. When he interviewed wet-nurses, the same candidates reappeared, with dyed hair and slightly familiar answers. The domestic accounts were laughable documents of petty larceny, informing Mrs. Sargent that she alone had consumed many pounds of sugar every day.

And expatriates reflexively ignored exactly where they were, as long as they were not at home in America. Likewise, their knowledge of home passed through a highly distorting filter. Though the expatriates' justification rested on a fundamental dissatisfaction with home, they endured a similar displeasure abroad, and had a near xenophobic addiction to mixing with their fellow nationals. It was a sociological fact. They were ruled by a weird patriotic compass. When Dr. and Mrs. Sargent reminded their children that they were American, they located in the atlas a country housing unknown quantities called grandparents, aunts, uncles, and cousins. They amplified such intelligence with stories and photographs. When they settled in Rome for a winter at the end of the 1860s, they gave their children the most perverse spectacle of what being American really meant. From their small house at 17, Trinità de' Monti, surveying the panorama of the city (near the house where Mrs. Sargent's mother had died in 1859), they watched the society of displaced Bostonians who a decade before had filled the pages of Hawthorne's novel *The Marble Faun*. They saw William Wetmore Story, lawyer turned sculptor, sculptor turned writer, who had buried himself in suffocatingly pretentious luxury at the Palazzo Barberini and whose life James later was obliged to understand: "his course . . . was almost the monotony of the great extremes of ease. Nothing really happened to him."[8] There was the sculptor Harriet Hosmer, who rode through the streets late at night to hounds imported from England, and her companion Charlotte Cushman, the actress who played male roles convincingly and gave farewell performances for over a decade. There was the sculptor Randolph Rogers, who busied himself with vast bronzes and marbles depicting abstract nouns — figures contorting to the tune of Hope, Glory, Grief, etc. — destined for Washington and Detroit. All told, these were people who stayed in Europe, gained recognition at home, tried to annex centuries of history, and only by employing those distinctly American qualities of brute perseverance and industry were they able to succeed. They came to Rome, as James explained in 1903, full of a "fine bewilderment," and because "the fineness of Rome was exactly in the quality of amusement."[9] Dr. Sargent put it a little more soberly: the place was hospitable to idleness — "'dolce far niente' is not understood in Boston as it is practiced here," he wrote to a friend.[10] In Rome the Sargents witnessed the supreme example of expatriate American life, and it eventually sent them packing.

Emily Sargent, c. 1875
Oil on panel, 12¼ × 9 (31.1 × 22.9)
Collection of the Ormond Family

Dr. Sargent clung to his patriotism with an intense urgency; for him it was the only palliative to homesickness, and it was about the only constant in their lives of perpetual motion. He followed the Civil War with mounting despair. He was incensed by the faulty reports he read in the English and French newspaper accounts. When he saw a neighbor in Nice unfurl the Confederate flag from her window to celebrate a Southern victory (months after the event), he shook off his characteristic lethargy and attempted to correct the errors by writing a long pamphlet on the real motives of the war, which he published in England and France, and which was totally ignored. He was a staunch member of the American Church in Nice; he was on the docks waiting for the visiting American navy. Such national pride as his children could claim was at best secondhand.

·When, in 1876, Mrs. Sargent took her son and eldest daughter to Philadelphia to see the Centennial Exhibition, they brought the heavy luggage of Europe with them. For them it was no journey home, but an extension of the generous itinerary they had always known. Sargent's cousins were amazed by his foreign ways. They were mystified by the fact that he and his mother went for long walks after lunch in the blazing heat. They were baffled by his accent and his sophistication.[11] He had strange manners for someone who was *supposed* to be a fellow American. After four months in America and Canada, Sargent, his mother, and sister took the boat back to Europe; they returned home.

Romantic mythology got it wrong. If Sargent had anything when he was born on that dreary Saturday, January 12, 1856, in the apartment next to the Palazzo Sperini in the Lungarno Acciaioli in Florence, it was his mother's well-thumbed *Baedeker*, and not a silver spoon, for he began his life much as he ended it — as a tourist. He was at home everywhere, and belonged nowhere.

By the time Sargent entered the atelier of Carolus-Duran in 1874,[12] the consequences of his childhood became apparent. His mother's unchallenged self-interest, the perpetual dislocation, the chronic mourning, and utter isolation had taken their revenge, working a subtly shaded pattern on his character. Suddenly, at the atelier on the Boulevard Montparnasse he found himself among his contemporaries, and he was totally unlike them: he was older than his years, he was better educated, he was more worldly, he was confident, and he had the high patina of sophistication. His fellow students were dazzled by him, and baffled (see p. 251). He had the misfortune to inspire awe, not intimacy. He was forbiddingly superior, yet modest; at best he was a perplexing enigma. No definition could help observers to negotiate his character.

And he was again among exiles. L'Atelier des Élèves de M. Carolus-Duran owed its foundation a year before much to the expatriate talent for imperialism. It was a fine irony that Carolus' striking and tamely unconventional showings at the Salon should also recommend him as a teacher, and only after he was approached a second time, by the Bostonian Robert C. Hinckley, did he agree to take on students.[13] Soon the studio at 81, Boulevard Montparnasse became a haven for

American pupils. Like Rome for the previous generation, Paris had a magnetic attraction for artists, and her natural pull was increased by financial and subsequent political ructions at the National Academy of Design in New York in the mid-1870s that seriously jeopardized the future of the Academy's schools. This turmoil, which went on for years and eventually closed down the Life School for the academic year 1876–77, naturally persuaded students and prospective students to look elsewhere for training, and they succumbed to the siren-call of Paris. By the time Sargent was established, the American population there was considerable, and the atelier Carolus-Duran was almost exclusively American.[14] The false patriotism of his youth — of mixing only with Americans abroad — was endorsed, and so, alas, was the wisdom of his mother's advocacy of a *Baedeker* education.

Sargent's relations with this band of refugees were governed by a delicate admixture of their uncertainty and his seemingly effortless mastery of purpose, their ignorance of Europe and his knowledge, their homesickness and his comfort, all of which produced an unbridgeable gulf between them and him. "Sargent, according to all accounts," Charteris wrote in his biography, "remained apart; not from any settled austerity of mind, but because he was absorbed in his work to the point of fanaticism."[15] This claim is slightly wide of the truth. His airs of reserve and absorption were the products of elements irreducible to mere single-mindedness. First, and most important, was the welcome novelty of formal education. He had waited a long time to be a student, and such a status had been hard won. And there was the novel peculiarity of finding himself surrounded by so many people. He had never experienced such society. This was an unexpected release from the private hospital of home. But mostly he remained apart because he was unschooled in anything else, and yet never sensed the omission or oddity.

The surprise of Paris could never topple years of habit, or erase a feature ingrained in his personality.

Hitherto Sargent's education had been yet another casualty in the exhausted old battle between America versus Europe; it had been lost in the overpowering energy of his mother's will. She avowed that Europe itself was sufficient education, that travel more than adequately made up for the schoolroom. Though she dismissed her husband's more orthodox views, Dr. Sargent had always returned to the issue of his son's education with a tenacity born of frustration: "We are exercised about sending Johnny to school," he wrote to his mother in 1869; "unfortunately where we are obliged to spend our winters there are no good schools, & so we must send him off somewhere. However, I don't think it is well, on many accounts, to keep a boy at home always; but Mary dreads the idea of sending her first-born son away from her. . . . "[16] Finally, two years later, Dr. Sargent shook himself into action, dragged the entire family off to Dresden for the winter while his son prepared for entry into the Gymnasium zum Heilige Kreuz. But before the young Sargent even took the entrance examinations, they were all back in Florence on account of Emily's health.

Like the romantic interpretation of the Sargents' expatriate existence, Mrs. Sargent's convenient system of education looked good enough on the surface. Her son played the piano with a rare fluency; he spoke, wrote, and read the major European languages with the adroitness of a native, and his talents as a draftsman and painter were precociously adept. Museums and capital cities were his playgrounds. And all this was born of the family's chronic itinerancy. Sargent benefited from an advantage not found in any schoolroom: the advantage of dullness. He learned to depend only on himself for entertainment and stimulation. If he was bored, it was his own fault. So, without much mental dexterity, he came to believe that work was not a duty, but fun. He played the piano for fun. He read for fun. He sketched for fun. All the usual starch of work had been laundered out. And because he had no notion of what was expected of him and had been denied any knowledge of what his contemporaries were doing, he concluded that there was nothing unusual about this attitude. It was the normal order of things.

But the solitary greenhouse which had bred these slightly distorted notions of normality used a sort of compost which also made him perfectly self-contained. He had flourished in a rarefied but highly intimate atmosphere, surrounded by people who knew all there was to know about him. To outsiders, however, he seemed austere and without much human warmth. If all of his friends were asked to pool their knowledge of the workings of his mind, they would draw one stupendous blank, and then give way to crossness, a crossness derived from having been shortchanged, which was scarcely rewarding for friendship. In 1899 one friend recorded his version of a tête-à-tête: "he talked about the necessity of independence & above all self-sufficiency[:] one shld be dependent on no one he said, least of all on friends of any sort. It is a mania with him isn't it? Horrid for his friends."[17]

The main features of Sargent's character had rotated into position by the time he was eighteen, when he started his studentship in Paris, and he never found any reason to question any of his homegrown values. Indeed, when finally put to the test, everything he had worked out for himself received a stunning confirmation. His fellow students were amazed. Sargent seemed to drop out of the sky, with no comprehensible history, and yet he was undeniably superior. His mother's selfishness was seen to have wrought a superbly and too eloquently prepared student. "I met this last week a young Mr. Sargent," J. Alden Weir informed his mother, ". . . one of the most talented fellows I have ever come across; his drawings are like the old masters, and his color is equally fine. . . . He speaks as well in French, German, Italian as he does in English, has a fine ear for music. etc. Such men wake one up, and, as his principles are equal to his talents, I hope to have his friendship. . . . "[18] Many years later, Will Low, another of these young Paris observers, tempered his initial enthusiasm: "Of course we are dealing with a phenomenal nature. . . . It may be simply a further indication of an exceptional temperament to record that . . . [he] had found time, even at this early age . . . to be much further advanced in his general education than most youths of his age. . . . an education thus gleaned . . . may leave curious lapses — lapses calculated to make a pedagogue weep."[19]

The first impression was bewildering enough, but his career as a student only amplified this original reaction. Sargent was perfect student material; he accepted every instruction like a majestic command. Any teacher would have been flattered by such a student, but Carolus' inexperience turned Sargent into a favorite — the outright, frank favorite of the studio. Sargent repaid the compliment with a string of successes, as if he were renewing his brilliant debut: in 1877 he placed second in the excruciatingly treacherous *concours* at the École des Beaux-Arts — "the first time that any pupil of Carolus-Duran's atelier had been rated so high," Dr. Sargent wrote to a friend, "the first time that any American Art Student in Paris had ever been so ranked [?]."[20] Then he was awarded a Third Class Medal for ornament drawing. Then there was his success in the Salon. The wonder which had clouded his fellow students' eyes had been justified. By outpacing everyone else at such cracking speed, Sargent was turned into a hero before he became human.

The forcing house of both the atelier system and European sophistication had produced in Sargent a perfect exponent of what these students sought. They were overwhelmed by him, and they carried the tales of his excellence home with them, forging the first link in the long chain of events which would establish Sargent's mighty reputation — a reputation that needed the cultivation of Americans. Sargent's fame during his studentship was a complicated crosscurrent of truth and romance which got hopelessly tangled, increasing in attractiveness with the distance of time and geography. Sargent was swept along on the tidal wave of all things continental that flooded over his generation of artists. He was a textbook realization of their ambitions. Yet they were never jealous; he was never the object of the usual competitiveness among students. He soon floated on the luxury

of being imported. Of course, had these American students in Paris, who eventually became the backbone of American art, been less intoxicated with the wonders of Europe, and had Sargent ever expressed a need for their help, they would have been less generous. Sargent never used them, though they were eager to show him their unflagging loyalty. They had this opportunity in the late 1880s, when they helped secure for Sargent portrait and large-scale decorative commissions in America.

Sargent eventually came to realize his father's hope that he make some claim on his nationality. Sargent finally became an American by a route as circuitous as that he had experienced from birth: he only became an American through the lens of Europe. After Dr. Sargent's death, his son accepted the commissions which would keep his thoughts in America for the best part of thirty years: the decoration of the Special Libraries Hall of the Boston Public Library, the Rotunda and staircase of the Museum of Fine Arts, and staircase panels of the Widener Memorial Library. Sargent came to these commitments as a result of a new civic pride that had sent American architects scurrying across Italy and France to poach the mature language of European art. Yet, when Sargent agreed to undertake these projects, with their biblical, mythological, and allegorical references, he was also betraying his artistic strengths.

Sargent had had the luck of the times to hurl him into prominence, even before these commissions. The students' gentle exodus across the Atlantic in the late 1870s had become a stampede — and a way of thinking. If something was European, it was bound to be good, or so the thinking went. Thus the American artists Edwin Austin Abbey and Frank Millet produced illustrations for two

American periodicals, *Scribner's* and *Harper's*, while living in Broadway, Worcestershire. From England they consolidated their reputations at home, to dizzying heights. When Henry James introduced Sargent to these men in the mid-1880s, he was broadening the American market for Sargent as well. The forces of Broadway encouraged their new tenant, John S. Sargent, and transformed his fortunes, converting him from a painter of tourists' portraits to the recorder of the blossoming vanities of America's rich. When his friends at Broadway engineered a commission for him to paint a portrait of Henry G. Marquand's wife (Fig. 102), Sargent was elevated beyond his wildest expectations. In America, he put on the butler's baize apron and set about polishing egos, egos of very clever men who had turned away from the challenge of amassing fortunes and faced the contests of more abstract ambitions. They wanted to import the traditions they had seen abroad, the occupations of leisure and, with any luck, the pastimes of a gentleman. They wanted portraits in order to acquire permanence. And the patriotic compass was set in motion, ultimately finding its magnetic attraction in Sargent. He had the sleekness of a perfect servant. "We lost our hearts to him," Robert Louis Stevenson wrote, "a person with a kind of exhibition manner and English accent, who proves on examination, simple, bashful, honest, enthusiastic and rude with a perfect (but quite inoffensive) English rudeness. *Pour comble*, he gives himself out to be an American."[21]

The quizzical conviviality that Stevenson noticed was part of the secret which made Sargent so pleasing to English and American sitters. The French, having marveled at his social and intellectual acquisitions, regarded him as a well-adapted curiosity; the English were wholly unembarrassed by his reserve; and the Americans were ready to employ these gifts of cosmopolitanism. And once his rather cautious portrait of Mrs. Marquand revealed that they had nothing to fear from his palette (as, in the early 1880s, they suspected they had), his career really became international. The Americans, however, gave him his start. The travelers' tales were, after all, true. When the Americans showed he was a worthy, trusty butler, the English took him over — the English upper middle class, however. And then, after a few years service with that class, he was invited to join the staff of the aristocracy, for once they saw he would not embarrass the past which lined their ancient walls, he was asked to immortalize them. They felt safe in his hands. The transit from Newport to Blenheim Palace, from Fifth Avenue to Chatsworth, from Beacon Hill to Welbeck Abbey took a decade and a half. And throughout this progress, Sargent really had no serious rival. He had the luck to sail in favorable winds.

The fact that he never liked his role as a portraitist was irrelevant. He was perfectly designed for the job. His *Baedeker* education had made him disinclined to peer below the surface of things. His mind did not turn on introspection. He was a born observer; he was a perpetual spectator. He once explained that he could only paint objects (scarcely a compliment to sitters): "I do not judge," he amplified, "I only chronicle."[22] This made him the ideal servant.

As he belonged nowhere, America showed every inclination to possess him — for unlike James, Whistler, Abbey, and Millet he never willingly abandoned the rights of birth. Though he chose to *live* in England, was thought to be English by almost everyone from Edward VII down, and had deep feelings about the Royal Academy, he was also very swift to correct anyone's impression that he was English. However, when England declared war in 1914, Sargent returned his Prussian Order of Merit. When America entered the war, he also resigned from the Berlin Academy. Unlike James, he did not find his wartime status in England — an alien obliged to register with the police — offensive to his feelings. Sargent nevertheless understood James' application for British citizenship as an act that brought nationality into concert with James' feelings and the facts. "I also was shocked," he wrote to Edith Wharton, "at the moment, on hearing of James' apostasy — but I soon admired the action as a protest against the apathy under kicks of the American Government — I think of him with awe. . . . "[23]

It would be easy to construe Sargent's loyalty as the expression of some higher motive, but that would be an enterprise which ignored his supreme powers of oblivion. He was never much aware of politics; he had failed to notice the Boer War altogether. He had never been seen to *read* a newspaper. If anything, he held on to the national classification of American out of habit, having borrowed his father's emotion. "As to the question of nationality," he once wrote to Whistler, "I have not been invited to retouch it and I keep my twang. If you should ever hear anything to the contrary, please state that there was no such transaction and that I am an American."[24] He had been tagged with the label "foreigner." He knew the inconvenience. When he entered the École des Beaux-Arts his father was unable to present any birth certificate and got a friend to submit an affidavit to the American Consul in Florence. He had trouble getting passports. But he had grown accustomed to the difficulty, having known nothing else. Yet, being an American was Dr. Sargent's proudest and only possession in exile — a legacy he passed on to his son. Had Sargent refused it, he also would have refused his father. His nationality was part of the tightly bound parcel marked family, and his family never left his side.

But it is fair to say he went one better than his father, who died no closer to home than he had lived reluctantly for the previous thirty-five years. Toward the end of his life, Sargent came to live in America for long stretches. From 1919 to 1924 he spent the best part of forty months in Boston, absorbed in his mural decorations for the Museum of Fine Arts. He repatriated himself in the same manner his father endured expatriation, living in hotels, dining in dining rooms full of people he did not like, sending long letters back to friends and family in England. Sargent returned "home" only to become an exile. He had turned the clock back, effected the correction which had eluded his father and, just like the expatriates of his childhood, found no comfort. And as if this irony did not carry sufficient sting, his beloved murals, worshiped fervently at the time by the general public at each unveiling, have become something lower than a joke — they have been ignored. Not only had Sargent failed in this bid for immortality, he failed to find any livable truth or meaning in that initial definition "American."

NOTES

1. Dr. FitzWilliam Sargent to Winthrop Sargent, February 21, 1865, Archives of American Art, Smithsonian Institution, Washington, D.C.

2. FitzWilliam Sargent, *On Bandaging, and Other Operations of Minor Surgery* (Philadelphia, 1848); *England, the United States and the Southern Confederacy* (London, 1863); *Les états confédérés et l'esclavage* (Paris, 1864).

3. Family tradition credits this event as the cause of Emily's illness. But Dr. Sargent, in his letters home, was careful to employ some unrevealing euphemism, such as "disease." From the symptoms he does reveal, it is possible Emily suffered from spinal rheumatism.

4. Dr. FitzWilliam Sargent described his daughter this way in a letter to his mother, Emily Haskell Sargent, n.d. [1865], Archives of American Art, Smithsonian Institution, Washington, D.C.

5. John S. Sargent to Ben del Castillo, April 16, 1865; quoted in Evan Charteris, *John Sargent* (New York, 1927), p. 7.

6. Dr. FitzWilliam Sargent to Winthrop Sargent, March 7, 1867, Archives of American Art, Smithsonian Institution, Washington, D.C.

7. Dr. FitzWilliam Sargent to Winthrop Sargent, November 24, [1869], Archives of American Art, Smithsonian Institution, Washington, D.C. For the Sargent's finances, see Stanley Olson, *John Singer Sargent: His Portrait* (New York, 1986), p. 4. Mrs. Sargent's finances, as far as can be discerned, were as follows: in 1850, after her father's death, she inherited a small trust, amounting to $10,000, which yielded approximately $700 per year in interest. Her mother died in 1859, leaving the rest of her father's estate to her, something around $45,000, which was made over to her in 1862 when she approved the inventory of the estate drawn up by her uncle in Philadelphia. The Sargents apparently could live comfortably, but without extravagance. Over the years, they also had to draw on the principle. Dr. Sargent, of course, had very little money, his salary having stopped once he left Philadelphia; his few investments in railways were of a very inconsequential order.

8. Henry James, *William Wetmore Story and His Friends* (New York, 1903), p. 34.

9. Ibid., pp. 6, 346.

10. Dr. FitzWilliam Sargent to George Bemis, August 20, 1867, Massachusetts Historical Society, Boston.

11. Recollection written by Mrs. Caroline Burche to David McKibbin, February 21, [1958–59], David McKibbin Papers, Collection of the Ormond Family, England.

12. Sargent enrolled in the studio of Carolus-Duran in May 1874: it was the culmination of a series of timely events, for he knew that if he did not seize the opportunity of the moment, his parents would grow restless and be off, postponing his studentship for yet another year. Sargent found out about the studio from Walter Launt Palmer, whom he had known in Florence; see Maybelle Mann, *Walter Launt Palmer: Poetic Reality* (Exton, Pennsylvania, 1984), p. 13; also p. 253, below.

13. The Frenchman who first suggested to Carolus-Duran that he serve as master of an atelier was Paul Batifaud-Vaur. For one account of the foundation of the studio, see James Carroll Beckwith's autobiographical fragment, pp. 88–89, Archives of the National Academy of Design, New York.

14. The American population at 81, Boulevard Montparnasse can only be guessed at as no records were kept and the studio was run on the most casual basis. The following were there when Sargent entered: Hinckley; Will Low (1853–1932), who was also a friend of the Palmers; Stephen Hills Parker (1852–1925); John M. Tracy (1844–1892); and Beckwith (1852–1917), who later became one of Sargent's best friends, sharing the studio at 73bis, Rue Notre-Dame-des-Champs. Others who *might* have been there were: Neville Cain (1855–1935); Eliot Gregory (1854–1915); C. M. Newton and Mountfort Coolidge (both unidentifiable).

For the best account of the independent teaching studios and the École des Beaux-Arts, see H. Barbara Weinberg, "Nineteenth-Century American Painters at the École des Beaux-Arts," *The American Art Journal*, 13 (Autumn 1981), pp. 66–84. And for the best account of the varying fortunes of the Academy schools, see Lois M. Fink and Joshua C. Taylor, *Academy: The Academic Tradition in American Art*, exhibition catalogue (Washington, D.C., National Collection of Fine Arts, 1975).

15. Charteris, *John Sargent*, p. 37.

16. Dr. FitzWilliam Sargent to Emily Haskell Sargent, October 18, [1869], Archives of American Art, Smithsonian Institution, Washington, D.C.

17. Flora Priestley to Vernon Lee (Violet Paget), n.d. [1899], The Miller Library, Colby College, Waterville, Maine.

18. J. Alden Weir to his mother, October 4, 1874, Archives of American Art, Smithsonian Institution, Washington, D.C.; also published in Dorothy Weir Young, *The Life and Letters of J. Alden Weir* (New Haven, 1960), p. 50.

19. Will Low, *A Painter's Progress* (New York, 1910), pp. 90–92.

20. Dr. FitzWilliam Sargent to George Bemis, March 24, [1877], Massachusetts Historical Society, Boston.

21. Robert Louis Stevenson to W. L. Henley, December 17, 1884, National Library of Scotland, Edinburgh.

22. Quoted in Charteris, *John Sargent*, p. 107.

23. John S. Sargent to Edith Wharton, August 6, [1915], Bienecke Rare Book and Manuscript Library, Yale University, New Haven, Connecticut.

24. John S. Sargent to James Abbott McNeill Whistler, n.d., Glasgow University Library, Glasgow.

The Formation of a Style and Sensibility

PATRICIA HILLS

John Sargent's art is brilliant in technique, dazzling in its radiant surface effects, and cosmopolitan in its range of subjects. It reflects, moreover, the outlook and ambition of the thoroughgoing professional practitioner — self-assured, unhesitant, and generally detached from personal, moral involvement with the subjects of his art. The appeal and elusiveness of Sargent's work derive from its technique, surface, cosmopolitan themes, and the artist's professionalism. To understand Sargent's artistic sensibility we must explore the meaning of these four qualities — for Sargent and for late nineteenth-century artists.

This fourfold constellation emerges in the earliest portrait paintings Sargent submitted to the Paris Salon in the late 1870s. *Frances Sherburne Ridley Watts* (Fig. 1), accepted by the jury in 1877 when he was just twenty-one years old, declared to the Parisian art world that he had mastered the technique of portraiture. This rendering of his close friend, the daughter of well-to-do Americans, is an exquisite display of feathery brushwork and sparkling accents over a solid armature of modeled form.[1] Her pose, the tilt of her head, her clothes, and the baronial armchair in which she is poised contribute to the image of a self-assured young woman. Two years later Sargent submitted a portrait of his teacher, Émile Auguste Carolus-Duran (Fig. 4), to the Salon and received some notice in the press, as well as an Honorable Mention.[2] Carolus-Duran is similarly posed and stylishly painted; the portrait has been succinctly described by Richard Ormond as "an almost text-book illustration of Carolus-Duran's own method."[3] *Madame Edouard Pailleron* (Fig. 3), which went to the 1880 Salon,[4] also won a degree of recognition. The outdoor background of a flower-strewn lawn folds up on the figure — a device often found in the paintings of Bastien-Lepage — and in the distance we glimpse a portion of her family country estate at Ronjoux in Savoy. With the outstanding exception of *The Oyster Gatherers of Cancale* (Fig. 9), Sargent rarely set his figures against the sky. He preferred to view them against solid matter. A series of long zigzag and S-rhythms ripple up and down Mme. Pailleron's black dress, with its petticoat of white net and its perky white bow. Through delicate layers of lace, she thrusts her fingers into the folds of the dress. The result is a virtuoso exhibition of caressing painterliness.

1.
Frances Sherburne Ridley Watts, 1877
Oil on canvas, 41⅝ × 32⅞ (105.7 × 83.5)
Philadelphia Museum of Art; The Mr. and
Mrs. Wharton Sinkler Collection

Sargent had entered Carolus-Duran's studio five years earlier, in 1874, and had learned well from the method, technique, and example of his teacher. By method, I mean the procedure whereby the artist plans the composition and then carries it through stages to completion; by technique, I mean the actual handling of wet or dry paint with the brush. Both were important aspects of Carolus-Duran's reputation as a teacher. According to Sargent, the method, inspired by studying tonal values in the works of Velázquez and Hals, was quite simple:

You must classify the values. If you begin with the middle-tone and work up from it towards the darks—so that you deal last with your highest lights and darkest darks—you avoid false accents. That's what Carolus taught me. And Franz Hals—it's hard to find anyone who knew more about oil-paint than Franz Hals—and that was his procedure.[5]

The method entailed a mastery of the art of perception within the studio — of seeing and then recording on canvas the nuances of light coming through a northern window as it illuminates the surface facets of a form. (With *Blonde Model* [Fig. 2], a studio exercise, Sargent has reduced the cheeks and the eye socket to just such small planes.) As a result of this process, the kind of drawing that demarcated the edges of forms played a subsidiary role.

Carolus-Duran also advocated the technique of painting *au premier coup*, or wet paint into wet paint. The results, in portraiture, could be pictures palpably realistic in their flesh tones.[6] Finally, the example of Carolus-Duran encouraged the display of virtuosity and placed a premium on the look of effortlessness. Finishing touches, such as the accents of color and the deft strokes defining the jewelry of the sitters, the wisps of hair, and the ruffles of the sleeves (Figs. 1, 3, 4) masked the deliberate pains Sargent took in the planning and execution of such portraits.[7]

Sargent's early subject pictures were also dazzling and equally acclaimed. In 1878, *The Oyster Gatherers of Cancale* (Fig. 9) went to the Salon, while Sargent sent the smaller version (Fig. 7) to the inaugural exhibition in New York of the Society of American Artists, where it generated praise from the critic for *The Art Journal*:

The silvery hue of this painting is what first attracts the attention, and immediately the eye rests upon a group of women and children, half in silhouette, rambling among the quiet pools left by the retreating tide. Their shadows, dark and vapoury, are cast on the ground, while the reflection of their figures appears in the still water around their feet. A little way off the ripples of the blue sea roll up against the steep shore, and luminous clouds shimmer with sunlight.[8]

In both the Society of American Artists version and the one shown at the Salon, Sargent emphasized light on objects rather than physical substance. What the figures lack in solidity, they make up for in a scintillating brilliance of light reflecting from the pools of water and bouncing off the edges of forms. These oyster harvesters have none of the earthy monumentality with which Millet or Courbet would have endowed them; they are, rather, part of a spectacle seen through the eyes of a passing tourist.[9]

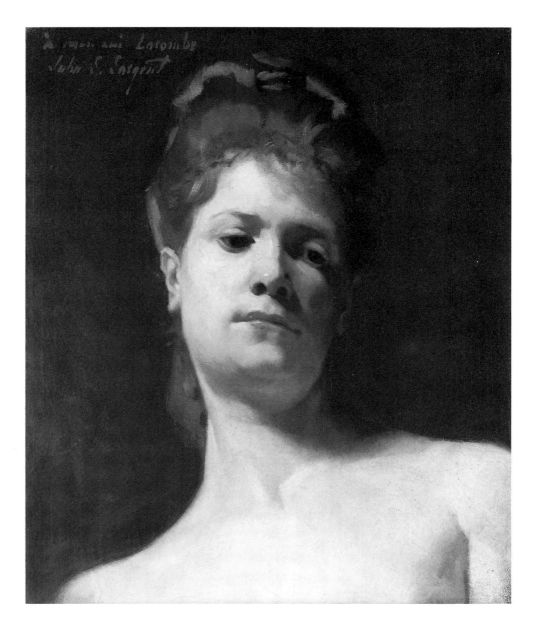

2.

Blond Model, c. 1877

Oil on canvas, $17^{15}/_{16} \times 14^{15}/_{16}$ (45.6×37.9)

Sterling and Francine Clark Art Institute,

Williamstown, Massachusetts

Indeed, raised as a member of a small but important class of international wanderers, Sargent was an intellectual tourist permanently on holiday. Therefore, breaks from Paris studio life were necessary for him, particularly when he could travel with family and friends, such as J. Carroll Beckwith, Paul Helleu, and his childhood friend Ralph Curtis (Fig. 11). *The Oyster Gatherers of Cancale* was the result of one such holiday in Brittany. Later, in the summer and fall of 1878, Sargent traveled to Naples and Capri, this time alone, but he quickly made friends among other artists visiting there. His favorite model in Capri was Rosina Ferrara, whom he described as, "an Ana Capri girl, a magnificent type, about seventeen years of age, her complexion a rich nut-brown, with a mass of blue-black hair, very beautiful, and of an Arab type."[10]

On these holidays he stretched his style to include the *plein-air* effects of outdoor painting. Yet he avoided the harsh light of the Mediterranean sun in the Capri pictures and instead chose a modulated light that would ensure fidelity to local color. In one of the paintings entitled *Capri* (Fig. 10) Rosina stands slightly off

3.
Madame Edouard Pailleron, 1879
Oil on canvas, 82 × 39 (208.3 × 99.1)
Corcoran Gallery of Art, Washington, D.C.;
Purchase and Gift of Katharine McCook Knox,
John A. Nevius, and Mr. and Mrs. Lansdell K.
Christie

center, leaning back into the twisted trunk of a tree, her arm draped over it.
Sargent meticulously rendered her figure as a precious flower amid the picturesque
thorniness of the thistle-strewn field.[11] In another work of the same title (Fig. 12),
she dances on the roof of a whitewashed house as late sunset casts a uniform glow
over the distant rooftops. Although the posture and mood of the *Young Man in
Reverie* (Fig. 13), leaning indolently against the white wall, commands our gaze,
Sargent was just as concerned with the contrast of tonal values — with the
difficulty of painting the bright whites of the wall and pottery against the dark
hair, cape, and shadows, and with the middle tones of the youth's face, naked
chest, and arm.[12]

In these years Sargent established what would become a lifelong pattern of
painting his subject pictures only while away on trips. There are only a few
exceptions, most notably *Rehearsal of the Pas de Loup Orchestra at the Cirque d'Hiver*
(Fig. 16) and *In the Luxembourg Gardens* (Fig. 17), both painted in Paris. Like

STYLE AND SENSIBILITY

Capri (Fig. 12), the latter is a twilight scene; the red glow of the strolling man's cigarette punctuates the hushed atmosphere, while the silvery reflection of the moon in the pool of water gives sparkle to the grayed lavender palette. Sargent's scene drew on the pictorial tradition of the *flâneur* ("stroller"), which had been developed by Manet and others in the 1860s. But his conception, with its deft strokes and miniaturizing quality, has more in common with the works of his own contemporary Giuseppe de Nittis (Fig. 18) than it does with the more broadly painted subjects of Manet, such as *La Musique aux Tuileries* (1862; National Gallery, London).[13]

The qualities which these subject pictures have in common with the portraits of the 1870s are technical brilliance, charm without nostalgia, and artifice modified by the actualities of the person or the site. Here there is no moodiness, nothing of the anecdotal or moralizing character seen in early nineteenth-century Romantic portraiture or mid-century sentimental genre painting of rustic life. Instead we have Sargent, the young cosmopolitan, manipulating technique in order to display the surface dazzle of forms. With the objective distancing of the professional he achieves a coherent and memorable image in each painting.

Many of Sargent's contemporaries noted his disengagement. The Englishman Charles H. Caffin, one of the most astute critics writing in America at the turn of the century, described the artist in 1903: "A self-contained man, of retiring disposition, he contemplates the 'passing show' with complete detachment and undisturbed scrutiny."[14] The artist's biographer, Evan Charteris, who knew him well, commented on the "detachment from events beyond the studio" which marked Sargent.[15]

Evan Mills in 1903 noted the link between Sargent's detachment and the cosmopolitan atmosphere in which he had been raised:

Mr. John S. Sargent is a typical example of the modern cosmopolitan man, the man whose habits of thought and life make him at home everywhere, and whose training has been such as to preclude the last touch of chauvinism. Such a man has become possible only during the last fifty years, and then only in the case of an occasional American. For the man born and bred in Europe of European parents must of necessity be influenced by national feelings that can not but make impossible any true detached cosmopolitanism. In the case of an American born and bred abroad, the only feelings that can possibly arise are those that come of cold selection; he is unattached to anything, and though living among and with the different European peoples, he never becomes one with them in sentiment or local bias.[16]

Sargent's cosmopolitanism created a sensibility whereby he was a perpetual sightseer in a world filled with the exotic "other." His childhood letters show a preoccupation with sightseeing, collecting photographs of views and buildings, and sketching animals and architecture at every opportunity. One single sentence, lodged in a letter dated October 13, 1865, particularly epitomizes the sensitive and inquisitive youth:

At the South Kensington Museum we saw some very fine paintings of Landseer, the celebrated animal painter, and a very fine picture by Rosa Bonheur called the horse fair, but the most curious thing there was an oyster forming a pearl; the oyster was in spirits of wine.[17]

"Curiosity" and a sense of wonder defined Sargent's approach to the world around him — as when his imagination was captured more by the sight of a preserved oyster-pearl than by a celebrated painting. Charteris' biography included the reminiscences of Sargent's childhood friend Violet Paget, who wrote under the pseudonym Vernon Lee. In her remarks, written after the artist's death, she tried to capture the essence of his character as she recalled him in the 1860s:

The words "strange, weird, fantastic" were already on his lips — and that adjective curious, *pronounced with a long and somehow aspirated* u, *accompanied by a particular expression half of wonder and half of self-irony.*[18]

The strange and the fantastic — the "otherness" of the world — were to have a continuing appeal to Sargent, who kept up the pace of traveling to exotic lands until the end of his life, and who numbered among his friends eccentric artists, colorful writers, and outrageous society women.

William Howe Downes, who wrote a biography of Sargent in 1925, summed up his impressions of a man who kept his sense of wonder while keeping his distance:

As to society, he neither sought nor avoided it. He was not gregarious; as Chase has pointed out, most of his friends were artists and literary folk. His supply of small talk was limited; the first impression of those who met him was that he was reserved and reticent; but, though he seldom spoke of himself or his work, he was keenly interested in music, the drama, literature, and the work of his colleagues in painting; in the right sort of company he could discuss such matters in a very original and interesting way. His taste in reading was broad and scholarly; he was a widely cultivated man; and to those whose privilege it was to enjoy his familiar friendship the genuineness and attractiveness of his character and personality were known. He was always most considerate and generous in his attitude towards the young and struggling members of his own profession.[19]

Although Sargent's disengaged cosmopolitanism has biographical roots, it coincided with, indeed it reflected, the aestheticizing tendencies of the later nineteenth century.[20] The international set of Henry James, Oscar Wilde, and Comte Robert de Montesquiou, as Albert Boime's essay reveals (pp. 75–81), was a more colorful manifestation of that aestheticization. But there was a larger context for the phenomenon, one imbedded in European and American thought. In this connection Matthew Arnold steps forth as a timely witness to the reevaluation of the role of art and culture then taking place. In *Culture and Anarchy* (1869) he offered his famous definition of culture as the "pursuit of our total perfection by means of getting to know, on all the matters which most concern us, the best which has been thought and said in the world."[21] His words, which have since

5.
Edouard Pailleron, 1879
Oil on canvas, 50 × 37 (127 × 94)
Musée National du Château de Versailles

6.
The Pailleron Children (Edouard and Marie-Louise), 1881
Oil on canvas, 60 × 69 (152.4 × 175.3)
Des Moines Art Center; Edith M. Usry
Bequest Fund in memory of her parents, Mr.
and Mrs. George Franklin Usry, and additional
funds from Dr. and Mrs. Peder T. Madsen and
the Anna K. Meredith Endowment Fund, 1976

grown to the proportions of a manifesto for many intellectuals and artists, differed
from earlier pronouncements that art and culture should teach and uplift the
morals and ideals of the population directly and didactically. It is no coincidence
that Arnold's views of culture were developed in the context of the sharp political
struggles surrounding the Reform bills being argued in the British Parliament in
the late 1860s,[22] and that they should have taken root in a period of reaction in
Europe to the Paris Commune and in America to the Civil War and its aftermath.
His advice was to remove culture from the sphere of political life. Arnold's
advocacy of "sweetness and light," therefore, can be seen as one expression of the
move toward beauty and moral detachment and away from the "fire and strength"
of moralizing.[23]

The waning influence of John Ruskin in the Anglo-American world of the
1870s and 1880s is another measure of these changed cultural attitudes — of the
rejection of moralizing and didacticism for an art exclusively concerned with
beauty.[24] Sargent's friend Vernon Lee (Figs. 19, 231) was in the forefront of the
attack on Ruskin's belief in the inseparability of aesthetics and ethics. In her 1881
essay "In Umbria," she argued for the independence of great art from morality or
sentiment.[25] In 1882, Sargent wrote to her about her book of essays. He was

*delighted with it and I think it is a book that will do a great deal of good, and I hope it is very
much read, for your view of art is the only true one. . . . I think your theory of the all-
importance of beauty and its independence of or its hostility to sentiment applies admirably to the*

*antique, and to the short great period of art in Italy. It is certain that at certain times talent
entirely overcomes thought or poetry. In decadence, this occurred to an outrageous extent. It is
another question and I suppose a matter of personal feeling whether that state of things is more
interesting than another.*[26]

In the realm of art criticism we can, of course, note parallel shifts toward the
direction of art-for-art's-sake. Oscar Reutersvard has traced a shift in French
criticism that began in the early 1870s. The critics at first defended the perceptual
naturalism of the Impressionists as the "optically exact reproduction from nature."
But by the late 1880s, Albert Aurier and others began to stress "the mark of the
brush" as having "its own stimulating role to excite the emotions."[27] Historians
today call this the shift away from the Impressionist to the Post-Impressionist
aesthetic — from the "matching" of painting to its model to the frank admission
that paintings are "made," that they are pictures composed of lines, planes, and
colors.[28]

However, among many Anglo-American critics the issues to discuss still
remained the *morality*, or didactic and expressive purposes of art; the differences
between Impressionism and Post-Impressionism remained unclear, at least until
the time of Roger Fry. American critics, aware of the provincialism of their own
country, knew that young painters would seek out the best technical training they
could find. They therefore cautioned that too much technique could lead to
paintings aesthetically pleasing but empty of purposeful content.[29] Gerard Baldwin
Brown, writing on "Modern French Art," for *Appletons' Journal* in 1880, observed
that France had come to represent the point of view that "a work of art . . . must
be judged on artistic grounds alone."[30] Brown reviewed the issues and finally
conceded: "Such things as awkward composition, unnatural posing, bad drawing,
slovenly execution, neither gods nor hanging committees can be asked to tolerate."[31]

John F. Weir, director of the Yale School of Art and older brother of Sargent's friend Julian Alden Weir, wrote a long article reviewing these issues for the May 1883 issue of *Harper's New Monthly Magazine*. To Weir: "Art is expression, and hitherto the student has merely been concerned with imitation, with *technique*, with means and principles — in short, with the mere grammar of art."[32] Weir understood that the history of American art had confirmed the continuing frustration of young Americans in their search for proper training facilities. To Weir, it was necessary for students to travel abroad for such training, but art should go beyond the mere grammar of technique and method:

It is perfectly natural that the neophyte should believe in the creed, Art for the sake of Art, for as yet he has known of no other; this alone has filled his thoughts, and only experience can give him larger views. Fresh from his disciplinary tasks, method and means form for him the beginning and the end of art; it is proper that they should, for this develops skill, which is always attractive. But granting skill, will the technical knowledge of the grammarian constitute a poet? Will the means usurp the end? Will method make the artist? We find in the works of enduring masters something more than this. They do not affect the superficial attractions of mere skill.[33]

While many feared that the embrace of technique and method would spell the rejection of content, message, and meaning, Whistler, the detached dandy if there ever was one, welcomed the elimination of extra-aesthetic concerns in works of art. In part, his downplay of message in art served as a healthy antidote to hackneyed content — be it sentimental, grandiose, romantic, or patriotic. Whistler's views were well known, and he later published them as *The Gentle Art of Making Enemies*:

Art should be independent of all clap-trap — should stand alone, and appeal to the artistic sense of eye or ear, without confounding this with emotions entirely foreign to it, as devotion, pity,

9.
The Oyster Gatherers of Cancale, 1878
Oil on canvas, 31 × 48 (78.7 × 121.9)
Corcoran Gallery of Art, Washington, D.C.;
Museum Purchase

*love, patriotism, and the like. All these have no kind of concern with it and that is why I insist
on calling my works "arrangements" and "harmonies."*[34]

It was Whistler's artistic audacity that lead John Ruskin to accuse him of "flinging
a pot of paint in the public's face." It was not just Whistler's hunger for self-
promotion that impelled him to sue Ruskin for slander; it was also his conviction
that his art was the art of the future. Ruskin lost the suit, and this proved to be a
near fatal blow to Ruskin and his view of art as a moral force.[35]

But Whistler's aesthetic viewpoint was perhaps too far ahead of its time,
more compatible with twentieth-century modernism than with the nineteenth
century's photographic perception of the visible world.[36] The painting of this
visible world he held beneath contempt: "The imitator is a poor kind of creature.
If the man who paints only the tree, or flower, or other surface he sees before him
were an artist, the king of artists would be the photographer. It is for the artist to
do something beyond this. . . . "[37]

Whistler would have categorized Sargent as "the imitator," because Sargent
subscribed to a perceptual naturalism. Sargent painted what he saw, what his eyes
told him was out there. He painted the surfaces Whistler deplored. He learned
from photography, as all nineteenth-century painters did, but choosing color and
wielding paint still made the painter's profession different in kind from the
photographer's.

38

10.

Capri, 1878

Oil on canvas, 30¼ × 25 (76.8 × 63.5)

Museum of Fine Arts, Boston; Bequest of
Helen Swift Neilson

11.

Ralph Curtis on the Beach at Scheveningen, 1880

Oil on board, 11 × 14 (27.9 × 35.6)

The High Museum of Art, Atlanta; Gift of the
Walter Clay Hill Family Foundation, 1973

Painting surfaces is what Sargent himself frankly advocated. His friend
Edmund Gosse (Fig. 20), the English novelist, told Charteris:

*One of Sargent's theories . . . was that modern painters made a mistake in showing that they
know too much about the substances they paint. . . . Sargent . . . thought that the artist ought to
know nothing whatever about the nature of the object before him ("Ruskin, don't you know —
rocks and clouds — silly old thing!"), but should concentrate all his powers on a representation
of its appearance. The picture was to be a consistent vision, a reproduction of the area filled by
the eye. Hence, in a very curious way, the aspect of a substance became much more real to him
than the substance itself.*[38]

Although Gosse was talking about a time in the mid-1880s, when he knew Sargent
in Broadway, Sargent would have advocated even earlier the approach that the
impersonal rendering of "the appearance," "a reproduction of the area filled by
the eye," was to be the conscious intention of the artist. To Sargent, when he was
painting his Venetian scenes of the early 1880s, it meant recording like a camera the
way that light flows over forms and catches in the irregularities of a textured surface
— reflecting back to the spectator not the semblance of texture but the light.

Light is not only the subject of the Venetian paintings, but of *El Jaleo* (Fig. 14),
which Sargent composed from sketches he may have made in 1879 in Spain. Here
light also functions as the visible manifestation of the rhythms of the music. The
irregular pattern of dark-suited men, lined up friezelike against the floodlit wall,
and the guitars and tambourine hanging from the ceiling at regular intervals

suggest the strumming beat of the musicians. The female dancer, her form punctuated by sharp contrasts of light and dark, becomes a tumultuous crescendo. Her extended arm points to the castanets held aloft by the two smiling women at the right — the castanets being both another musical accent as the dance proceeds and a secondary point of focus for the spectator of Sargent's scene.

When Sargent sent *El Jaleo* to the Salon of 1882, John Forbes-Robertson, writing for the London *Magazine of Art*, rhapsodized:

John S. Sargent . . . a pupil of Carolus Duran, has not hitherto signalised himself; but this year his 'El Jaleo,' a dancing gipsy, has attracted universal attention. She is a magnificent creature in a rich white satin dress, and, with her left arm outstretched, and her right grotesquely akimbo, as is the custom with Andalusian gipsies, she figures on the stage of a small theatre to the rapturous delight of a row of guitar-players behind, whose shadows are thrown upon the wall by the unseen footlights. Although the execution is rough to a degree, and several passages are little more than suggested, the touch is never uncertain, and the chiaroscuro is as telling as that of Goya, after he had blended the manners of Velasquez and Rembrandt.[39]

The following year the editor for the same magazine had less enthusiasm for *El Jaleo*; but he, too, focused on the drama of the scene, created in part by the manipulations of light.

It is preposterously clever — far too clever, in fact, for a decent work of art. It is of great size, and not an inch of it but is touched with trickiness and chic. At the first glance, no doubt, a general impression of the subject is conveyed. The spectator is dazzled by a general glare of light, and bewildered by a whirl of tumbled drapery, so that he has no time to consider what may be the function of those uncouth blacknesses behind.[40]

However, he ends by praising the effects of light: "Throughout the work drawing is immolated to value; but, on the other hand Mr. Sargent's values are thoroughly studied, and his atmospheric effect is well-nigh irreproachable."[41]

What he means when he says that "drawing is immolated to value" can be demonstrated by Sargent's preparatory sketches presumably made when he visited Spain in the autumn and winter of 1879.[42] The drawings in a scrapbook in the Isabella Stewart Gardner Museum (Figs. 15, 222–224) reveal Sargent's primary concerns, to draw light and shadow, not form. In these charcoal sketches he obliterates contours — replacing them with strokes that represent the shadows caught in the hollows of the planes. The fact that light comes from below — from presumed footlights — creates a *tour de force* of accentuated physiognomy.

This perceptual naturalism was to guide Sargent for the rest of his career. However, the sites of his pictures would change from the darkened streets and interiors of the early 1880s to the sunlit English gardens and riverbanks of the mid-1880s, when, influenced by Monet and the Impressionists, he chose subjects fully surrounded by light. His later renderings of Venetian canals, Mediterranean olive groves, and Alpine meadows continued to be light-filled paintings.

12.
Capri, 1878
Oil on canvas, 20 × 25 (50.8 × 63.5)
The Warner Collection of Gulf States Paper
Corporation, Tuscaloosa, Alabama

13.
Young Man in Reverie, 1878 (inscribed 1876)
Oil on canvas, 30 × 24 (76.2 × 61)
Private collection

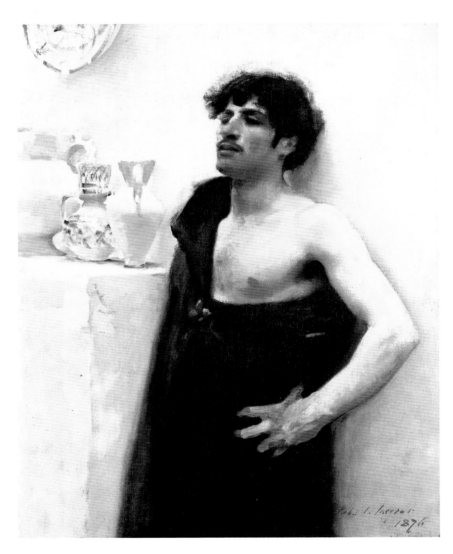

14.
El Jaleo, 1882
Oil on canvas, 94½ × 137 (240 × 348)
Isabella Stewart Gardner Museum, Boston

Sargent's ongoing concern for pictorial method was paralleled by his effort to establish a professional working routine, which became more pronounced by the turn of the century. He developed an air of objectivity, often noted by such sitters as the poet William Butler Yeats (Fig. 249). Disarmed by Sargent's particular charm, Yeats wrote to the American collector and lawyer John Quinn in 1908: "Sargent is good company, not so much like an artist as like some wise, wealthy man of business who has lived with artists. He looks on at the enthusiasts with an ironical tolerance which is very engaging. . . ."[43]

When Sargent was not traveling, he followed a regular work routine. His valet for twenty years, Nicola d'Inverno, recalled Sargent's working habits: "His life was as orderly as that of a bishop." He awoke at 7, breakfasted at 8, then had a bath; at about 9 A.M. he handled his correspondence, and by 10 was in the studio; following a 1 P.M. lunch break, he returned to the studio and painted from 2 or 2:30 to 5 P.M.[44] Visitors never interrupted his schedule of painting. The American painter William A. Coffin reported in 1896:

Sargent's studio is always a sociable place. Unlike many artists, the presence of visitors or companions does not disturb him when he is painting. He seems to work without obvious exertion even in his intensest activity. "When his models are resting, he fills up the gap by strumming on the piano or guitar," says one of his friends; "his manner while at work is that of a man of

consummate address, and does not show physical or mental effort." . . . *Skill and accomplishment in every field excite his admiration, but his own creed is stable and unaffected by transitory influences.*[45]

As years passed, Sargent tired of commissioned portraiture, even though his fees provided a handsome income. He vowed to give it up, expressing to friends that he wanted no more ladies nagging him about their daughters' looks: "No more paughtraits whether refreshed or not. I abhor and abjure them and hope never to do another especially of the Upper Classes."[46] However, he did turn out portrait drawings, both as commissions and as mementos for friends and hostesses.

History will nevertheless remember Sargent as a portrait painter in the grand tradition of Van Dyck and Gainsborough. Like his famous predecessors, he mastered the art of capturing the poise, authority, and confidence of the prominent and powerful. But Sargent also recorded the failure of confidence that characterized upper-class life in the late nineteenth century, an insecurity subtly but unmistakably reflected in his portraits of women. The best of these exhibit a fascinating tension between the sitter's external self-assurance and inner anxiety. As Charles Caffin remarked, the women Sargent portrayed "are, to a certain extent, the product of an age of nerves, and in his portraits of them there is perceptible an equivalent restlessness of manner, a highly strung intention, almost a stringiness of nervous expression."[47]

However great was Sargent's skill at imbuing his sitters with the psychological character of their era, he was still burdened by the obligation to flatter a patron. For this reason, it was his subject pictures that prepared the way for modernism no less than Whistler's paintings did. Sargent's dazzling paintings of Venice, Cancale, and later Egypt, Corfu, and Switzerland anticipated an attitude that sees art as the expression of a mind on holiday, disengaged from real objects, from the people and things of the world.

16.

Rehearsal of the Pas de Loup Orchestra at the Cirque d'Hiver, 1878

Oil on canvas, 36⅝ × 28¾ (92.1 × 71.9)

Private collection; on loan to The Art Institute of Chicago

17.
In the Luxembourg Gardens, 1879
Oil on canvas, 25½ × 36 (64.8 × 91.4)
John G. Johnson Collection at the Philadelphia
Museum of Art

18.
Giuseppe de Nittis, *Return from the Races*, 1875
Oil on canvas, 22⅞ × 45⅛ (58.1 × 114.6)
Philadelphia Museum of Art; The W. P.
Wilstach Collection, given by John G. Johnson

19.
Vernon Lee, 1881
Oil on canvas, 21⅛ × 17 (53.7 × 43.2)
The Tate Gallery, London; Bequeathed
by Miss Vernon Lee through
Miss Cooper Willis, 1935

NOTES

1. For information on Frances Sherburne
Ridley Watts as well as other well-known
Sargent sitters, see James Lomax and
Richard Ormond, *John Singer Sargent and the
Edwardian Age*, exhibition catalogue (Leeds,
England, Leeds Art Galleries; London,
National Portrait Gallery; and The Detroit
Institute of Arts, 1979).

2. Trevor Fairbrother has clarified the
confusion regarding when and for which
picture Sargent received an Honorable
Mention at the Salon. It was for this
portrait of *Carolus-Duran* in 1879, not for
*The Oyster Gatherers of Cancale [En Route pour
la Pêche]* in 1878; see Trevor J. Fairbrother,
John Singer Sargent and America (New York,
1986), pp. 32, 40.

3. Richard Ormond, *John Singer Sargent:
Paintings, Drawings, Watercolors* (New York,
1970), p. 18.

4. See pp. 83–84, below.

5. Quoted in Evan Charteris, *John Sargent*
(New York, 1927), p. 29.

6. Regarding the teaching methods of
Carolus-Duran, see R. A. M. Stevenson,
The Art of Velasquez (London, 1895),
pp. 102–10; also Carolus-Duran, "A
French Painter and His Pupils," *The Century
Magazine*, 31 (January 1886), pp. 372–76.

7. Most nineteenth-century writers comment
on the hard work Sargent put into his
portraits; see, for example, John La Farge,
"Sargent, the Artist," *The Independent*,
April 27, 1899, p. 1141.

8. S. N. Carter, "First Exhibition of the
American Art Association," *The Art
Journal*, 4 (April 1878), p. 126. The version
sent to New York, now in the Museum of
Fine Arts, Boston, was then called *Fishing
for Oysters at Cancale*. For the early
exhibitions of the Society of American
Artists, see Jennifer A. Martin Bienenstock,
"The Formation and Early Years of the
Society of American Artists: 1877–1884,"
Ph.D. dissertation (The City University of
New York, 1983). See also Meg Robertson,
"John Singer Sargent: His Early Success in
America, 1878–1879," *Archives of American
Art Journal*, 22, no. 4 (1982), pp. 20–26;
and Fairbrother, *John Singer Sargent and
America*, pp. 28–44.

9. See the discussion of the concept of
"spectacle" in T. J. Clark, *The Painting of
Modern Life: Paris in the Art of Manet and His
Followers* (New York, 1985), p. 9.

10. Quoted in Charteris, *John Sargent*, p. 48.

11. *Capri* was exhibited at the Society of
American Artists in 1879 with the title *A
Capriote*; the version sent to the Salon in
1879 (private collection, New York) was
then called *Dans les Oliviers, à Capri (Italie)*.

12. I am grateful to Odile Duff, researcher for
the Sargent catalogue raisonné being
prepared by the Coe Kerr Gallery, Inc., for
verifying that the painting was done in
1878, rather than 1876 as inscribed on the
canvas. Duff also very kindly let me read
her unpublished manuscript on the Capri
paintings.

13. Regarding Manet and the concept of the *flâneur*,
see N. G. Sandblad, *Manet: Three Studies in
Artistic Conception* (Lund, Sweden, 1954).

14. Charles H. Caffin, "John S. Sargent: The
Greatest Contemporary Portrait Painter,"
World's Work, 7 (November 1903), p. 4099.

15. Charteris, *John Sargent*, p. 202.

16. Evan Mills, "A Personal Sketch of Mr.
Sargent," *World's Work*, 7 (November
1903), p. 4116. Although called "A
Personal Sketch," Mills did not really know
Sargent well; he thought, for example, that
the lifelong bachelor was married.

17. Quoted in Charteris, *John Sargent*, p. 9.

18. Vernon Lee, "J. S. S. *In Memoriam*," quoted
in Charteris, *John Sargent*, p. 249.

19. William Howe Downes, *John S. Sargent: His
Life and Work* (Boston, 1925), pp. 21–22.

20. Sargent was in the right place at the right
time with the right kind of predispositions.
George Kubler's notion of entrance (*The
Shape of Time: Remarks on the History of Things*
[New Haven, 1962], pp. 6–7) is relevant
here: "Talent is a predisposition: a
talented pupil begins younger; he masters
the tradition more quickly; his inventions
come more fluently than those of his
untalented fellows.... The quality
talented people share is a matter of kind
more than degree, because the gradations
of talent signify less than its presence. It is
meaningless to debate whether Leonardo
was more talented than Raphael. Both
were talented. Bernardino Luini and Giulio
Romano also were talented. But the followers
had bad luck. They came late when the feast
was over through no fault of their own."

21. Matthew Arnold, *Culture and Anarchy*, ed.
J. Dover Wilson (Cambridge, England,
1963), p. 6. I am indebted to
David C. Huntington's essay for turning
my attention to Arnold at this time; see
David C. Huntington in *The Quest for Unity:*

20.
Edmund Gosse, c. 1886
Oil on canvas, 21½ × 17½ (54.6 × 44.5)
National Portrait Gallery, London

American Art Between World's Fairs 1876–1893, exhibition catalogue (The Detroit Institute of Arts, 1983), pp. 11–12.

22. See the introduction by J. Dover Wilson in Arnold, *Culture and Anarchy*, pp. vii–xl.

23. See Arnold's chapters "Sweetness and Light," ibid., pp. 43–71; and "Hebraism and Hellenism," pp. 129–44.

24. See Roger Stein, *John Ruskin and Aesthetic Thought in America: 1840–1900* (Cambridge, Massachusetts, 1967). Stein quotes (p. 221) John F. Weir, writing in 1871, who compared Ruskin to Hippolyte Taine: "Mr. Ruskin affects the subjective, moral aspect, the influences, and motives of art; while M. Taine is more concerned with its objective phase, its sensuous, positive characteristics, and its physical causes and relations." During these years Taine lectured at the École des Beaux-Arts.

25. Vernon Lee, *Belcaro: Being Essays on Sundry Aesthetical Questions* (London, 1881).

26. Quoted in Charteris, *John Sargent*, p. 56.

27. Oscar Reutersvard, "The Accentuated Brush Stroke of the Impressionists: The Debate Concerning Decomposition in Impressionism," *The Journal of Aesthetics & Art Criticism*, 10 (March 1952), p. 373. This article was brought to my attention by Grace Seiberling's "The Evolution of an Impressionist," in *Paintings by Monet*, exhibition catalogue (The Art Institute of Chicago, 1975).

28. Regarding matching and making, see E. H. Gombrich, "The Analysis of Vision in Art," in *Art and Illusion: A Study in the Psychology of Pictorial Representation* (Princeton, 1960), pp. 291–329.

29. This criticism largely focused on such French artists as Carolus-Duran, Jules Bastien-Lepage, Georges Clairin, Tony Robert-Fleury, and Giuseppe de Nittis, rather than on those — Manet, Monet, Degas — whom we would consider the avant-garde of French painting in the early 1880s. A good Anglo-American view is provided by Henry Bacon, *Parisian Art and Artists* (Boston, 1883). Bacon's experiences as an American expatriate have been investigated by Sara Caldwell Junkin, "The Europeanization of Henry Bacon (1839–1912): American Expatriate Painter," Ph.D. dissertation (Boston University, 1986). Professor H. Barbara Weinberg's scholarship has done much to inform us of the situation of Americans abroad, as has the work of Dr. Lois Fink.

30. Gerard Baldwin Brown, "Modern French Art," *Appletons' Journal*, 9 (September 1880), p. 271.

31. Ibid, p. 272.

32. John F. Weir, "Art Study at Home and Abroad," *Harper's New Monthly Magazine*, 66 (May 1883), p. 947.

33. Ibid., p. 951.

34. James Abbott McNeill Whistler, *The Gentle Art of Making Enemies* (New York, 1890), pp. 127–28.

35. Excerpts from the proceedings of the trial were published by Whistler, *The Gentle Art of Making Enemies*, pp. 2–10.

36. There is much recent work on the "photographic vision" of nineteenth-century painting; Peter Galassi, *Before Photography: Painting and the Invention of Photography*, exhibition catalogue (New York, The Museum of Modern Art, 1981), explored the roots of "photographic vision"; see his notes and bibliography for references to post-1839 painting.

37. Whistler, *The Gentle Art of Making Enemies*, p. 128. I briefly reviewed these issues, as they continued to engage artists and writers at the turn of the century, in *Turn-of-the-Century America: Paintings, Graphics, Photographs, 1890–1910*, exhibition catalogue (New York, Whitney Museum of American Art, 1977), pp. 9–13.

38. Quoted in Charteris, *John Sargent*, pp. 77–78.

39. John Forbes-Robertson, "The Salon of 1882," *Magazine of Art*, 5 (1882), p. 414.

40. [Editor], "America in Europe," *Magazine of Art*, 6 (1883), p. 6.

41. Ibid.

42. The sketches may have been done later, after he had returned to Paris. See Richard Ormond, "Sargent's *El Jaleo*," in *Fenway Court: Isabella Stewart Gardner Museum, 1970* (Boston, 1971), pp. 2–18.

43. Letter dated April 27, 1908, quoted in Allan Wade, ed., *Letters of W. B. Yeats* (New York, 1955), p. 509; also quoted in Ormond, *John Singer Sargent*, p. 256.

44. "The Real John Singer Sargent as His Valet Saw Him," *Boston Sunday Advertiser*, February 7, 1926.

45. William A. Coffin, "Sargent and His Painting: With Special Reference to His Decorations in the Boston Public Library," *The Century Magazine*, 52 (June 1896), pp. 172, 175.

46. Quoted in Charteris, *John Sargent*, p. 155.

47. Caffin, "John S. Sargent: The Greatest Contemporary Portrait Painter," p. 4116.

Sargent in Venice

LINDA AYRES

John Singer Sargent's striking vision of Venice has been eloquently demonstrated by two recent exhibitions devoted to American artists in Venice,[1] as well as by the present retrospective, which places Sargent's work in Venice in the context of his oeuvre. Thanks to all three exhibitions, Sargent's Venetian works, which had previously received scant attention in the literature, have emerged as a powerful and important group.[2] Indeed, Venice had a strong and lasting appeal for Sargent: he created more than 125 paintings and watercolors during his many trips there over four decades.

This essay focuses on a portion of that production — a dozen figure paintings that resulted from two visits Sargent made to Venice in the early 1880s. These paintings provided him with the opportunity to explore the lessons in tonal painting he had learned from Carolus-Duran and to experiment with figure groupings. But these Venice works also show the extraordinary powers of a painter who would be lauded in his own lifetime for an unequaled brilliance of technique.

Sargent was no stranger to Venice when he arrived there in September 1880 at age twenty-four to join his parents at the Hotel d'Italie (now the Bauer-Grunwald) on Campo San Moisè.[3] His sister Emily reported:

He expects to remain on here indefinitely, as long as he finds he can work with advantage, & has taken a Studio in the Palazzo Rezzonico, Canal Grande, an immense house where several artists are installed, & where one of his Paris friends has also taken a room to work in.[4]

Sargent stayed into the winter months, at least through January and possibly until late February or early March 1881, moving to 290, Piazza San Marco, next to the Clock Tower, after his parents left Venice.[5]

The second trip to Venice occurred in the late summer of 1882, and Sargent remained for several months.[6] This time he lived in the sumptuous fifteenth-century Palazzo Barbaro, on the Grand Canal near the Accademia bridge, with his Boston relatives, the Daniel Sargent Curtis family.

During these two stays in Venice, Sargent created a remarkable series of figure paintings that are distinct in subject matter and style from those of other American artists. He avoided the well-known scenes of contemporary art — the

21.
The Sulphur Match, 1882
Oil on canvas, 23 × 16 (58.4 × 40.6)
Collection of Jo Ann and Julian Ganz, Jr.

49

22.
Robert Blum, *Venetian Lace Makers*, 1887
Oil on canvas, 30⅛ × 41¼ (76.5 × 104.8)
Cincinnati Art Museum; Gift of Mrs. Elizabeth
S. Potter

depictions of the water, the festive and colorful crowds, and the grand architecture for which Venice was famous. Already familiar with the city's monuments, he offers us Venice as seen by the local inhabitants — scenes of working-class men and women meeting in obscure streets or occupied with indoor tasks.

The Venetian paintings share several characteristics. Generally monochromatic, these black and gray works are infused with the overall silvery tonality of Venetian light. A sense of mystery and exoticism seen in other paintings by Sargent pervades this Venetian work, the same effect that characterizes his *Fumée d'Ambre Gris* of 1880 (Fig. 50).[7] Figures are placed in steeply receding spaces and against unornamented architectural elements. Many of the same models — particularly a woman named Gigia Viani and an unidentified man — appear repeatedly in his compositions of this period, making it more difficult to differentiate the 1880 from the 1882 paintings.[8]

There are some clues as to chronology, however. We know, for instance, that Sargent exhibited two oils entitled *Venetian Interior* at the Grosvenor Gallery, London, in May 1882, indicating that interior scenes were among the works he completed during the first, 1880–81 visit. In fact, any or all of three paintings, each depicting a group of women working and talking in the same hall on the *piano nobile* of an old palazzo, may have been produced during that first Venetian sojourn: *Venetian Bead Stringers* (Fig. 23), *A Venetian Interior* (Fig. 24), and *Venetian Interior* (Fig. 25).

It is difficult to know which of these three interiors Henry James had in mind when he described a painting by Sargent he had seen in the 1882 Grosvenor Gallery as:

a pure gem, a small picture . . . representing a small group of Venetian girls of the lower class, sitting in gossip together one summer's day in the big, dim hall of a shabby old palazzo. The shutters let in a clink of light; the scagliola pavement gleams faintly in it; the whole place is bathed in a kind of transparent shade; the tone of the picture is dark and cool. . . . The figures are extraordinarily natural and vivid . . . [and] the whole thing free from that element of humbug which has ever attended most attempts to reproduce the Italian picturesque.[9]

The palazzo that forms the setting for this series was one of the once-beautiful palaces on the Grand Canal that by the 1880s were either inhabited by the poor or converted into glass works.[10] The long central hall, or *portego*, pictured in this group, ran the length of the palazzo, with windows on each end providing light.[11] The halls had stone floors and were sparsely furnished with a few stone benches or long wooden settees.

Unlike the coquettish and gaily dressed workers seen in other artists' Venetian genre scenes — for instance, Robert Blum's *Venetian Lace Makers* (Fig. 22) — the women in Sargent's painting are aloof and melancholy, bored by the tedious task of threading thousands of small beads for export. They appear detached, not only from the viewer, but also from each other.

The most austere and perhaps the most subtle rendering is the Albright-

23.
Venetian Bead Stringers, 1880–82
Oil on canvas, 26¾ × 30¾ (68 × 78.1)
Albright-Knox Art Gallery, Buffalo, New
York; Friends of the Albright Art Gallery
Fund, 1916

Knox painting *Venetian Bead Stringers* (Fig. 23). Three women — two sitting and one standing — occupy a nearly empty and steeply receding hall. Sargent positions the group of darkly clad women off center, but deftly balances them with the strong light coming through the center rear windows and doorway to the left. It is a carefully planned arrangement. The stepped white highlights in the painting lead one's eye from the upper left stair landing diagonally to the lower right corner and the creamy gown worn by the standing woman. The monochromatic tonality imparts a visual stillness to the work, broken only by the fluttering of the delicately colored fan sketchily rendered in a mixture of blue, purple, and pink. The black shawls silhouetted against light walls bring to mind the studies for the dancers in *El Jaleo* (Figs. 175, 222–225) that Sargent most likely made on a trip to Spain during the winter of 1879.

24.

A Venetian Interior, 1880–82

Oil on canvas, 19¹⁄₁₆ × 23¹⁵⁄₁₆ (48.4 × 60.8)

Sterling and Francine Clark Art Institute, Williamstown, Massachusetts

The Clark Art Institute's *A Venetian Interior* (Fig. 24), probably executed during Sargent's first trip, is smaller than *Venetian Bead Stringers* (Fig. 23), but contains a larger and more complex arrangement of figures.[12] The group is farther away from the land end of the *portego*, providing us with a longer view of the hallway to whose walls have been added a substantial number of dark rectangles representing pictures. The figures to the right, while smaller and more distant than those on the left, are accented with red clothing which captures our attention. Bead stringers are again at work, here more conspicuously so. The eye is especially drawn to the standing figure at the far right who holds up a luminous strand. Oblique sources of light, seen in the Albright-Knox version, are here as well, with a splash of light from the left doorway taking on a heavy impasto.

Of the three interior scenes, the Carnegie Institute's *Venetian Interior* (Fig. 25) is the largest, and, in many ways, the most felicitous. Sargent reportedly considered this among the best works of his career.[13] Although the painting

25.
Venetian Interior, 1880–82
Oil on canvas, 27 × 34 (68.6 × 86.4)
Museum of Art, Carnegie Institute,
Pittsburgh; Museum Purchase, 1920

contains the same number of figures as the Clark's *Interior*, the feeling here is less crowded and also lighter in atmosphere. Looking toward the Grand Canal side of the palazzo, the work has several different light sources. Sargent, in a virtuoso performance as a painter of light, indicates one source by a rich streak of yellowish impasto on the floor to the right of the woman strolling toward us. In addition, white light is reflected in freely painted brushstrokes on the dark settee and other furniture, on the picture frames lining the cool gray walls, and on the stone floor in front of the open doorway leading to the balcony.

The figures in the Carnegie's *Interior* are even less industrious than those in the other two scenes. One woman, freely rendered and very casual, leans back in her chair, engaged in some sort of manual craft (perhaps bead stringing). Two others sit with a young child, another gazes out onto the canal, and two stroll toward us. It is the black-shawled pair nearest us who are the most arresting; one woman's pink skirt and the other's pink fan command attention. Gigia Viani, one of the pair, confronts us with her gaze. Her graceful pose, one arm akimbo, is reminiscent of the Greek Tanagra figurines (fourth century B.C.) which inspired late nineteenth-century artists such as James McNeill Whistler.[14] Like the figurines, Sargent's attenuated models epitomize feminine elegance and rhythmic movement.

Sargent's debt to Whistler is evident when one compares the Carnegie's *Venetian Interior* to Whistler's nocturnal pastel, *Palace in Rags* (Fig. 28). We see the same *portego* of the same palazzo and the same set of windows leading to the balcony around which a group of people sit. Although it is tempting to think that the interiors depict the Palazzo Rezzonico, where both Whistler and Sargent had studios at different times, visitors to the Rezzonico agree that its proportions are grander than those depicted in Sargent's and Whistler's pictures.[15]

It is unclear when Sargent first met the famous Whistler, though the two seem likely to have met during Sargent's 1880 Venetian visit, if not before. By the time Sargent reached the city in September 1880, Whistler had been there a year and had taken a room at the Casa Jankowitz, attracting a group of other Americans, including a young etcher named Otto Bacher who, like Sargent, had been a pupil of Carolus-Duran in Paris. Whistler was extremely prolific in Venice, producing not only fifty etchings and a number of paintings, but between ninety and a hundred innovative pastels which he thought particularly good. They pleased the public as well; the pastels received high critical praise and sold well when exhibited in London in January 1881.[16] In any event, we know from Charteris that Sargent admired the older artist's work: "Sargent used to say that Whistler's use of paint was so exquisite that if a piece of canvas were cut out of one of his pictures one would find that it was in itself a thing of beauty. . . ."[17]

Whistler's effect on Sargent can be seen in subtle ways. Sargent's delicate panoramic view of c. 1882, *Venise par Temps Gris* (National Trust, England) calls to mind Whistler's *The Lagoon, Venice: Nocturne in Blue and Silver* (Fig. 27). At the same time, Whistler's small-scale etchings (Fig. 29) and pastels of obscure Venetian alleys and his monochromatic vignettes of contemporary Venetian domestic life influenced Sargent's figure paintings. Whistler's interest in working-class subjects, the sense of alienation and detachment in his Venetian work, and his prevalent use of apertures all have parallels in Sargent's Venetian paintings.

However, many of the characteristics that attracted Sargent to Whistler's work can be found, too, in the work of Velázquez, an artist profoundly admired not only by Sargent and Whistler but also by Sargent's teacher, Carolus-Duran, and many other late nineteenth-century French artists. Sargent traveled to Madrid in 1879 specifically to study the Spanish master, copying a number of Velázquez's paintings (including *Las Meninas* and *Las Hilanderas*). The experience seems to have affected him greatly. Following his Madrid trip, Sargent moved from painting portraiture in the French academic tradition (for instance, *Madame Edouard Pailleron*, Fig. 3), and adopted a more restrained, refined brushwork. As Richard Ormond has noted, Sargent's new technique relied on delicate, silvery color harmonies, effective use of blacks and grays, simplified settings and accessories, and a sense of evocative space.[18]

Sargent's debt to Velázquez was pointed out as early as 1882,[19] and the early Venetian scenes are manifestations of the aesthetics of the Spanish master. As Trevor Fairbrother noted, a painting like the Carnegie Institute's *Venetian Interior* (Fig. 25) emulates Velázquez in the placement of its figures and its use of light and shadow.[20] There are other references to Velázquez in this painting: to the dwarf in *Las Meninas* who, like the woman in the Carnegie's *Venetian Interior*, boldly confronts the viewer; and to such Velázquez portraits as *Philip IV* (Fig. 26) and *Pablo de Valladolid* (Museo del Prado, Madrid), which relate to Sargent's darkly clad figures in front of austere, light backgrounds.

A fourth interior scene — *Venetian Glass Workers* (Fig. 30) — may have been a product of either the 1880 or 1882 visit. It is a somber depiction of working conditions among the lower-class Venetians. Two men (the first we have seen in Sargent's interior genre paintings) and three women emerge ghostlike from the extremely dark background. But the glass workers are not the true subjects of the painting.[21] Light — vibrant, shimmering light — is Sargent's focus in this work. A window to the left and another, unseen window admit light to the workroom. Light reflects dramatically on white and pale blue glass. Sargent freely wielded his brush throughout the painting, especially on the thin glass bundles. In a technical *tour de force*, he rendered each bundle with just one brushstroke, the individual bristles of his brush creating separate rods. The virtuoso play of light is so startling that one almost overlooks the subtle color harmonies in the workers' clothing (such as the center figure's grape-colored dress and scarf of red and salmon).

The Bead Stringers of Venice (Fig. 31), set outdoors,[22] is similar to the Albright-Knox's *Venetian Bead Stringers* (Fig. 23) in its empty left foreground and group of uncommunicative figures to the right. Most of the asymmetrical composition is bathed in shadow, but a bright bolt of light slashes through the background near a group of summarily painted women. Sargent cut out the upper right section of the canvas, deleting the top portion of another woman who leans back in her chair (as in *The Sulphur Match*, Fig. 21). It has been suggested that Cecil Van Haanen's *Pearl Stringers of Paris* (exhibited at the Royal Academy in 1880) is the source for the uncut version of Sargent's painting of bead stringers. But as Margaretta Lovell has pointed out, the source is just as likely to have been Velázquez's *Las Hilanderas*, a portion of which Sargent copied during his 1879 visit to Madrid. The spirit of the painting is more akin to Velázquez than to Van Haanen, although both earlier paintings are more crowded and anecdotal than the Sargent.[23]

The palette in *The Bead Stringers of Venice* is markedly lighter and brighter than in many of Sargent's Venetian paintings. Orange, turquoise, and mustard create a more colorful work, one closer to the Venetian scenes by European artists such as Giacomo Favretto (1849–1887). Similar in its lighter palette is *Venetian Courtyard* (Fig. 34), a scene neither indoors nor outside, but set in the loggia of a palazzo. The predominant terracotta tonality is punctuated by lively splashes of

26.
Diego Velázquez, *Philip IV*, 1624
Oil on canvas, 78¾ × 40½ (200 × 102.9)
The Metropolitan Museum of Art, New York;
Bequest of Benjamin Altman, 1913

color: Gigia Viani's pink skirt and vermilion fan, the turquoise and red scarves worn by the women sewing at the rear, and the plant with red flowers on the balustrade.

A number of outdoor genre scenes, created by Sargent in Venice during the two visits, relate in formal and thematic terms to the Venetian interiors. These include *Venetian Street* (Fig. 32), *A Street in Venice* (Fig. 33), *Street in Venice* (Fig. 35), and *Venetian Water Carriers* (Fig. 36).

Venetian Water Carriers differs from the others in this group and from the majority of Sargent's Venetian scenes in that it does not depict deeply receding space.[24] The rear wall halts spatial recession at the sides and the open door reveals only an interior completely black save for a glimmer of light coming through the window blinds — a conceit reminiscent of Whistler's use of apertures in his Venetian work. Sargent has caught two women in mid-action as if captured by a photograph. In this fascinating study of asymmetrical balance, one woman leans over to lower her bucket into the well while another, her back turned to us, shifts her weight in order to balance the full copper pail she carries. The door hanging on its hinges at the right balances her figure straining to the left. The freely painted wall and pavement have touches of salmon and green, but the most colorful section of this largely monochromatic painting is the dark pink sash worn by the woman on the left.

The three other outdoor genre scenes depict men and women meeting and talking in the *calles*, the back streets of Venice which William Dean Howells called "the narrowest . . . and most inconsequent little streets in the world."[25] The setting for only one painting (Fig. 35) has been identified — the Calle Larga dei Proverbi (behind the church of SS. Apostoli off the Grand Canal). But the others may well have been painted in one of the numerous, similar looking *calles* in that area.[26]

Street in Venice (Fig. 35) depicts two bearded men in an alley as they pause to watch a young woman who clutches her shawl tightly around her as if to ward off their glances. The figures inhabit a mysterious world bathed in autumnal light and uneasy stillness and cloistered by cool stone buildings. Sargent keeps the architectural details to a minimum, as he did in the group of small-scale architectural scenes — studies of sunlight and shadow — painted on his visit to Tangier in early 1880.

The same male and female models and costumes are used again in *Venetian Street* (Fig. 32), which Sargent's cousin and fellow artist Ralph Curtis called "Flirtation Lugubre." The scene is a deeply receding space — even more contained than that in the National Gallery's *Street in Venice* — the street's narrowness emphasized by the vertical canvas. We focus on an enigmatic encounter in a *calle*. Strong light and dark contrasts are created by the figures juxtaposed against light walls and by the black aperture at top center between light curtains.

Venetian Street is arguably the most hauntingly beautiful of Sargent's intimate and romantic Venetian street scenes. Filled with reflected light, it has the

27.
James Abbott McNeill Whistler, *The Lagoon,
Venice: Nocturne in Blue and Silver*, 1879–80
Oil on canvas, 20 × 25¾ (50.8 × 65.4)
Museum of Fine Arts, Boston; Emily L.
Ainsley Fund

28.
James Abbott McNeill Whistler,
Palace in Rags, c. 1879–80
Pastel on paper, 11⅛ × 6⅞ (28.3 × 17.5)
Private collection

29.
James Abbott McNeill Whistler, *The
Beadstringers* (2nd Venice set), 1879–80
Etching, 9¼ × 5¹⁵⁄₁₆ (23.5 × 15.1) irregular
Isabella Stewart Gardner Museum, Boston

30.
Venetian Glass Workers, 1880 or 1882
Oil on canvas, 22 × 33 (55.9 × 83.8)
The Art Institute of Chicago; Mr. and Mrs.
Martin A. Ryerson Collection

luminosity of a pearl. Sargent's brushwork is painterly, yet thinly applied in many areas, giving us an indication of his working methods. Close study of the cloaked man suggests that the artist first created the architectural framework for the painting, probably working from nature, and then applied the figures on top of this backdrop. *A Street in Venice* (Fig. 37), while not a study for a specific painting, exemplifies the intriguingly empty architectural renderings Sargent occasionally made of Venice's obscure alleys, inhabited only by sunshine and shadow.

The Clark Art Institute's *A Street in Venice* (Fig. 33) gives an unusual tunnel-like view of a Venetian street. Inscribed "Venise," the painting depicts a man and woman meeting outside a wine cellar, indicated at its entrance by a leaf branch, wine bottle, and the names of the wines Cipro and Valpoli[cella]. The steeply receding *calle* is in shadow, while brightly lit buildings at the rear provide a strong contrast. Influenced perhaps by contemporary photographs and by the painter Giovanni Boldini, who also had a studio in the Palazzo Rezzonico in 1880, Sargent blurred the foreground and placed more sharply focused objects in the middle ground and distance;[27] as a result, the eye moves quickly toward the back of the painting. The lines of the exposed bricks to the left reinforce the strong perspective. Painterly brushwork and the salmon hues in the brickwork and in the woman's skirt enliven the otherwise monochromatic scene. The dimly lit, narrow space and figures dressed in ominous black lend a disturbing air to the scene, a

31.
The Bead Stringers of Venice, 1880 or 1882
Oil on canvas laid on board, $22\frac{1}{8} \times 32\frac{1}{4}$
(56.2 × 81.9)
The National Gallery of Ireland, Dublin

feeling increased by the woman's stare. Whether her gaze is hostile or a simple acknowledgment, her awareness of the observer makes this — and *Venetian Interior* (Fig. 25) — a different sort of genre painting from those of Sargent's contemporaries.

Sargent successfully captures Venetian life in these street scenes. But the men and women talking, flirting, and observing one another belong to the *demimonde*. The intimate encounters that Sargent depicts represent situations that would have been forbidden to Venice's upper-class women. "For her to walk alone with a young man would be vastly more scandalous [in Venice] than much worse things, and is, consequently, unheard of," William Dean Howells wrote in 1867.[28] Others have suggested that the women in Sargent's Venetian interiors, lounging in decaying palazzos, may be prostitutes.[29] In any event, Sargent's women clearly exist outside polite society.

The most sensually provocative of Sargent's Venetian paintings is *The Sulphur Match* (Fig. 21). It appears to be set in a tavern. The man and woman — whom we recognize as the models in various street scenes — sit directly before a cool stone wall and bench. Gigia Viani, in a bright red shawl, leans back coquettishly in her chair as her companion lights a cigarette. This exquisite painting ideally captures the drowsiness and dreamlike qualities that Americans of the late nineteenth century thought typically Venetian. Venice, said Howells, is a society in which people "seemed to have nothing to do, and . . . nobody seemed to be driven by any inward or outward impulse."[30] Nowhere is that spirit better illustrated than in the languor of Gigia's pose — her body propped indifferently against the wall, the casual clutter of an overturned wine bottle and a broken glass at her feet.

The largest oil to emerge from Sargent's Venetian period of the early 1880s is *Italian Girl with Fan* (Fig. 39). In this monumental painting (almost 8 feet high), Gigia — wearing the same cream dress as in *The Sulphur Match* — faces the viewer

32.
Venetian Street, 1880–82
Oil on canvas, 29 × 23¾ (73.7 × 60.3)
Collection of Rita and Daniel Fraad

33.
A Street in Venice, 1880–82
Oil on canvas, 27⁹⁄₁₆ × 20⅝ (70 × 52.4)
Sterling and Francine Clark Art Institute,
Williamstown, Massachusetts

34.
Venetian Courtyard, c. 1882
Oil on canvas, 27½ × 31¾ (69.9 × 80.6)
Collection of Mrs. John Hay Whitney

35.
Street in Venice, c. 1882
Oil on wood, 17¾ × 21¼ (45.1 × 54)
National Gallery of Art, Washington, D.C.;
Gift of the Avalon Foundation

36.
Venetian Water Carriers, c. 1882
Oil on canvas, 25⅜ × 27¾ (64.5 × 70.5)
Worcester Art Museum, Massachusetts

with a direct expression not unlike that in the Carnegie Institute's *Venetian Interior* (Fig. 25). Her large blue fan and burgundy shawl enliven the monochromatic background, which is pierced by the dark voids of a door and two pictures.[31]

The large size of *Italian Girl with Fan* suggests that Sargent intended to submit it to the Salon. As early as September 1880, he expressed concern about creating a Salon painting in Venice. As he wrote to Vernon Lee's mother from that city: "there may be only a few more weeks of pleasant season here and I must make the most of them. . . . I must do something for the Salon and have determined to stay as late as possible in Venice."[32] Writing to her again in mid-August 1882, Sargent felt "bound to stay another month or better two in this place so as not to return to Paris with empty hands."[33]

37.
A Street in Venice, c. 1882
Oil on canvas, 18 × 21½ (45.7 × 54.6)
Collection of the Ormond Family

Several of Sargent's large, full-length paintings depicting a single standing female had been well received at previous Salons (*Madame Edouard Pailleron*, Fig. 3, and *Fumée d'Ambre Gris*, Fig. 50, in 1880, *Madame Ramón Subercaseaux* [private collection], in 1881, and *Lady with the Rose [Charlotte Louise Burckhardt]*, Fig. 98, in 1882), and it is logical to think that Sargent intended this impressive life-size figure study to follow in that tradition. He did not, however, send *Italian Girl with Fan* to the 1883 Salon. Instead, he submitted *The Daughters of Edward D. Boit* (Fig. 48), begun on his return to Paris in the winter of 1882, and closely related to his Venetian work of the period. Its unconventional composition, use of oblique light sources, and the way in which the foreground figures are blurred while those in the middle ground are clearly focused — all these features bring to mind Sargent's early Venetian paintings. In its sense of mystery and the lack of communication among the young girls, it harks back to the interiors depicting bead stringers in a Venetian palazzo. The two Boit girls in the background shadow remind us of the men huddled in conversation in the National Gallery's *Street in Venice* (Fig. 35).

Sargent painted a number of informal portraits of friends while he lived in Venice during the early 1880s, including *Mrs. Charles Gifford Dyer* (Fig. 41) and *Mrs. Daniel Sargent Curtis* (Fig. 40), whose faces emerge from plain backgrounds and are brought to life with the bravura brushwork Sargent admired in the work of Frans Hals.[34] Sargent also created two outdoor scenes of shrouded women in a Venetian *campo*: *Campo Behind the Scuola di San Rocco, Venice* (Fig. 42) and *Sortie de l'Église* (whereabouts unknown), depicting the Campo San Canciano.

38.
Gigia Viani, 1880
Oil on canvas, 13½ × 10½ (34.3 × 26.7)
Harvard University Art Museums, Fogg Art
Museum, Cambridge, Massachusetts;
Bequest of Grenville L. Winthrop

In later trips to Venice, Sargent abandoned the dark *calles* and interiors that had first fascinated him and turned to sunlit architectural subjects in both oil (Figs. 157, 159) and watercolor (Figs. 182–187). However, the influence of his earlier Venetian period remained. *The Pavement* (Fig. 43), an unusual view of San Marco, brings to mind the dark, cool interior scenes of Sargent's early 1880s work. And it conveys the sense of space, stillness, and strong light-dark contrasts seen in such paintings as *Venetian Glass Workers* (Fig. 30).

Sargent's early 1880s paintings of Venice are subtle and somber, and his subject matter — itself different from that rendered by most American artists — is viewed with objectivity and detachment, with his own air of reserve reflected in the pictures' inhabitants. But should we compare Sargent with American artists during this period of his career? Henry James asked the same question in 1887, noting that Sargent was born and bred in Europe and that his art "might easily be mistaken for [that of] a Frenchman."[35] And a writer for *The Daily Graphic*, reviewing the 1888 National Academy of Design exhibition, groused: "Sargent is practically a French painter. He doesn't live here, nor come here if he can help it."[36] The one American with whose Venetian work Sargent's can be compared is Whistler, himself an expatriate artist trained in Europe.

While only a few nineteenth-century Americans (Whistler, Robert Blum, and Frank Duveneck) painted genre scenes in Venice, many European artists exhibited such work in London and Paris, among them, Cecil Van Haanen, Eugène de Blaas, William Logsdail, Henry Woods, and Luke Fildes. Their work, unlike Sargent's, was colorful, sometimes garish, and their sitters were fashionably dressed, but they did establish Venetian genre scenes as a highly popular subject.[37] Similarly, Giacomo Favretto, the leader of the nineteenth-century Italian genre school, was an acute observer of the Venetian people. His *Idillio* (c. 1880; Vercelli, Museo Civico Borgogna), depicting a man and woman talking in a *calle*, reminds us of Sargent's depictions of such couples. Yet another genre painter, Mariano Fortuny, a Barcelona artist popular in Paris in the 1860s and 1870s, also influenced Sargent's work. Fortuny showed Italian peasants posing against brightly lit walls — as in several of Sargent's Venetian works, including *Young Woman with Black Skirt* (Fig. 171).[38] Above all, one should not overlook the obvious influence on Sargent of Carolus-Duran. He encouraged his student to study Velázquez and taught him to paint directly from observation, *au premier coup*, which gives such scenes as *The Sulphur Match* an incredible sense of immediacy.

Nineteenth-century photography probably also influenced Sargent in terms of technique and subject matter. The foreground blurring that he employed in many of his Venetian scenes had the effect of focusing like a camera lens on a specific point, leaving the contours of other areas intentionally vague (see, for instance, the columns in *Venetian Courtyard*, Fig. 34). As for subject matter, Venice was one of the most photographed of nineteenth-century cities.[39] Everyone sought picturesque views of the city, and the numerous photographers who established

41.
Mrs. Charles Gifford Dyer, 1880
Oil on canvas, 24 × 17 (61 × 43.2)
The Art Institute of Chicago; Friends of
American Art Collections

40.
Mrs. Daniel Sargent Curtis, 1882
Oil on canvas, 28 × 21 (71.1 × 53.3)
Helen Foresman Spencer Museum of Art,
University of Kansas, Lawrence; Samuel H.
Kress Study Collection

studios in Venice (beginning in the early 1850s) obliged them with photographs made for export.

Carlo Naya (1816–1882), especially known for his genre scenes, photographed women at the *campo* well with their copper buckets, as well as a drab group of bead stringers in an alley, appearing weary and bored by their labors (Fig. 46). A photograph of c. 1884 from Brogi Studios (Fig. 45) also represents bead stringers outdoors in a shadowed narrow *calle* leading to a sunlit background façade, a composition seen frequently in Sargent's outdoor scenes. These are but a few examples of the thousands of monochromatic images produced in Venice in the mid- to late nineteenth century that popularized genre scenes of the Venetian working class.[40]

Although Sargent's representations of Venice differed from those of American artists, his perceptions of the city and its people were similar to those of American writers familiar with Venice. What fascinated Sargent and his literary counterparts was what they considered to be the indolence of the Venetian people and in particular the relationship between the sexes. In addition to William Dean Howells, other American writers were struck by the *dolce far niente* of Venetian life. Samuel Isham remarked on "the gentle lassitude of the loafers leaning against the wall draped in their dark cloaks," a sight depicted in such paintings as the

42.

Campo Behind the Scuola di San Rocco, Venice,
c. 1880–82

Oil on canvas, 26 × 25½ (66 × 64.8)

Private collection

National Gallery's *Street in Venice* (Fig. 35).[41] The loafers, in Leporello hats, ogled the "bewitching creatures . . . with restless butterfly fans, and restless, wicked eyes too, that flash and coax as they saunter along."[42] Howells recalled how "men of all ages and conditions" exercised "a rude license of glance" toward women. He reported that they stared at them as they approached, "and I have seen them turn and contemplate ladies as they passed them."[43] *Street in Venice* also documents this phenomenon, which Mark Twain considered a Venetian custom.[44]

While many American artists widely exhibited and successfully sold their Venetian work, Sargent's paintings were not at first as favorably received. Martin Brimmer, a Boston collector, saw what he called Sargent's "half-finished" pictures on a visit to the Curtis family in Venice in the fall of 1882:

They are very clever, but a good deal inspired by the desire of finding what no one else sought here — unpicturesque subjects, absence of color, absence of sunlight. It seems hardly worthwhile to travel so far for these.[45]

In addition to sending two Venetian interior scenes to the Grosvenor Gallery in May 1882 (see p. 50), Sargent submitted *Street in Venice*, two Venetian interiors, and *Sortie de l'Église* to the 1882 Exposition de la Société Internationale des Peintres

et Sculpteurs in Paris. A reviewer found the group "trite and unoriginal," and also expressed sentiments similar to Brimmer's, stating that Sargent

leads us into obscure squares and dark streets where only a single ray of light falls. The women of his Venice, with their messy hair and ragged clothes, are no descendents of Titian's beauties. Why go to Italy if it is only to gather impressions like these?[46]

The problem was, as one critic noted, that Sargent was not painting the "Venice of our dreams."[47]

However, opinions on the Venetian paintings were not universally unfavorable, as formerly believed. American reviewers, in fact, were generally positive about this aspect of Sargent's work. The paintings were praised by New York critics when they were first seen in the annual exhibition of the National Academy of Design in 1888. A writer for *Frank Leslie's Illustrated Newspaper* cited the Venetian scenes as an example of what the younger artists were accomplishing, while a *New York Herald* critic called *Street in Venice* (Fig. 35) and *Venetian Bead Stringers* (Fig. 23) "masterly."[48]

The New York Times writer agreed, stating that he would rather have one Venetian sketch than ten portraits like that of *Mrs. Charles Inches* (Sargent's other entry in the Academy annual [1887; private collection]). "Observe the difference when Mr. Sargent paints Venetian women of the middle class under his old inspiration — Velasquez and Spain," the critic wrote. "How delightfully he catches the slouchy picturesqueness of the Venetian girls! How well he paints the curves inside the inevitable shawl drawn closely round the figure!"[49]

Later critics were even more enthusiastic in their comments. Samuel Isham, writing in 1916, felt that while Venice's canals and monuments had been painted tens of thousands of times, Sargent's *Street in Venice* "*is* Venice as none of the other

44.

An Interior in Venice, 1899

Oil on canvas, 25 × 31 (63.5 × 78.7)

Royal Academy of Arts, London

representations are." He considered Sargent's monochromatic paintings to be infinitely more beautiful than "the customary blaze of orange and red," adding that while they did not depict intricate carving or Gothic arches, they "somehow give the grace and mystery of Venice as Ruskin's painfully elaborated drawings do not."[50] And Royal Cortissoz, admitting that Sargent's Venice was "a totally different world" from that rendered by other Americans, considered it "one of the most interesting that I know . . . the vivid record of a Venice that every one can see and touch."[51]

Sargent's Venetian paintings disappeared into private collections at first, only gradually making their way into public institutions. Although a Miss Chanler appears to have purchased *Street in Venice* after Sargent's 1880 exhibition at Boston's St. Botolph Club, and the renowned French actor Benoît-Constant Coquelin probably bought *Venetian Street*, the Venetian works at first rarely sold.[52] Many were given to friends or exchanged for goods and services. *Venetian Water Carriers* and *Venetian Glass Workers* were traded to the piano maker Friedrich

45.
Brogi Studios, *Calle dell'Angiolo a San Martino (Venezia)*, n.d.
Photograph

46.
Carlo Naya, *Bead-Worker*, n.d.
Photograph

Bechstein around 1886 for one of his instruments. The Clark Art Institute's *A Street in Venice* was given to J. Nicolopoulo, Greek minister to France, while its *Venetian Interior* was presented to Jean Cazin. Sargent gave Dublin's *The Bead Stringers of Venice* to Valentine Lawless, Lord Cloncurry, and presented Buffalo's *Venetian Bead Stringers* as a wedding gift to J. Carroll Beckwith in 1887.

Although Sargent's Venetian work was controversial, many now concur with William Howe Downes, the artist's early biographer:

When one contemplates such pictures as the "Street Scene in Venice," the "Venetian Bead Stringers," the "Venetian Water Carriers," and the "Venetian Glass Workers," some regret must be felt that so much of his time and energy were given to portrait painting. . . . [The Venetian scenes] have as distinct a cachet of their own as a Vermeer or a Chardin. In other words, they are in their kind of a perfection that leaves little to be desired. Slight, sketchy, almost casual these scenes seem at first glance, yet as they are examined they impress and charm us more and more, and in the end convince us that no painter succeeds better than he in attaining, through the unity of form and color, the very aspect of life itself.[53]

Sargent's best-known Venetian scene — typical of the portraiture that made him famous — may well be *An Interior in Venice* (Fig. 44), an elaborate and richly painted depiction of the Curtis family in their elegant Palazzo Barbaro.[54] Yet it is the austere figural paintings of 1880–82 that comprise some of the artist's most innovative work. These were his halcyon days, before he was perpetually hounded by potential sitters. For the young artist, acclaimed by critics, it was a fascinating time of exploration in the study of light and composition and of observation of the exotic Venetian working class. The paintings are neither typically Sargent in technique nor, insofar as artistic tradition is concerned, typically Venetian in subject, but their power and beauty are undeniable.

My research on Sargent's Venetian work of the early 1880s began in 1982 as an independent project at the National Gallery of Art, Washington, D.C., and I am grateful for the encouragement and support provided by my colleagues there. I also extend my gratitude to David Brewster and Milan Hughston for their generous assistance.

1. Donna Seldin, *Americans in Venice: 1879–1913*, exhibition catalogue (New York, Coe Kerr Gallery, Inc., 1983); and Margaretta M. Lovell, *Venice: The American View, 1860–1920*, exhibition catalogue (The Fine Arts Museums of San Francisco, 1984).

2. The chronology of Sargent's Venetian works is confused due to a lack of documentation and his repeated visits to the city. This difficulty, together with the belief that these works were almost an aberration for him, may have led writers to ignore them in favor of the fashionable portraiture for which the artist is best remembered. Most monographs on Sargent, including the latest by Carter Ratcliff, *John Singer Sargent* (New York, 1982), give short shrift to the Venetian work, although Richard Ormond's *John Singer Sargent: Paintings, Drawings, Watercolors* (New York, 1970), includes a discussion of the Venetian period (pp. 29–30). Charles Merrill Mount, "Carolus-Duran and the Development of Sargent," *The Art Quarterly*, 26 (Winter 1963), pp. 385–417, first isolated for discussion a number of Sargent's Venetian figure paintings.

3. We know that he visited the city briefly in 1870 and again in 1874, when he studied the works of Titian and Tintoretto; see Evan Charteris, *John Sargent* (New York, 1927), p. 18.

4. Emily Sargent to Vernon Lee (Violet Paget), September 22, 1880, The Miller Library, Colby College, Waterville, Maine; quoted in Ormond, *John Singer Sargent*, p. 95 n. 32. The Paris friend mentioned in the letter was Ramón Subercaseaux, Chilean consul to Paris, who was an amateur painter.

5. Donna Seldin, *Americans in Venice*, p. 17, gives the January date, while Stanley Olson, *John Singer Sargent: His Portrait* (New York, 1986), p. 95, states that

Sargent left at the end of February 1881. L. V. Fildes, in the memoir of his father, *Luke Fildes, R.A.: A Victorian Painter* (London, 1968), pp. 68–69, states that the elder Fildes arrived in Venice on January 10, 1881, and saw Sargent frequently during the next two months. If his recollection is accurate, this would place Sargent in Venice until as late as March 1881.

6. Margaretta M. Lovell, *Venice: The American View*, p. 95, believes that Sargent remained in Venice until the early weeks of 1883.

7. *Fumée d'Ambre Gris*, a monochromatic anthropological study of a North African woman painted during a trip to Tangier, was admired at the 1880 Paris Salon for its mystery. For a discussion of Sargent's attraction to the bizarre, see Vernon Lee, "J. S. S. *In Memoriam*," in Charteris, *John Sargent*, pp. 250–52. Sargent's interest in exotic subjects continued throughout his life, as in *Dolce Far Niente* (c. 1908–09; The Brooklyn Museum, New York) and *Javanese Dancer* (1889; collection of the Ormond Family).

8. Ormond, *John Singer Sargent*, p. 29, and David McKibbin to William Campbell, September 24, 1963, curatorial files, National Gallery of Art, Washington, D.C., identify the woman as Gigia Viani, Sargent's favorite Venetian model; they do not, however, provide evidence for this identification. Although the male model was once thought to be the American artist J. Frank Currier, this identification is most likely incorrect. Gigia apparently also posed for Sargent's cousin Ralph Curtis, and Curtis' Venetian paintings have sometimes been mistaken as Sargent's work.

9. Henry James, "John S. Sargent," *Harper's New Monthly Magazine*, 75 (October 1887), p. 689.

10. William Dean Howells, *Venetian Life* (1867; ed. Boston, 1894), p. 181. The glass industry was an important one to Venice at this time and figures not only in the three paintings in this group, but also in Sargent's *The Bead Stringers of Venice* (Fig. 31) and *Venetian Glass Workers* (Fig. 30).

11. Figs. 23 and 24 depict the view toward the land side of the palazzo, while the orientation of Fig. 25 is to the water side.

12. M. Knoedler & Co., New York, invoice to Robert Sterling Clark, October 21, 1913,

quotes a letter from the wife of the French Impressionist artist Jean Charles Cazin: "I remember the picture quite well. It was presented to me by Sargent about 1881–1882." Since Sargent did not return to Paris until late 1882 or early 1883 (see n. 6, above), the painting is most likely the product of the earlier trip. Cazin and Sargent admired each other's work. Cazin eventually sold the painting to the French actor Coquelin, who also owned *Venetian Street* (Fig. 32), and *Sortie de l'Église* (whereabouts unknown).

13. Sargent's opinion is cited in a letter from Walter L. Clark to Edward D. Balken, January 22, 1924, records of the Carnegie International, Archives of American Art, Smithsonian Institution, Washington, D.C.

14. Sargent also used this pose in *A Street in Venice* and *Venetian Courtyard* (Figs. 33, 34). Whistler, who collected Tanagra figurines, painted a work entitled *Tanagra* (c. 1869; Maier Museum of Art, Randolph-Macon Woman's College, Lynchburg, Virginia).

15. Memoranda in the files of the Sterling and Francine Clark Art Institute and the National Gallery of Art. Douglas Lewis of the National Gallery has suggested the early Renaissance Palazzo Corner-Spinelli as a likely candidate.

16. The Fine Art Society, "Venetian Pastels"; Whistler's *Palace in Rags* was no. 33.

17. Charteris, *John Sargent*, p. 21.

18. Ormond, *John Singer Sargent*, p. 27.

19. "The Salon: From an Englishman's Point of View," *The Art Journal*, 44 (July 1882), p. 219.

20. Trevor J. Fairbrother in Theodore E. Stebbens, Jr., Carol Troyen, and Trevor J. Fairbrother, *A New World: Masterpieces of American Painting 1760–1910*, exhibition catalogue (Museum of Fine Arts, Boston, 1983), p. 311.

21. The workers sort glass tubes and cut them into bead-size pieces which later go to the bead stringers. Lovell, *Venice: The American View*, pp. 102–04, discusses the importance of the glass industry in Venice, the alienating nature of this tedious labor, and the popularity of the glass works as a tourist attraction.

22. Otto Bacher, *With Whistler in Venice* (New York, 1909), pp. 97–98, reported that groups of bead stringers were seen daily in the *calles*, and Whistler drew them from life for his pastels and etchings.

23. Lovell, *Venice: The American View*, p. 102. Van Haanen was one of the many artists in Venice when Sargent was there during the winter of 1880–81. Mount, "Carolus-Duran and the Development of Sargent," p. 400, noted the connection between Van Haanen's painting and the Dublin painting (Fig. 31). Lovell observed that the worker in the foreground of *Las Hilanderas*, like Sargent's bead stringer, turns her back to us, and sunlight draws our attention to the figures in the background.

24. Because this flattening of space is seen in two works dated 1882 (*Italian Girl with Fan*, Fig. 39, and *The Sulphur Match*, Fig. 21), *Venetian Water Carriers* may also date from Sargent's later visit to Venice.

   Other artists depicted the daily morning ritual of the water carriers; see Frank Duveneck's *Water Carriers, Venice* (1884; National Museum of American Art, Smithsonian Institution, Washington, D.C.) and a group of monotypes by Maurice Prendergast, including *Venice* and *Venetian Well* (both from Prendergast's 1898–99 trip to Venice and now in the Daniel J. Terra Collection, Terra Museum of American Art, Chicago).

25. Howells, *Venetian Life*, p. 32.

26. The National Gallery painting (Fig. 35) looks toward Salizzada del Pistor. The street entering from the left, where a cluster of figures sit in conversation, is Calle Vincenzo Manzini. Proverbi is the neighborhood. X-rays reveal that underneath *Street in Venice* is a bust-length portrait of Gigia Viani.

27. Mount, "Carolus-Duran and the Development of Sargent," p. 399.

28. No girl could venture into the streets alone — even during daylight hours — without being insulted. Howells understood, then, why Venetian men go to the "pleasant women of the *demi-monde*, who only exact from them that they shall be natural and agreeable"; Howells, *Venetian Life*, pp. 362, 369.

29. Margaretta M. Lovell, "A Visitable Past: Views of Venice by American Artists, 1860–1915," Ph.D. dissertation (Yale University, New Haven, 1980), p. 115.

30. Howells, *Venetian Life*, p. 37.

31. David McKibbin's notes on this painting (photocopies in the curatorial files of the Cincinnati Art Museum) indicate that he wondered if the "fan" was not actually a bundle of glass materials. McKibbin also records that Ralph Latimer (a nephew of the Curtises) reported that Sargent left

Italian Girl with Fan unfinished at the Palazzo Barbaro, although he subsequently worked on it further. According to Latimer, Sargent commented, upon seeing the painting again at the palazzo in 1913, "I have never painted a better *head*."

32. John Singer Sargent to Mrs. Paget, September 27, 1880; quoted in Ormond, *John Singer Sargent*, p. 29.

33. John Singer Sargent to Mrs. Paget, August 16, 1882; quoted in Ormond, *John Singer Sargent*, p. 29.

34. Sargent studied Hals' work on a trip to Haarlem in the summer of 1880.

35. James, "John S. Sargent," p. 683. Until the late 1880s Sargent made only one brief visit to America, in 1876, in order to retain his citizenship.

36. "Painters and Pictures," *The Daily Graphic*, April 2, 1888, p. 242.

37. Anne Coffin Hanson, *Manet and the Modern Tradition* (New Haven and London, 1977), pp. 9–10, discusses the increased interest in genre painting in mid-nineteenth-century France. Large numbers of works at the Salon depicted peasants, gypsies, beggars, and fishermen — people of the lower class.

38. Favretto's *Idillio* is fig. 33 in *Venezia nell'ottocento: immagini e mito*, exhibition catalogue (Venice, Museo Correr, 1983), p. 197. Kathleen Foster, in a paper presented before the College Art Association in 1983, made the connection between the Sargent watercolor and Fortuny's figural work. The American collector William H. Stewart's collection of Fortuny was shown at the 1878 Paris Exposition Universelle.

39. Henry James, "Venice," *The Century Magazine*, 25 (November 1882), p. 3, asserted that, because it had been photographed so extensively, Venice was the easiest city in the world to visit without actually going there.

40. Italo Zannier, *Venice: The Naya Collection* (Venice, 1981) includes a good discussion of Carlo Naya and other photographers (his figs. 14–61) active in Venice during this period.

41. Samuel Isham, *The History of American Painting* (1916; ed. New York, 1927), p. 437.

42. Francis Hopkinson Smith, *Gondola Days* (Boston and New York, 1899), p. 30.

43. Howells, *Venetian Life*, p. 360.

44. Mark Twain, *The Innocents Abroad or The New Pilgrim's Progress* (1869; ed. New York and London, 1911), I, p. 237.

45. Martin Brimmer to Sarah Wyman Whitman, October 26, 1882, Martin Brimmer Papers, Archives of American Art, Smithsonian Institution, Washington, D.C.

46. Arthur Baignères, "Première exposition de la Société des Peintres et Sculpteurs," *Gazette des Beaux-Arts*, 26 (February 1883), p. 190; trans. in Ormond, *John Singer Sargent*, p. 29, and Ratcliff, *John Singer Sargent*, p. 73.

47. "An Exhibition of American Paintings," *The Art Amateur*, 27 (November 1892), p. 138. The critic, however, considered the painting on exhibition, the National Gallery's *Street in Venice*, an "excellent picture."

48. "The Academy Exhibition," *Frank Leslie's Illustrated Newspaper*, 66 (April 14, 1888), p. 131, and "Catholicity in Art," *New York Herald*, March 31, 1888, p. 4.

49. "Portraits at the Academy," *The New York Times*, April 8, 1888, p. 10. The Sargent portrait in the 1888 Academy annual was listed erroneously as *Mrs. Charles Vurches*.

50. Isham, *The History of American Painting*, p. 437.

51. Royal Cortissoz, *Personalities in Art* (New York and London, 1925), pp. 118–19.

52. A review of the St. Botolph Club exhibition illustrated *Street in Venice* and *Sortie de l'Église*; see Greta, "The Art Season in Boston," *The Art Amateur*, 19 (June 1888), p. 5. Charles Merrill Mount to William Campbell, July 17, 1962, curatorial files, National Gallery of Art, Washington, D.C., states that the National Gallery, Carnegie, and Albright-Knox paintings came to America in 1888 for the Boston exhibition. The Boston newspapers listed a few figure pieces of Spanish subjects (David McKibbin to William Campbell, August 20, 1971, curatorial files, National Gallery of Art). Several of the Venetian scenes have been mistaken over the years for Spanish works. *Venetian Courtyard* was known until recently as *Spanish Courtyard*; *Venetian Street* was auctioned in 1893 as *À Seville* and *Sortie de l'Église* was auctioned in 1909 as *Sortie de l'Église en Espagne*.

53. William Howe Downes, *John S. Sargent: His Life and Work* (Boston, 1925), pp. 30, 93.

54. Mrs. Curtis, reportedly offended by the informal pose of her son Ralph (at left), rejected this painting. However, Sargent was so fond of *An Interior in Venice* that he substituted it for his original diploma painting at the Royal Academy.

Sargent in Paris and London: A Portrait of the Artist as Dorian Gray

ALBERT BOIME

Following the volatile reception of *Madame X* (*Madame Pierre Gautreau*) at the Paris Salon of 1884 — "Detestable! Boring! Curious! Monstrous!" — Sargent did not exhibit the portrait again publicly until 1905.[1] That year the aristocratic Aesthete Robert de Montesquiou proclaimed it as Sargent's masterpiece, praising it as the high point of his career. Looking back to the period of the first reaction to the work, Montesquiou concluded that Sargent should have blithely ignored the commotion instead of shifting his base to London, where he sold out to the aristocracy and never again reached the same lofty level of achievement.[2] Montesquiou's evaluation of the work was confirmed by the painter himself, who wrote later in life that it was "the best thing" he had ever done.

This concurrence between Montesquiou and Sargent over the merits of *Madame X* is one of the most telling statements about the painter's early career and his dramatic shift from Paris to London. In the decade prior to the presentation of *Madame X*, he had been gradually defining his social role as an artist. His progress unfolded within the context of the *beau monde*, the realm of high society and fashion which began to close the gap with Bohemia in the last quarter of the nineteenth century. Montesquiou and Sargent embody this development: the former was a descendant of old French nobility who lived out his aesthetic fantasies among the Parisian nouveau riche and in the *demimonde*, and the latter was the son of expatriate Americans living out their fantasies in the make-believe world of a high society then besieged by the economic and social transformations of the period. Montesquiou, the so-called "Prince of Decadence," was well known in Paris for his eccentric and dandified existence.[3] He and his circle exerted a profound influence on Sargent and his art, especially during the early 1880s.

Sargent was not only involved with Montesquiou at this time, but both men also had close associations with Henry James and Oscar Wilde through a set of quotidian social connections among the English and French literati and Aesthetes, as well as American expatriates who hosted salons and dinner parties. At Sargent's request, for example, his friend James received Montesquiou, accompanied by Dr. Samuel Jean Pozzi, in London. "One," Sargent wrote to James in his letter of introduction, "is Dr. S. Pozzi, the man in the red gown (not always), a very

47.
Madame X (*Madame Pierre Gautreau*), 1884
Oil on canvas, 82⅛ × 43¼ (208.6 × 109.9)
The Metropolitan Museum of Art, New York;
A. H. Hearn Fund, 1916

brilliant creature, and the other is the unique extra-human Montesquiou . . . who was to Bourget . . . what Whistler is to Oscar Wilde."[4] In Paris during 1883–84, Sargent and Wilde frequented the salon of Henrietta Reubell, an elegant American expatriate; they also dined together, along with Paul Bourget. Bourget, a novelist and James' good friend, was fascinated with the theme of decadence and the super-refinement of the Aesthetes.[5] Sargent had in fact introduced Bourget to James, as well as to Vernon Lee.[6]

Sargent's letter to James also notes that he has given Montesquiou a card of introduction to Burne-Jones and the Comyns Carrs. Alice and J. Comyns Carr were prominent figures in London's bohemian circles. Carr was director of the Grosvenor Gallery, the showplace of artists affiliated with the Aesthetic Movement. This affiliation was often mediated through the friendship of these artists with Oscar Wilde. And Alice Comyns Carr's sister, Alma Strettell, was not only Sargent's friend, but also Montesquiou's, and she considered the Frenchman "very Pre-Raphaelite and precious."[7] The exotic, artificial taste of this group is best understood through the description of Montesquiou's apartment, as recorded by Sargent's friend, the artist and set designer Walford Graham Robertson (Fig. 69). Robertson recalled the extraordinary atmosphere of Montesquiou's rooms in the Quai d'Orsay:

the room of all shades of red, one wall deep crimson, the next rose colour, the third paler rose, and the last the faintest almond pink; the grey room where all was grey and for which he used to ransack Paris weekly to find grey flowers; the bedroom, where a black dragon was apparently waddling away with the bed on his back, carrying the pillow in a coil of his tail and peering out at the foot with glassy, rolling eyes. . . . "[8]

It should now be clear that the lives of Wilde, Montesquiou, James, and Sargent overlap, and I hope to show that they shared fundamental ideas about art. Sargent's key portraits of the 1880s and 1890s are often associated with anecdotes or remarks involving Wilde and Montesquiou, suggesting a common background of ideas. While Sargent and his friends Edmund Gosse and Henry James criticized Wilde's life-style, they were entranced by his personality. They all knew one another well enough to trade barbs, and Wilde occasionally sniped at what he considered the meretriciousness of Sargent's paintings and the tortured prose of James' novels. Yet Wilde's genuine affection for the young Sargent is demonstrated in his inscription to the painter in a collection of poems by James Rennell Rodd, *Rose Leaf and Apple Leaf*, published in 1882 with an introduction by Wilde. The dedication reads: "To my friend John S. Sargent, in deep admiration of his work." On the title page Wilde added, "rien n'est vrai, que le beau"; "nothing is true except the beautiful" — the watchword of the Aesthetes.[9]

The Aesthetes generally accepted the idea of art as an activity for asserting the personality and gaining mastery over experience. James and Wilde often echo one another's values and theoretical judgments. They believed that culture consists of the perpetual cultivation of the self, of eking out the artistic personality from life. Wilde believed that art should not imitate life but other art, and James claimed that it is "art that *makes* life, makes interest, makes importance. . . ."[10] While James insisted that the real and the actual were critical to the art experience, the actual had to be refined and intensified for the spectator. Both essentially cultivated artificiality and conscious style with the idea of creating their own unique selves. Their vocabulary, echoed by Sargent, resounds with terms like "exquisite," "intense," and they make liberal use of the term "creature" to describe their soul mates. Even James' initial impression of Sargent emphasizes the painter's refinement:

The only Franco-American product of importance here strikes me as young John Sargent the painter, who has high talent, a charming nature, artistic and personal, and is civilized to his finger-tips. He is perhaps spoilable — though I don't think he is spoiled. But I hope not, for I like him extremely; and the best of his work seems to me to have in it something exquisite.[11]

Oscar Wilde's *The Picture of Dorian Gray* (1891) is a clinical description of a dandy — of the kind of life-style both he and Montesquiou advocated. Indeed, Montesquiou had furnished the model for des Esseintes, the decadent protagonist of Joris-Karl Huysmans' novel *À rebours* (1884). Wilde drew heavily upon *À rebours* for *Dorian Gray*, which recounts the growth, education, and development of an exceptional youth whose attempt to make himself an aesthetic being carries him to the farthest reaches of excess. He throws himself into this effort under the influence of Lord Henry Wotton, an Anglified version of Montesquiou who profoundly attracts and corrupts Dorian. Neither Lord Henry nor Dorian wish to get too involved with people or things, but merely want to find them "exquisite." Meanwhile, the portrait of Dorian painted by the artist Basil Hallward traces in its features the corruption of Dorian — the real Dorian remains young and inviolate. The mysterious projection of his soul onto the canvas becomes a mocking mirror, and when in the end Dorian attempts to kill the portrait — his conscience — he kills himself. The picture painted by Hallward is then restored to its original likeness, while Dorian dies a withered and debauched human being. The portrait usurps life, while Dorian's life usurps the properties of the portrait.

The background and setting of the novel is drawn from the fashionable world of James and Sargent. It opens with a studio "filled with the rich odor of roses . . . the heavy scent of lilac."[12] A "Japanese effect" is created by the shadows of birds in flight on the silk curtains stretched in front of the huge window. Lord Henry tries to convince Basil to send the portrait to the Grosvenor Gallery rather than to the stuffy Royal Academy exhibition. Like Sargent, Dorian Gray plays the piano and performs at musical parties; Basil Hallward paints like Sargent, for we hear "the sweep and dash of the brush on the canvas." The "color scheme" underlying the story mood is lilac and purple — Sargent's favorites. Hallward is later invited to exhibit his portraits at the Galerie Georges Petit in Paris — where Sargent exhibited in 1884. The society in which Sargent moves is sharply exposed: Lord

48.

The Daughters of Edward D. Boit, 1882
Oil on canvas, 87 × 87 (221 × 221)
Museum of Fine Arts, Boston; Gift of Mary
Louisa Boit, Florence D. Boit, Jane Hubbard
Boit, and Julia Overing Boit, in memory of
their father

Henry and his uncle, Lord Fermor, discuss the "rather fashionable" tendency of English aristocrats to marry American heiresses. Lord Henry lives in the Mayfair district, the exclusive area of London where Sargent found his sitters and participated in the numerous receptions of the London "season," lasting from May to July. In addition, the novel abounds in allusions to Sargent and James' favorite authors, such as William Beckford, Théophile Gautier, Richard Wagner, Gustave Flaubert, Walter Pater, and Huysmans — all heroes of the Aesthetes.

Dorian Gray amuses himself with the study of perfume and the secrets of their manufacture, including ambergris, which stirs one's passions (see p. 84). On

another occasion he devotes himself entirely to music, organizing "curious" concerts in which mad gypsies tear wild music from little zithers, and "grave yellow-shawled Tunisians" pluck "at the strained strings of monstrous lutes. . . ." Several of these motifs echo themes in Sargent's paintings: the exotic *Fumée d'Ambre Gris* (Fig. 50), the theatrical *El Jaleo* (Fig. 14), with its steamy, drugged atmosphere, and *The Daughters of Edward D. Boit* (Fig. 48), with its mysterious shadows and decorative reduction of the dispersed sisters to the level of the blue and white Chinese vases — all take popular Salon subjects and give them a psychological twist that anticipates the hothouse world of *Dorian Gray*.

But it is especially in the concepts of art and in the treatment of the figure that Wilde evokes the personality of Sargent. The artist Hallward says that "Dorian Gray is to me simply a motive in art." He finds him in "the curves of certain lines, in the loveliness and subtleties of certain colors." His is the search for an abstract sense of beauty which is based on life but is neither biographical nor historical. Compare this to Sargent's remark about Mme. Gautreau to Vernon Lee in 1883: "she has the most beautiful lines, and if the lavender or chlorate of potash-lozenge colour be pretty in itself I should be more than pleased."[13]

Henry James' mature novels and stories about artists share an outlook similar to that in *Dorian Gray*. In James' novel *The Tragic Muse* (1890), as in *Dorian Gray*, a young actress — named "Vane" in both works — rivets the attention of the male characters and succeeds in developing herself into a brilliant performer by sheer dint of aesthetic commitment.[14] James' Gabriel Nash, analogous to, though less

50.
Fumée d'Ambre Gris, 1880
Oil on canvas, 54¾ × 37 (139.1 × 94)
Sterling and Francine Clark Art Institute,
Williamstown, Massachusetts

cynical than, Lord Henry Wotton, seeks to conform his life to an aesthetic ideal
and incarnates the point of view of the Aesthetes Walter Pater and Wilde. Nash
encourages both the actress and the artistic pretensions of Nick Dormer, who
waivers between a career in public life and one as a portraitist. Like Dorian Gray,
Nash's aestheticism is a protest against crass middle-class respectability and
philistinism. Under his influence, the actress transforms herself into a work of art,
"an exquisite harmony of line and motion and attitude and tone."[15] Still another
connection is Nick's offer to paint Nash, who feels uncomfortable in the role of
sitter. The painting is never completed; Nash eventually disappears from the
story and the unfinished portrait gradually fades from the canvas.

What makes the character of Gabriel Nash especially significant is his
uncanny resemblance to Sargent. During a stay in Sicily, Nash lives for many days
in a Saracenic tower "where his principal occupation was to watch for the flushing
of the west."[16] Charteris tells us that during a trip to Capri in 1878 Sargent
organized a fête on the flat roof of his hotel and stayed up all night with his friends
watching "the figures of the dancers silhouetted against the violet darkness of the
night . . . when the stars are giving place before the first orange splash of day."[17]

Indeed, by the late eighties and early nineties James was using Sargent as a character in several of his stories. "The Pupil" (1891) is based to a large extent on Sargent's youth; the child-hero grows up with neurotic expatriate parents who are anxious to appear in all the "good places," to be seen at official parties, and whose pretensions at being "people of fashion" have something of the pathetic about them. Like Sargent's parents, the willful mother and passive husband of the story inhabit a villa at Nice, have trouble paying their bills, and transmit the insecurity of their life-style to their precocious adolescent boy. "The Real Thing" (1892) concentrates on a portraitist who interviews an impoverished highborn couple as models for a series of illustrations on aristocratic society. But the presence of "the real thing" actually stifles the artist's creativity and he is forced to turn once again to vulgar professional models to stimulate his imagination.

These stories reflect James' deepened awareness of the fundamental aims of the Aesthetic Movement. He does not ask whether the work of art means something, but asserts its existence by virtue of the way in which the artist has transformed reality and infused it with his imaginative powers.[18]

This evolution of his conception of art was influenced by Sargent, who figures in so many of these later stories. Above all, in "The Real Thing" James intended to exemplify the futility in art of "amateurishness," the way "superficial, untrained, unprofessional effort goes to the wall when confronted with trained, competitive, intelligent, *qualified* art." Finally, the artist-narrator affirms the participation of James and Sargent in the Aesthetic Movement when he states that he possessed "an innate preference for the represented subject over the real one: the defect of the real one was so apt to be a lack of representation."[19]

Thus Sargent's influence on James in these pivotal years seems to have been related to their participation in the movement arising in France and England in opposition to extreme realism and naturalism. This opposition is even reflected in Sargent's Impressionism, which neither Monet nor Charteris found to be in accord with the French version. Indeed, Sargent's use of prismatic color in outdoor scenes always had an unnatural, artificial quality to it, particularly evident in such works as *Carnation, Lily, Lily, Rose* (Fig. 72), where the stifling environment and decorative quality have the look more of a William Morris wallpaper than of a Monet. Even the later *Paul Helleu Sketching with His Wife* (Fig. 89) makes use of the grassy carpet of bright colors as no more than a foil for elegantly painted figures, a decision which manifests a greater concern for style than for realism.

Sargent's preference for style over realism originated in his student days with Carolus-Duran and with the elite society to which the master belonged and for which he took on portrait commissions. Carolus-Duran was one of the most sought-after portraitists in France from the 1860s on, a time when having a portrait painted was a requirement of fashionable life. I believe that the vast ambitions the Sargents had for their son prompted them to move to Paris in May 1874 in order to ensure him the best instruction. They had carefully weighed their

L'ILLUSTRATION

JOURNAL UNIVERSEL

PRIX DU NUMÉRO: 75 CENTIMES   SAMEDI 17 JANVIER 1880   PRIX D'ABONNEMENT

51.
Engraving after Sargent's *Carolus-Duran*
L'Illustration, 75 (January 17, 1880), cover

plans and decided to enter him in the atelier of Carolus-Duran, whose reputation was known to them through their social contacts. They wanted Sargent to acquire the skills needed to make a living doing fashionable portraits — and thus move up the social and economic ladder.

It was not simply that Carolus-Duran's technique appealed to those dissatisfied with the typical academic grind (although Sargent also entered the École des Beaux-Arts in 1874), but that his ideas about art were infinitely marketable at the moment. Carolus-Duran's motto was: "Love glory more than money, art more than glory, nature more than art."[20] He made his career, however, by ignoring this formula. Despite his origins as a disciple of Courbet during the Second Empire, he threw in with the elite of the Third Republic who wanted an elegant image of themselves at the time they were recovering from the blows of the Franco-Prussian War and the Commune. In the 1870s there was an urgency to form fashionable social circles modeled after the English, which included a "season" of balls, dinner parties, country-house weekends, hunts, and regattas. This was not the exclusive society of the great landowning aristocrats, but one which made its peace with entrepreneurs and financial wizards, and which also took the world of Bohemia into its company.

The ideals of this elite were embodied in the magazine *L'Illustration*, a right-of-center periodical which subscribed to the new social hierarchy and supported scientific and industrial progress. It attacked Zola and the Impressionists in the 1870s (although it modified this position in the next decade) and reported weekly on the comings and goings of the elite in the sections entitled "Courrier de Paris" and "Bulletin du Sport et de High Life" — the use of the English term pointing to the model of inspiration for the new social alliances. A study of this journal during the time of Sargent's apprenticeship reveals that Carolus-Duran was its favored painter, his work constantly singled out and praised. His portraits were particularly lauded for their skill in translating the social state of the sitter. For example, a portrait shown at the 1879 Salon (*Madame la Comtesse V . . .*), which emphasizes outward appearances rather than emotional depths, was hailed by *L'Illustration*'s critic: "what dignity in the bearing of the Comtesse, what disdain in her attitude. . . . "[21]

Sargent's presentation of his portrait of *Carolus-Duran* (Fig. 4) at the same Salon could not have been better timed. Well aware of Carolus-Duran's popularity with the editorial board of *L'Illustration*, Sargent deliberately chose a subject he knew would appeal to the journal. That he succeeded is shown by the cover of the January 17, 1880 issue of *L'Illustration*, which reproduces the portrait (Fig. 51) — a rare honor accorded a foreign artist. The critic in the accompanying article considered it "one of the most popular portraits of the last Salon."[22]

The appeal of Sargent's portrait is in its studied air of nonchalance, which puts it somewhere between modernity and tradition. Carolus-Duran sits with knees spread apart, his upper body tilted to the left. His right elbow rests on his knee and his hand casually holds a metal-tipped cane. The dandified costume is

52.
Engraving after Sargent's *Edouard Pailleron*
L'Illustration, 80 (December 9, 1882), p. 377

highlighted by the flashing whiteness of lace cuffs, collar, and handkerchief. But the bent left arm is posed tautly and the left hand twisted outward against the thigh. Adding to this sense of tense control is the sitter's direct gaze and the conspicuous presence of the Legion of Honor award in his buttonhole. This dual reading of the portrait — informality and rigor, nonchalance and fastidiousness — is appropriate for the painter, who changed his name from the plain Charles-Émile-Auguste Durand to the latinized Carolus-Duran when he achieved prosperity and fame. His students recalled his eccentric clothing and love of shock value; it was not unusual to see him in a black velvet coat, an orange silk shirt with ruffles, a green tie, and ample gold jewelry. He cultivated an artificial self-image — from his name to his exotic furnishings — which won approval in his fashionable and influential social circle.

Among Carolus-Duran's friends was Edouard Pailleron, a prominent playwright and poet and one of those who commissioned a portrait from Sargent in the wake of his 1879 Salon success (Fig. 5). Sargent depicted Pailleron standing and looking out at the spectator, but the effect is strikingly close to that of the *Carolus-Duran*. Pailleron's costume is a picture of studied negligence: a string tie with tassels around the neck outlined against a bright red scarf; a loosely fitting silk shirt slips out beneath the dark jacket buttoned close to the top. Pailleron stands with his left hand on his hip, his right holding a pamphlet whose page he marks with his forefinger. His sensitive head is framed by carefully groomed hair and an elegant beard parted in the middle. This is a far cry from the stuffy, conventional portraits painted by leading French artists of the time such as Bonnat and Bouguereau. The Pailleron portrait — although not shown at the Salon — enjoyed as much publicity as the *Carolus-Duran*, and was reproduced on the cover of the December 9, 1882 issue of *L'Illustration* (Fig. 52).

The reproduction of Sargent's portrait coincided with the celebration of Pailleron's recent election to the Académie Française, an event predicted by the magazine the previous month. *L'Illustration*'s regard for Pailleron was analogous to that shown for Carolus-Duran; he was a darling of the journal and the focus of regular feature articles and comments. Pailleron represents one of the new breed of Parisians who commissioned young Sargent — a fashionable social leader who broke no new ground but who pushed to the limits the conventions of Parisian high society. He was especially known for his Monday evening dinners, at which he assembled his friends in an immense dining room decorated with Turkish textiles and Japanese panels "with fantastic faces."[23]

During the summer of 1879, Pailleron invited Sargent to his wife's estate at Ronjoux in Savoy to paint Mme. Pailleron and their two children. This was Sargent's first experience with the country-house institution that later became familiar to him in England. The Paillerons hosted writers and artists at their residence, and Sargent benefited from this contact. He posed Mme. Pailleron out-of-doors, facing the viewer, and lifting the flounce of her dress (Fig. 3). She is set against a bright, sunlit meadow and well below the horizon, where we glimpse an ancient stone balustrade opening up to the wooded area of the estate. She is thus identified with her property, which she had inherited two years before.

Sargent nevertheless deprives the portrait of its inherent naturalism, in part through decorative effect, but primarily through the black satin dress and the tenseness of posture he imposes in an ostensibly relaxed outdoor setting. Mme. Pailleron twists her left arm while holding up her flounce and supports this grip with her right hand, which crosses in front of her body. Only two fingers of the right hand actually sustain the left and there is a nervous tension in the quivering fingers. While she maintains her gaze, the struggle to support this pose is evident and yields a sense of discomfiture. All around her Sargent paints a pattern of flowering crocuses growing in the meadow. Mme. Pailleron too is treated as a kind of floral ensemble, from the whisked-in scarf and the bright red flower pinned on her left shoulder to the gauzy fabric of her black satin dress. Sargent has cleverly manipulated the folds of the flounce to flow into an undulating rhythm taken up by the right arm and accentuated by the see-through texture of the sleeve. Her auburn hair picks up the red from the corsage, transforming the picture into a decorative panel — an approach Sargent would amplify in his later *Carnation, Lily, Lily, Rose*.

Sargent's *Madame Pailleron* was exhibited together with the *Fumée d'Ambre Gris* (Fig. 50) at the Salon of 1880, and *L'Illustration* continued to give him publicity by reproducing the latter picture in its composite of the exhibition (Fig. 68). Sargent had painted *Fumée d'Ambre Gris* from a sketch he made during a trip to Morocco in the winter of 1879; in Tangier he was struck by the architecture and costumes of the indigenous people. The figure in *Fumée* stands under a Moorish arch in the private sanctuary of a courtyard, the embodiment of Sargent's fantasy of exotic, faraway lands and the women that inhabit them. In her own way, as a member of upper-class Moroccan society, she complements Mme. Pailleron, although she is even more stately and ritualized. She is most likely in the process of perfuming her garments and body in preparation for a social engagement. Henry James, whose plots are as nuanced and intricate as Sargent's pictorial themes, saw in this work something related to a religious rite:

I know not who this stately Mohammedan may be, nor in what mysterious domestic or religious rite she may be engaged; but in her muffled contemplation and her pearl-colored robes, under her plastered arcade, which shines in the Eastern light, she is beautiful and memorable.[24]

The "mysterious" ritual in which the woman is engaged is the inhaling of ambergris, a resinous substance originating in the intestines of the sperm whale and thrown out as debris on the shores of Africa, China, India, Ireland, and the Bahama Islands. It had an aroma analogous to musk, and was added to perfume oils, soap, and other toiletries. Taken internally — usually through inhalation — it supposedly acted as an aphrodisiac and exhilarant. Sargent's figure is clearly entrapping the fumes not only for the aroma of ambergris but for its quickening qualities: the tentlike shelter she creates ensures that she will inhale the fumes from the smoldering resin in the censer.

SOLEARES

Come home with me, sweetheart ;
And I will tell my mother
That our Lady of Grace thou art !

— 9 —

Sargent's fascination with this subject may at first glance seem comparable to the numerous Orientalist themes pervading the Salons of the 1880s. Similar works by Gérôme and Benjamin Constant proved popular in the late 1870s and early 1880s, in direct response to the growing imperialistic and colonializing objectives of the Third Republic. Sargent thus produced a work he knew would have an instant appeal. But at the same time, the subject testifies to the interest of his friends in sensual experiences and gratification. Both Montesquiou and Huysman's character des Esseintes surrounded themselves with exotic plants and perfumes whose odors they drank in deeply. Montesquiou also experimented with a variety of drugs in his thirst for new and complex sensations. It is no coincidence that the protagonists of *À rebours* and *Picture of Dorian Gray* both relish the intoxicating delights of ambergris. When James calls the picture "exquisite, a radiant effect of white upon white," he demonstrates a taste for these exotic fantasies. The woman is in fact a Muslim analogue to the canopied Spanish Madonnas that Sargent sketched during the same voyage, combining hieratical imagery, exotic ritual, and eroticism in what was to become commonplace fin-de-siècle symbolism (Fig. 53).

These connections again point to Sargent's involvement with the Aesthetes who began to play a major role in Parisian culture. One of them was Dr Samuel Jean Pozzi, whose remarkable portrait Sargent completed the following year (Fig. 55). Pozzi actually owned a watercolor study by Sargent related to *Fumée d'Ambre Gris* and entitled *Incensing the Veil* (c. 1880; Isabella Stewart Gardner Museum, Boston). Soon to become an internationally respected surgeon and gynecologist, Pozzi was already an established medical practitioner at the time Sargent executed his portrait.[25] Sargent had described him as "a very brilliant creature," and Montesquiou — no slouch himself — called Pozzi the "most seductive" personality he had ever encountered.[26] These remarks epitomize the ideal of the dandified,

54.
Charles Nadar, *Samuel Jean Pozzi*, n.d.
Photograph reproduced in M. Laignel-
Lavastine, ed., *Histoire générale de la médecine*
(Paris, 1936), III, p. 62

charismatic, and anti-philistine Aesthete of the period. The ideal corresponds to a fabricated self-image that a friend and colleague of Pozzi's had in mind when he said that "he sincerely loved art and science, being himself a kind of beautiful work of art."[27] This concept — the individual perceiving his body and his personality as a work of art — answers to the highest ideal of English and French Aestheticism.

Dr. Pozzi intentionally adopted an aesthetic stance both for his life-style and his professional activities. Striking in Sargent's portrait are Pozzi's delicate hands, which nervously tug at the collar of his robe and the drawstring. His long, tapering fingers — separated and individuated like those in the portrait of *Madame Pailleron* (Fig. 3) — seem consciously arranged. In the Pozzi portrait, however, the hands may also reflect the doctor's renowned gynecological methods: Pozzi emphasized the "immaculate purity" of the hands, especially for "operations performed in the interior of the vaginal or uterine cavities." He established his reputation with a practice known as "bi-manual exploration," in which the physician placed one hand on the belly of the patient and introduced "one or several fingers of the other hand into the vagina."[28]

Even the environment Pozzi inhabits — in the portrait and in real life — is artfully conceived, a closeted niche of velvety curtains and lush carpets, painted in reds, mauves and magentas. Pozzi himself wears a vibrant scarlet dressing gown and white lace accessories, including the ruffled collar and embroidered red and white slippers. The spellbinding effect of this red-on-red color scheme imparts to the contemplative Pozzi a majestic and preternatural presence akin to that of a mage or a Renaissance prince. It is a far cry from the official photograph of Pozzi taken around the same time (Fig. 54). Moreover, the red-on-red scheme, which unites figure and ground like the white-on-white of *Fumée d'Ambre Gris*, manifested the preoccupation of the Aesthetes not only with interior decor, but specifically with red interiors.[29]

The fact that Pozzi commissioned an American to paint his portrait attests to his cosmopolitanism as well as to the shared tastes and opinions of artist and patron. In addition to *Incensing the Veil*, Pozzi also owned an oil study by Sargent of Virginie Gautreau. The wife of a prominent Parisian banker, Gautreau was reputed to be Pozzi's mistress. And she was, of course, the subject of Sargent's *Madame X* (Fig. 47), which touched off the scandal that drastically altered the course of the artist's life. While this picture has been exhaustively discussed, I want to argue two main points that come within the ken of my discussion: the aestheticizing of the human being — an extension of the real-life process exemplified in the life-styles of Montesquiou and Pozzi — and the social implications of the controversy surrounding the reception of the picture. Both, I believe, are interrelated and help explain the wellsprings of the public outrage and negative reviews that greeted the work.

Despite the fact that Sargent and Mme. Gautreau fell out over the portrait and even earlier had displayed strained relations, the work is the result of their mutual collaboration. Both stood in similar relationship to French society: they

56.
Jean Alexandre Joseph Falguière, *Diana*,
after 1887 (plaster model, 1882)
Bronze, 18⅜ (46.7) high
Private collection

were American superstars who worshiped at the shrine of French culture. Mme. Gautreau was born Virginie Avegno in New Orleans to Anatole Placide Avegno, an attorney, and Marie Virginie de Ternant, descended from French nobility. Anatole Avegno, a major in the Thirteenth Louisiana Regiment of the Confederacy, died of a wound received at the Battle of Shiloh, and the mother, bitter over the Civil War's outcome, took her daughters, Virginie and Louise, to Paris. A large number of Southern aristocrats had moved to Paris and established themselves in a colony which, through relatives, had good connections with upper-class French circles.[30]

Virginie's mother functioned like a stage mother, managing the career of her daughter as a "professional beauty." This term was taken from a category of upper-class English society and designated a woman who served as a kind of ornament at balls and dinner parties connected with the social timetable known as the "season." Lillie Langtry functioned in this role for English society, approximating our idea of the Hollywood glamour queen. Yet the very term suggested middle-class origins, an acknowledgment on the part of the upper classes of the rising power of the bourgeoisie. The professional beauty gained a reputation for her sumptuous fashions and the wealth that supported them. Although the wife of a banker, Mme. Gautreau preserved in her person the special rank traditionally accorded to courtly women celebrated for their looks. The professional beauty, a person as skilled in her own way as an artist or actor, formed part of the new alignment of Bohemia and society that marked the social world of Paris and London in the last quarter of the nineteenth century.

Eagerly followed in the society columns of the day, Mme. Gautreau pushed the boundaries of the aristocratic social code to the limit. She deliberately accentuated her physical attributes with an array of exotic cosmetics: she covered her body with a lavender powder, dyed her hair with henna that gave it an auburn-mahogany color, tinted her ears rose, and traced her eyebrows with two heavy mahogany lines. She wore daring low-cut gowns, exposing her neck and shoulders and, except for diamonds in her hair, hated to wear jewelry because it detracted from her alabaster-looking skin. Virginie Gautreau molded and shaped herself into a painted object, a veritable work of art.[31]

Sargent perceived her this way: his letters outlining the plans for her portrait suggest an infatuation less with the person than with the "creature." When he asked a mutual friend to urge Mme. Gautreau to allow him to paint her, he said that he intended an "homage to her beauty," and that she should know him to be "a man of prodigious talent."[32] Sargent means here that he and Mme. Gautreau, with their exceptional skills, were clearly made for each other. Judging from his letter to Vernon Lee in February 1883, he obviously saw her in aesthetic terms: "Do you object to people who are 'fardées' [made up] to the extent of being a uniform lavender or blotting-paper colour all over? If so you would not care for my sitter; but she has the most beautiful lines and if the lavender or chlorate of potash-lozenge colour be pretty in itself I should be more than pleased."[33]

57.
Engraving after Charles Chaplin's *Portrait de Mme. La Comtesse de L.R.* L'Illustration, 73 (April 26, 1879), p. 265

Sargent's response to Mme. Gautreau, like his general response to people, was predicated on his reduction of her person to mere line and color.

The final painting abstracts these formal qualities from the sitter and transforms her into a highly stylized design. It is less a portrait of a particular person than a work that could be called "Portrait of a Great Beauty." Sargent treated her profile in cameo while at the same time fixing the silhouette of her figure in a nearly frontal view. As in his previous portraits, he gave a tense look to the body to ensure an exaggerated pictorial effect. This tension is conspicuous in the strained neck muscles and tendons which support the sharp profile, while the bizarre, twisting right arm that grasps the edge of the coffee table could only have been a source of cramps in real life. Mme. Gautreau's left hand holds a fan and simultaneously raises slightly the flounce of her gown, but the thumb and ring finger are doing no work, putting all the pressure on the two middle fingers. In short, Mme. Gautreau's portrait projects a profound sense of self-consciousness and strain. It is a prime example of the Aesthetic Movement's love of the exaggerated posture and transformation of the body into a decorative object.

Sargent deftly brushed Mme. Gautreau's diamond tiara into the shape of a crescent moon, the symbol of the antique goddess Diana. This was immediately picked up by the critics, one of whom recalled that when Mme. Gautreau made her remarkable debut in high society several years earlier, she had been compared to Diana by virtue of her "elegant litheness."[34] Diana, chaste and remote huntress, whose effigies in the Louvre showed her with bare shoulders, was a ubiquitous metaphor for the professional beauty of the Third Republic. While by the end of the century the Diana type was to take its place in the pantheon of *femmes fatales*, in this period it designated the elegant aristocratic woman of high fashion (Figs. 56, 57).[35] Indeed, so commonplace did this association become that Wilde, in *The Picture of Dorian Gray*, describes the entrance of the Duchess of Monmouth, "looking like Artemis in a tailor-made gown." Gautreau's tiara thus identifies her with this tradition, revealing her self-conscious attempt to emulate and even upstage the aristocracy.

The identification of the upper-class woman with the Diana motif parallels the anti-philistine attitudes of the Aesthetes and Symbolists: the *femme froide*, the sterile woman resplendent in her own useless beauty, echoes the male's haughty refusal to contaminate himself with mundane activities and pursuits. Her inaccessibility and objecthood are inseparable; worshiped as a goddess, she maintains herself as a kind of des Esseintes whose whole life is centered on the rare, the outlandish, and the artificial.

This goes right to the heart of the well-known statement on *Madame X* by Louis de Fourcaud in the conservative *Gazette des Beaux-Arts*.[36] De Fourcaud's disquisition has been rightfully singled out for its rare perception of Sargent's portrait, but what has not been emphasized enough are his reasons for praising the work. He began the portrait section of his review by observing that the Salon's offerings in this category demonstrate that "the principle of egalitarianism, the growing ease of communications, the development of industry and commerce, the immense speculation which results from these factors, have multiplied the number of *parvenus*." The *parvenu*, he continues, is someone who wishes to accommodate himself to the flow of life from one day to the next, to the "refinement of pleasures," who has engendered a new type of person that may be defined as "*l'homme du monde*" — the man of the world. This type is neither the great feudal lord of yesteryear nor even the traditional commoner; but "a newly rich man of affairs, roughed out on the wing, slicked up in a jiffy, to become suddenly, not a nobleman, but — as we say at present — a *gentleman*" (English in original). The gentleman makes an instant display of his riches and his hastily assimilated culture, quickly building and furnishing his townhouse and organizing a salon, setting up a private drawing room and a storehouse of curios.[37] When he commissions a portrait of himself he wishes to see himself projected with an aura of profundity, canniness, happiness, and especially wealth. The task of the portraitist is to paint this aura, and at the same time somehow retain the individuality of the sitter.

When it comes to painting the women of this class, de Fourcaud went on, the difficulty for the portraitist increases. Wives of millionaire industrialists, well-heeled notaries, fashionable physicians, nabob ambassadors, and *arriviste* painters, the actress creating a storm, and the *demimondaine* in the limelight, all adorn themselves with similar gowns, diamonds, laces and frills — all made by the same firms and following the latest fashion. The attempt to recover "the natural" under the artificial trappings, to bring out the authentic personality from beneath the various disguises, would drive anyone crazy. Few portraitists measure up to the task, and in an effort to find a way of pleasing clients most of them wind up adopting a formula.

De Fourcaud concluded, however, that the thrust toward realism and the analysis of everyday life has nevertheless created possibilities for achieving a breakthrough in the art of portraiture. The current tendency to depict sitters in their actual domestic or professional milieu predisposes them to behave much more naturally and convey to the painter their authentic personality. Even the ambience itself has a physiognomy which complements that of the model. Those artists who paint sitters in their quotidian spaces, with all the attributes of class, taste and life-style, can succeed to the level of the great portraitists of former ages who characterized for perpetuity the types and mores of their period.

Judging the portraits in the Salon of 1884 by this criterion, de Fourcaud predictably found that there were a scant fourteen which fit the model he described. Not surprisingly, the focus of de Fourcaud's discussion was Sargent's full-length portrait. The critic chose to disregard the violent epithets hurled at the work, and allowed himself to be blown away by its "curious intentions and bizarre refinements." While normally he did not harbor a taste for complications, in this instance the complex nature of Sargent's treatment was appropriate to the subject. He was referring to

*the physiology of the Parisian woman of foreign extraction, elevated from childhood to be an idol
and to be constantly discussed in the fashionable journals with the title of beauty queen or, as the
English put it, the* professional beauty. *Know that in a person of this type everything relates
to the cult of self and the increasing concern to captivate those around her. She ends by being
more than a woman: she becomes a sort of canon of worldly beauty. Her sole purpose in life is to
demonstrate her skills in contriving incredible outfits which shape her and exhibit her and which she
can carry off with bravado and even a touch of innocence, like Diana sporting her loose tunic. . . .
Her character of plastic idol, almost superhuman, soon despoils herself of the inconvenience of all
her eccentricities.*

In this astonishing statement de Fourcaud provides an insight into the psychology
of an aristocratic observer trying to make sense of the impact of economic and
social transformations on Salon art. His singular preference for portraiture not only
testifies to his "refined" artistic taste, but declares his conservative social position.
He admires Sargent for clinically and ruthlessly dissecting the types of *parvenus*
that now threaten his own social position. By supporting realism and
Impressionism, de Fourcaud became somewhat of an anomaly, but he admired
these styles out of a perverted predilection for images that offered a picture of the
decline of French society, that mirrored the anxieties caused by the onrush of
modernity and capitalism.

 Madame X symbolically points to the ascendance of the new economic elite,
through the extraordinary display of purchasing power in the form of high fashion.
She is the emblem of "conspicuous consumption." De Fourcaud adores Sargent for
his capacity to seize the emblematic expression of the idol and its social role. He
grasped Sargent's "purity of lines," which transformed the portrait into a kind of
life-size cameo. He acutely described the tortured and strained position of arms
and head and their purposeful assimilation to the exigencies of the design.
Ultimately, Gautreau was a "figure disposed by a heraldist" on a coat of arms. For
this reason de Fourcaud led off his review with an inset of Mme. Gautreau's profile,
reproduced after Sargent's sketch (Fig. 58); it served both as the leitmotif of his
essay and as an indication of the heraldic character of the portrait.

 De Fourcaud, however, erred when he claimed that Sargent was unaware of
the full range of the social implications of his approach. Despite the strain in their
partnership, Sargent and Mme. Gautreau clearly shared a similar concept about
the final work. Sargent felt confident enough to try for a *succès de scandal* —
motivated by his admiration for Manet's *Olympia*, which he had viewed at the
French painter's posthumous exhibition in 1884 — and had even moved to a more
fashionably located studio in anticipation of a growing clientele. Gautreau, on her
part, recognized the opportunity to display her own originality and to outshine
her rivals. The painting is a testament to a compact between two cocky Americans
to thumb their noses at envious foreign hosts. The fact that Gautreau turns her
head away from the viewer — in violation of the standard Salon portrait type for
fashionable women (Fig. 57) — reinforces the arrogance of her body language. The
startling innovation of the pose had to have been arranged between them.

Study for *Madame X*
Reproduced in Louis de Fourcaud, "Le Salon de 1884," *Gazette des Beaux-Arts*, 29 (June 1884), p. 465

LE SALON DE 1884[1]

(DEUXIÈME ARTICLE)

VI.

LE trait distinctif de la nouvelle école française, c'est, incontestablement, l'amour de la vie réelle, de la vie familière, de la vie vivante. Nos artistes cherchent à rendre ce qu'ils voient. Celui-ci nous donne un coin de boulevard, celui-là un chantier de construction, ce troisième un intérieur de brasserie, ce quatrième une soirée dans le monde, ces autres une gare de chemin de fer, un conciliabule de gamins auprès d'une barrière, la parade des lutteurs à la fête de Neuilly, des porteurs de viande, des hommes de métier... que sais-je? Il n'y a plus de petits sujets, il n'y a que des sujets vrais ou des sujets conventionnels et des œuvres plus ou moins expressives. On me dira qu'il ne se produit pas plus de tableaux de marque que par le passé : j'en demeure d'accord, mais cela ne prouve rien contre la tendance moderne et le goût de l'humble vérité qui nous ramène, par-dessus les complications quintessenciées de la Renaissance, au pur principe de bonhomie de l'art du moyen âge.

Trois grands signes caractérisent, à mon jugement, la production moderne : le nombre toujours croissant des scènes populaires, l'importance de plus en plus grande du portrait, et le rôle de plus en plus

1. Voir *Gazette des Beaux-Arts*, t. XXIX, 2e période, p. 377.
XXIX. — 2e PÉRIODE.   59

Unfortunately, their gesture was ill-timed. For several years after the Franco-Prussian War and the Commune, which ended French hegemony on the Continent, the younger generation indulged itself in a kind of effervescent cosmopolitanism. As we have seen, there was a greater openness on the part of the French elite to sample foreign culture. Weary of the idea of a monopoly on artistic, literary, or musical excellence, they took the broad view that their country formed but one component in the European cultural complex. This was abetted by the exciting prospects of developing technology and, consequently, a greater disposition to take seriously any novelty, however bizarre in appearance and origin. The growing use of anglicized or outright English terms is an important index to this new receptivity. The influx of prosperous North and South Americans and Russians also contributed to the cosmopolitan atmosphere of the period. The impact of the Russian novel, Wagnerian music (although rejected in the wave of Germanophobia immediately following the war), American invention, and the English Aesthetic Movement all attested to a readiness to accept foreign innovations. The spectacular success of Gautreau and Sargent in their respective spheres during the 1870s and early 1880s would not have been possible without this cultural climate.

But in 1882 the crash of the Union Générale bank touched off a long depression that compromised this cultural openness. Latent hostility aroused by English and North American economic power, agricultural competition, and colonial rivalries had already introduced a note of xenophobia into the French community and this flared up dramatically after 1882. And it was directed to a new kind of American, one no longer dismissed as crude and uncultivated, but one recognized as culturally sophisticated.[38]

The critic Perdican couched his alarm over Yankee economic prowess in cultural terms, and in this context neither Sargent nor Gautreau were spared.[39] In June 1881, he began his usual diatribe about American aggressiveness, this time by noting the victory of the American thoroughbred Foxhall in Sunday's races. He then used this example to demonstrate the American takeover of French life: "They have painters who grab all our medals like M. Sargent, gorgeous women who eclipse our own like Mme. Gauthereau [*sic*] — and horses who defeat our *steeds* as Foxhall did . . . last Sunday!"[40]

Here we get a sense of the smoldering tensions in Franco-American relations which erupted into outrage when Sargent and Gautreau flaunted their talents in the portrait of *Madame X*. Sargent's bold and daring experiment and the arrogant demeanor of Gautreau proved too much for the French public by 1884. Just as the gossip columnists concealed their concern with American economic hegemony within a cultural context, so the art critics articulated their irritation and resentment in the adjectives and epithets overheard by de Fourcaud.

Once we agree on the social and political implications of Sargent's work, the public's response to its sexuality assumes a deeper significance. Gautreau's sexual power worked its magic in direct proportion to the political power wielded by her class, which now dominated the worldwide economy. Thus for the aristocratic Decadents and their acolytes she also represented the *femme fatale* of colossal deeds and depravity, the cruel and aloof Diana whom men approached with mingled fear, disgust, and desire. It was the ascendancy of the middle class to power that produced this monstrous female offshoot who now symbolized the degeneracy of "mankind."

That Sargent himself shared these misogynist feelings is evident from Paul Bourget's interpretation of the portrait of *Isabella Stewart Gardner*, painted in 1888 (Fig. 59). An eccentric yet dominant force in Boston society, Gardner wanted a portrait of herself as sensational as that of Mme. Gautreau.[41] Sargent now carried the idea of the female idol to its extreme, making his sitter face full front, her hands clasped together. This presentation of Mrs. Gardner recalls the frontally oriented female figure in Piero della Francesca's *Death of Adam* fresco at Arezzo. Sargent placed Mrs. Gardner so that a red and black brocade tapestry behind her formed an irregular circle just behind her head like an aureole. She wears a stunning close-fitting black dress with a plunging neckline, and two strands of pearls around her

59.
Isabella Stewart Gardner, 1888
Oil on canvas, 74¾ × 31½ (189.9 × 80)
Isabella Stewart Gardner Museum, Boston

waist echo the curve of her arms and repeat those of the aureole-like circle. To accentuate the line of her figure, the painter tied a black shawl tightly around her hips, letting the ends hang down in front. Typically, he manipulated the human body to make it conform to a stylistic hybrid.

The bizarre quality of this portrait had an instant appeal to the French Decadents whom Sargent knew intimately in the early 1880s. A striking passage in Bourget's *Outre-mer (Notes sur l'Amérique)* (1895), a book about America that he published after a journey around the country, articulates male fears of the "new woman." Having praised Sargent as one of the great artists of the epoch, he proceeded to analyze the portrait of what he calls the "*Idole Américaine*":

Rubies, like drops of blood, sparkle on her shoes. . . . The head, intellectual and daring, with a countenance as of one who had understood everything, has for a sort of aureole, the vaguely gilded design of one of those Renaissance stuffs. The rounded arms . . . are joined by the clasped hands — firm hands . . . which might guide four horses with the precision of an English coachman. It is the picture of an energy, at once delicate and invincible, momentarily in repose, and there is something of the Byzantine Madonna in that face, with its wide-open eyes. Yes, this woman is an idol, for whose service man labors, whom he has decked with the jewels of a queen, behind each of whose whims lie days and days spent in the ardent battle of Wall Street. Frenzy of speculation in land, cities undertaken and constructed by strokes of millions of dollars, trains launched at full speed over bridges built on a Babel-like sweep of arch, the creaking of cable cars, the quivering of electric cars, sliding along their wires with a crackle and a spark, the dizzy ascent of elevators in buildings twenty stories high . . . these are what have made possible this woman, this living orchid, unexpected masterpiece of this civilization.

And Bourget concludes with the sacred ideal of the Aesthetes and Decadents: "She is like a living *objet d'art.*"[42]

It is in this context, the woman as a dehumanized object of dread, that one can understand Sargent's *Astarte* (Fig. 60) for the Boston Public Library — his own version of the *femme fatale*. Like Wilde in *Salomé*, Sargent was inspired by Flaubert's *Salammbô* and *Hérodiade*. Vernon Lee, who alone among Sargent's close friends always emphasized his taste for the "strange, weird, fantastic," characterized it with the prose of the Decadents:

She is, so to speak, the main smoke wreath of unseen fires, and the strange winged creatures surrounding her as in a cocoon, whirling in slow crab movements are the inner smoke spirals; they form wings to her head and wings to her garment, vague whirling night creatures swathed chrysalislike in her blue veil — "a mystic opium vision" — the night, muffled, expectant, so lurid and yet so vague, full of possible dangers.[43]

Lee's nightmarish description points to a Sargent liberated from his sitter's demands and allowing his fantasies to run their course. Here he freely indulged in the psychological material only hinted at in the remarkable portraits of the early 1880s.

60.

Pagan Deities: Astarte and Neith, 1895–1916
Oil on canvas
North ceiling, Boston Public Library

After the scandal of *Madame X*, Sargent's days in Paris were numbered. He and Gautreau had pressed their advantages and talents too far at the wrong time and had violated the code of French social decorum. They had been tolerated for their ability to bring something new to the fashionable set, but they had failed to maintain the rules of etiquette that preserved the dignity and sense of upper-class solidarity. By having gone to excess in showcasing their singularities, they no longer acted the part of talented foreigners laying their all on the altar of French culture. It cannot be a coincidence that Sargent's Parisian social circle dropped him entirely after the scandal.

Montesquiou, moreover, castigated Sargent for his abrupt withdrawal from Paris culture and his sell-out to English aristocracy. But while there is much truth in Montesquiou's assessment, Sargent did not wholly forget the ideas and techniques he learned in Paris when he turned to painting the English upper classes. There was even initial resistance in England to his methods. His ability to survive the English bias against French influence depended on an acceptance of his psychological eccentricities. He learned how to control his gifts and tendencies to conform to the demands of high society, giving his portraits the novelty they required but never venturing out again beyond the social code.

Sargent's entry into English high society had been facilitated by Henry James and James' friend Margaret Stuyvesant White (née Rutherfurd), the wife of Henry White, recently attached to the U.S. Embassy in London. "Daisy" White had commissioned her portrait from Sargent in the spring of 1883, and it was exhibited the following year in London. She was a highly intelligent and attractive woman, admired by society hostesses, and proved instrumental in mediating Sargent's entrance into London high society. The Whites hosted such Aesthetes as Oscar Wilde and Herbert Beerbohm Tree, and participated in the group later known as the Souls — a clique of high-powered men and women influenced by Walter Pater and Aestheticism.[44] In addition to the Whites, the Souls included many individuals later painted by Sargent — among them, George Nathaniel Curzon (later Viceroy and Governor-General of India), Margot Tennant, Lord and Lady Elcho, Alfred Balfour, Lady Aline Sassoon, and Lord Ribblesdale. Another member of the group, Evan Charteris, son of Lord Elcho, became Sargent's first authoritative biographer.

The Souls formed an elite association within the larger body of some 4,000 British families that made up London "society" in the late nineteenth century, families that were united in their social and political ambitions, and whose interests and connections were national and imperial in scope.[45] Half of the group had parents who had been MPs for some period, and several had court positions or were career diplomats. The five families of Charteris, Wyndham, Tennant, Balfour, and Lyttleton supplied eleven members of the group. They celebrated the works of Burne-Jones and William Morris and supported the Aesthetic Movement. Their socially mixed clique corresponded to the fragmentation of the London upper crust as it expanded to incorporate wealthy industrialists and merchants. In 1884, the Reform Act extended the franchise to working-class people, which made the upper classes more afraid of the proletariat than of the middle classes — with whom they formed an alliance in response to the perceived threat.[46]

The aristocrats took in as well artists, actors, and writers. Artists and writers such as Sargent, James, and Gosse, professional beauties like Lillie Langtry, and actresses like Ellen Terry were people of no family, but they had claims to recognition through their specialized and professional skills, or through their distinctive beauty, wit, culture, and even sheer entertainment value. Although the highest social circles had always had their bohemian fringe, by the 1880s commentators could observe that society had become so overgrown and socially integrated that it was no longer possible to distinguish between entertainers and aristos.[47] With this expansion and fragmentation came vulgarization and the worship of mere wealth, reflected in the Prince of Wales' associations with self-made types and actresses. In a more general sense, material success became one sure sign of security — hence the swift popularization of a fashion or a style: it was necessary to keep coming up with something new and even outrageous to prove such success.

61.

The Misses Vickers, 1884
Oil on canvas, 54 × 72 (137.2 × 182.9)
Sheffield City Art Galleries, England

But before Sargent could enter this privileged domain, he had to establish his credentials as the right sort of person, especially in the wake of the Paris scandal. It is fascinating to observe the extent to which London critics concerned themselves with the way he depicted the social rank of the sitters. The reviewer for *The Athenaeum* attacked the "ungracefulness" of his portrait of *Mrs. Thomas Wodehouse Legh* (private collection) at the Grosvenor Gallery in 1884, and his sad neglect of "taste" in rendering *Mrs. Henry White* (Fig. 64) at the Royal Academy the following month. The next year, the same reviewer faulted *The Misses Vickers* (Fig. 61), then showing at the Paris Salon, as an insult "to their evident high culture and intelligence." Sargent's *Edith, Lady Playfair* (Fig. 65), exhibited at the Royal Academy in June 1885, was seen as "almost vulgar in its demonstrativeness." In 1886, the portrait of *Mrs. Robert Harrison* (private collection) was deemed a "decidedly unpleasant . . . household companion, and, for the owner's sake, we hope unjust to the lady."[48]

Sargent had to confront and overcome a suspicious English art establishment not quite ready to accept his French techniques and mannerisms, which lacked the

62.

A Dinner Table at Night (Mr. and Mrs. Albert
Vickers), 1884

Oil on canvas, 20¼ × 26¼ (51.4 × 66.7)

The Fine Arts Museums of San Francisco; Gift
of the Atholl McBean Foundation

63.

Fête Familiale: The Birthday Party (The Albert
Besnard Family), 1885

Oil on canvas, 24 × 29 (61 × 73.7)

The Minneapolis Institute of Arts; The Ethel
Morrison and John R. Van Derlip Funds

64.
Mrs. Henry White, 1883
Oil on canvas, 87 × 55 (221 × 139.7)
Corcoran Gallery of Art, Washington, D.C.;
Gift of John Campbell White

65.
Edith, Lady Playfair, 1884
Oil on canvas, 59 × 38 (149.9 × 96.5)
Museum of Fine Arts, Boston; Gift of Edith
Russell, Lady Playfair

grace of high fashion portraits. The turning point was the popular reception of *Carnation, Lily, Lily, Rose* (Fig. 72), purchased by the Council of the Royal Academy with the Chantrey Fund. This gesture was deplored by the conservative critic of *The Athenaeum*, but met with critical approval almost everywhere else. Ironically, the work attests to Sargent's profound awareness of the Aesthetic Movement. What is most striking about this outdoor scene is its wholly unalloyed decorative effect; the lily and rose blossoms are dispersed like wallpaper patterns and, while the two children are naturalistically portrayed, they are absorbed into the general play of floral blossoms, Japanese lanterns, and the suffused twilight glow of mauve and lilac. The marked presence of the lily manifests the passion of the Aesthetes for this flower, which they promoted as an outstanding example of natural design.

The artificiality of the composition is amply documented: not only were the flowers and the lanterns arranged daily for the effect, but so were the children. The first model Sargent used had dark hair, so he supplied her with a blond wig. His fascination for hair, which bordered on the fetishistic, is seen in his encounter with Edmund Gosse during the period in which he was painting the picture. When Gosse approached him at the easel the reflection on his hair made Sargent stop and

66.
Lord Ribblesdale, 1902
Oil on canvas, 101¾ × 56½ (258.4 × 143.5)
The Tate Gallery, London

exclaim: "Oh! what lovely lilac hair, no one ever saw such beautiful lilac hair!" This statement could almost have been lifted from du Maurier's jibes at the Aesthetes in the pages of *Punch*, but for Sargent it was no laughing matter. When discussing his planned portrait of Ellen Terry (Fig. 67), he said that from the purely pictorial point of view it could not fail — "magenta hair!" And several critics observed his obsession with Mme. Gautreau's dyed hair. Oscar Wilde's Lord Henry was similarly entranced by the dyed hair and painted faces of actresses.[49]

Sargent's proclivity for the objectification of certain bodily parts related him to the Aesthetic Movement and is a hallmark of his outlook. Thus for Consuelo's portrait in the group composition *The Marlborough Family* (Fig. 120) he asked her not to wear her pearl necklace because it concealed the line of her neck, which he compared to the "trunk of a tree."[50] The question is: why did the English aristocracy allow Sargent to paint them as he did? First of all, he represented something totally new, a breath of fresh air into the traditional culture. While there was initial irritation at his Frenchness, this had less to do with the clever and chic than with the current anti-French feelings of jingoistic Britons watching the extensions of French overseas power. But French ideas gradually won over the main art-buying group, which wanted something new, yet within the stable framework of tradition. Sargent certainly worked to please them, and by 1888 even the critic of *The Athenaeum* could admit that his portrait of *Elizabeth Allen Marquand (Mrs. Henry G. Marquand)* (Fig. 102) "shows that he is bent upon refining his painting in every way."[51]

Osbert Sitwell, recalling the history of Sargent's portrait of his family, understood the artist's role in London society during the last two decades of the century.[52] His clients demanded the "sort of Gainsborough" owned by their grandfather, but at the same time something "not so old-fashioned." Sargent supplied the skill of the Old Masters but added to it "the skin-thin glint of the French Impressionists," then still novel to the English public. At the same time, Sitwell sensed in the outlandish accessories and atmospheric effects Sargent's greater fascination for the decorative ensemble than for the sitters themselves. But Sargent's interpretation mirrored the way his sitters saw themselves in this period and thus represented something true and genuine. The lurking shadows, the intense gazes, the nervous hand gestures objectively visualized the undercurrent of anxiety that began to appear in London high society in the mid-1880s.

Sargent got sucked into the vortex of this society, becoming widely known among the fashionable and the influential — a renown that propelled him to the top of his profession. He even took to the country side of society life, hunting and shooting with the rest of the pack. Both his own innate need for a community to give him a sense of identity and the elite's need for novel appearances put him within distance of the aristocratic outreach program. We can find an apt analogy in the growing custom of the declining nobility to marry American heiresses. Sargent's portraits of *Edith, Lady Playfair* and *The Marlborough Family* show his awareness of the Yankee energy and animation infusing the upper classes with new

67.
Ellen Terry as Lady Macbeth, 1889
Oil on canvas, 87 × 45 (221 × 114.3)
The Tate Gallery, London; Presented by
Sir Joseph Duveen (the elder), 1906

life. *The Marlborough Family* makes Consuelo (née Vanderbilt) dominate the composition — and rightfully so since it was her money that the Duke of Marlborough desperately needed at the time.

Lord Ribblesdale is a case study of the liberal-minded aristocrat willing to make concessions. He married one of the Tennants — an heir to an industrial fortune — and, when she died, married the widow of John Jacob Astor. He voted consistently in the House of Lords with the Liberals in Parliament, and warned of dire consequences if the rest of the aristocracy failed to follow his lead. He kept company with the Whites, Gosse, Terry, and Henry Irving, belonged to the Souls, and commissioned Sargent to portray him in a dandified hunting costume (Fig. 66). Lord Ribblesdale, who measured his friends by their fashions and was fastidious about his own clothing, actually recedes behind his outfit. The accumulation of riding accessories imparts an absurd, almost caricatural, look to a classical type known to the French as "milord anglais."[53]

Sargent painted the portraits of the George Henry Lewises (private collection), who represented the commoners moving up into the aristocratic domain — in Lewis' case, even more of an achievement since he was Jewish. Lewis was a lawyer who specialized in criminal litigation. He made his reputation handling those cases involving the intimate side of aristocratic life, where behavior might risk scandal and social disaster. Like Sargent in his sphere, Lewis was absorbed by the aristocratic classes to secure them against legal proceedings and exposure. He and Sargent became close friends, and it was Lewis who enabled Sargent to escape a lawsuit when he destroyed a farmer's crop while out hunting.[54]

The Lewises were familiar figures in the artistic and theatrical worlds and had close ties with the Prince of Wales. When the latter ascended the throne as Edward VII they were admitted into his intimate circle and Lewis was knighted. Already in the 1880s, Lady Lewis had established a reputation as one of London's most notable hostesses, and did much to break down the barriers between the fashionable and bohemian branches of London society. Her parties comprised the most cosmopolitan assemblies in town; here Wilde entertained the company with sparkling conversation and Langtry displayed her skills as a professional beauty. Sargent had painted several of the regulars, including Ellen Terry (Fig. 67), Henry Irving, Walford Graham Robertson (Fig. 69), George Henschel (Fig. 71), the Comyns Carrs, and Dr. William Playfair and his wife.[55] The English side of Sargent's relationship to Wilde and the Aesthetic Movement is documented in part by Alice Comyns Carr, who recalled that she saw Wilde frequently at the Lewises in the early 1880s, where he would often come in the company of Burne-Jones.[56]

The role of Wilde and Sargent in this upper-class milieu becomes clearer in the context of the aristocracy's sense of impending crisis. Urgent warnings were issued against the neglect of that cultural patronage which ensures appearances and reinvigorates tradition. One defender of the aristocracy in crisis proclaimed the need for the landed elite to remain "vigilant and alert" by absorbing "all those elements of ability and of exceptional proficiency among the population in which taste, good judgement and a certain instinctive knowledge of good and evil are inherent."[57]

This stern warning to honor the artist yields an insight into Sargent's role in English high society. His task was to give material form to aristocratic ideals, fantasies and — inadvertently, of course — its fears. Once permitted his French *trucs* and his links with the Aesthetic Movement, he found himself in an unbeatable situation. The new rich and the old elite gladly accepted his image of them, although perhaps for different reasons. Wertheimer was willing to take a risk on Sargent and his future worth, just as the Duke of Marlborough and Sir George Sitwell employed him to grant them immortality in the bosom of their ancestors. Both took a chance on the image of newness that he bestowed upon their effigies. He translated their anxieties in a highly stylized manner, assimilating them to his devices of disjuncture, contorted bodily gestures, intent gazes, and heavy shadows.

What Sargent did on canvas, Wilde and Montesquiou did with their entertainment skills. They had the ability to sum up in their persons the essence of modern culture. Their appeal was mainly to salons like those of the Lewises, the Whites, and the Tennants, whose pretensions to high culture required "instant" recognition. The Aesthetes in France and England appealed to the new social alliance in imparting to their host's environment a brilliant and almost absurd image of culture.[58] They embellished the residences of the *parvenus* and the landed elite with the over-refinement that characterized their own interiors. They provided a guide to *culture* which needed no explanation and no apology. They were literally walking examples of all that was modern and artistic in contemporary life.

Sargent felt most at home in this artificial world. Lacking an authentic national identity, he had to forge one for himself. English friends noted his affected British accent, while his correspondence (like that of his alter ego Henry James) is shot through with Gallicisms and foreign phrases. Sargent created for himself a world based on art, an extra-refined environment that evaded the philistinism and crassness of modern life. At the same time, he was dependent upon the whims of a privileged elite whose wealth alone could subsidize his existence. His attachment first to the Franco-American colony in Paris and next to English high society was a function of his cosmopolitanism — a dirty word in James' lexicon for the very reason that it hinted at rootlessness. Lacking a secure authentic culture, both James and Sargent found themselves most at ease among an elite which had international connections. This group felt more at home with others of the same class in foreign countries than with people lower on the social ladder in their native lands. Sargent threw in with this culture, its receptions, soirées, dinners, balls, clubs, shooting parties, and country-house weekends. And this acculturation process dovetailed with the rarefied view of himself and his environment that he so brilliantly captured on canvas.

68.
Engraving of paintings in the 1880 Salon, including Sargent's *Fumée d'Ambre Gris*
L'Illustration, 75 (May 22, 1880), pp. 333–34

NOTES

I am grateful to a number of wonderful people who have given generously of their time, ideas and skills to help guide my faltering steps on unfamiliar, but richly fertile terrain: Irene Bierman, Myra Boime, David Cannadine, Ron Cobb, Joan DelPlato, Phil Freshman, Peter Fusco, Peter Haidu, Colleen Hill, Iris Jackson, Alfred E. Lemmon, Cynthia Jaffee McCabe, Stanley Olson, Richard Ormond, Ray Reece, Debora Silverman, Jeanne C. Fawtier Stone, Lawrence Stone, Harmon Taber, John Tagg, Grace Wax, Stanley Weintraub, Ruth Yeazell, and Stephen Yenser. Finally, I want to express my gratitude to Patricia Hills for her bountiful moral as well as research support, to Bram Dikstra for letting me see the manuscript for his forthcoming book, *Idols of Perversity: War on Woman in Turn of the Century Culture*, and to Stephen Tabachnick for his inspired suggestion to read *The Picture of Dorian Gray*.

1. Recorded by Louis de Fourcaud, "Le Salon de 1884," *Gazette des Beaux-Arts*, 29 (June 1884), p. 483. For discussions of the critical reception of *Madame X*, see Richard Ormond, *John Singer Sargent: Paintings, Drawings, Watercolors* (New York, 1970), pp. 31–32; and Carter Ratcliff, *John Singer Sargent* (New York, 1982), pp. 84–88. The general response to *Madame X* was hostile, although there were sympathetic critics such as de Fourcaud; see above, pp. 89–91.
2. Robert de Montesquiou, "Le pavé rouge: quelques réflexions sur 'l'oeuvre' de M. Sargent," *Les arts de la vie*, 3 (June 1905), pp. 329–48.
3. Philippe Jullian, *Prince of Aesthetes: Count Robert de Montesquiou, 1885–1921* (New York, 1968).
4. See Leon Edel, *Henry James: The Middle Years 1882–1895* (Philadelphia, 1962), pp. 149–53.
5. See, for example, the account in Rupert Hart-Davis, ed., *The Letters of Oscar Wilde* (London, 1962), pp. 157–58.
6. In 1885, Bourget reviewed Lee's first novel, *Miss Brown*, and defended the Aesthetes against the lampooning treatment she had there accorded the movement; see

Bourget, "L'esthéticisme anglais," in *Études anglaises* (Paris, n.d.), pp. 305–18.
7. Eve Adam, ed., *Mrs. J. Comyns Carr's Reminiscences* (London, 1926), pp. 190–91.
8. Walford Graham Robertson, *Life Was Worth Living* (New York and London, 1931), p. 157.
9. Sargent's copy of the Rennell Rodd book is now in the collection of Richard Ormond, who kindly sent me a photocopy of the dedicatory page. For Wilde's barbs at Sargent and James, see Hart-Davis, ed., *The Letters of Oscar Wilde*, p. 158; E. H. Mikhail, ed., *Oscar Wilde: Interviews and Recollections*, 2 vols. (New York, 1979), I, p. 178.
10. Quoted in Stephen Donadio, *Nietzsche, Henry James, and the Artistic Will* (New York, 1978), p. 204.
11. Edel, *Henry James*, p. 108.
12. I am using Oscar Wilde, *The Picture of Dorian Gray*, ed. Isobel Murray (Oxford, 1974).
13. Quoted in Evan Charteris, *John Sargent* (New York, 1927), p. 59.
14. *Dorian Gray* was serialized in *Lippincott's Monthly Magazine* in 1890 and published as a novel the following year; *The Tragic Muse* appeared in serialized form in *Atlantic Monthly Magazine* in 1889 and was published as a novel in 1890.
15. Henry James, *The Tragic Muse*, 2 vols. (ed. Fairfield, Connecticut, 1976), II, p. 141.
16. Ibid., p. 22.
17. Charteris, *John Sargent*, p. 48. Nash's flamboyant language is not unlike that of Sargent, who expressed his delight with the publication of James' letters by describing them as "such beautiful flutters — it is like watching the evolutions of a bird of paradise in a tropical jungle"; ibid., p. 218.
18. By this time James had discarded the moralizing and conventional interpretations of his earlier stories in which artists figure as key characters. "A Landscape Painter" (1866), "The Story of a Masterpiece" (1868), "The Madonna of the Future" (1873), and his first novel, *Roderick Hudson* (1875), generally depict the artist in the context of James' firsthand experience of art processes and styles gained from his contact with French and French-influenced American painting. The painters or sculptors struggle with the synthesis of the ideal and the real in the interest of some higher aim, which eludes them. The artworks themselves have either an allegorical content or speak to some "essential truth."

69.
W. Graham Robertson, 1894
Oil on canvas, 90¾ × 46¾ (230.5 × 118.7)
The Tate Gallery, London; Presented by
W. Graham Robertson, 1940

19. The genteel couple in "The Real Thing" have been recommended to the artist by his friend Claude Rivet, a landscape painter who is surely based on Claude Monet. At the end of the story, the portraitist turns with relief to his Italian servant for a model. In either 1892, the date of "The Real Thing," or the following year (accounts vary), Nicola d'Inverno became Sargent's valet and model; for the next quarter century, Sargent was devoted to him.

20. Quoted in Jules Claretie, *Peintres & sculpteurs contemporains*, 2 vols. (Paris, 1882–84), II, p. 176.

21. Lucien Paté, "Salon de 1879," *L'Illustration*, 73 (May 26, 1879), p. 331.

22. "Nos gravures: portrait de M. Carolus-Duran par M. Sargent," *L'Illustration*, 75 (January 17, 1880), p. 42.

23. For a short biography of Pailleron, see Jules Claretie, *Edouard Pailleron* (Paris, 1883). The same author, in the article accompanying the reproduction of Sargent's portrait, described Pailleron's book collecting, dueling and hunting skills, his gifts as a conversationalist, and his popularity in all the salons; see Claretie, "Nos gravures: Edouard Pailleron," *L'Illustration*, 80 (December 9, 1882), p. 392. Among the articles in *L'Illustration* devoted to Pailleron was one praising his new play, *Le monde où l'on s'ennuie*, as one of the season's entertainment hits and describing the playwright as "one of the liveliest and most candid minds of our theater . . . a poet of the right school, a Gaul of the right race, a Parisian to his fingertips and French to his bones"; Perdican, "Courrier de Paris," *L'Illustration*, 77 (April 30, 1881), p. 278.

24. Henry James, "John S. Sargent," *Harper's New Monthly Magazine*, 75 (October 1887), p. 688.

25. See Pierre Larousse, *Grand dictionnaire universel du XIXe siècle*, 17 vols. (Paris, 1866ff.), XVII, p. 1735, s.v. "Pozzi."

26. For Sargent's description, see pp. 75–76, above; Robert de Montesquiou, *Les pas effacés: mémoires*, 3 vols. (Paris, 1923), II, pp. 195–96.

27. Horace Blanchon, "Assassinat du Professeur Pozzi," *Le Figaro*, June 14, 1918. Pozzi was tragically murdered in his drawing room by a former male patient.

28. Samuel Jean Pozzi, *A Treatise on Gynaecology, Clinical and Operative*, 3 vols. (London, 1892–93), I, pp. 2, 116–20.

29. In addition to the red interior in Montesquiou's apartment, recalled by Graham Robertson (p. 76, above), Oscar Wilde, who wrote that *Dorian Gray* is an essay on decorative art, wanted E. W. Godwin's decoration for his Tite Street house to include a vermilion scheme or some "shade of red" for his drawing room; see Hart-Davis, ed., *The Letters of Oscar Wilde*, p. 165.

30. For the complex interrelationships in the Avegno and Gautreau families, see George F. Jordan, "John Singer Sargent Captured the Mystique of 'Madame X,'" [New Orleans] *Times Picayune*, June 22, 1975; "Parlange, Eshleman Family Records Uncover Story of Immortal 'Madame X,'" *Times Picayune*, June 29, 1975.

31. Even the press responded to Mme. Gautreau as a work of art. One gossip columnist, reporting on the season at a seaside resort in Brittany, singled out Mme. Gautreau in this way: "At Saint-Mâlo-Paramé, the famous and exquisite shoulders of the beautiful Mme. Gautherot [*sic*] are inevitably, at the time of bathing, the subject of everyone's gaze. I know a painter, enamoured of the Greek splendors, who has taken up opera glasses and a canvas in order to see and paint from afar the shoulders of the beautiful Mme. Gautherot"; Perdican, "Courrier de Paris," *L'Illustration*, 82 (August 11, 1883), p. 83.

32. Charteris, *John Sargent*, p. 59.

33. Ibid.

34. Jules Comte, "Salon de 1884: la peinture," *L'Illustration*, 73 (April 26, 1879), pp. 267, 270.

35. In the 1878 Salon, the portrait painter Charles Chaplin exhibited a portrait of a countess with a crescent tiara (Fig. 57), which a critic claimed possessed such elegance and exquisite refinement that it suffices the painter to add only a "crescent of diamonds in her hair in order to recall the evanescent apparitions glimpsed by the ancient poets of the goddess with the silver bow"; Perdican, "Courrier de Paris," *L'Illustration*, 81 (February 24, 1883), p. 115. Perdican described another Chaplin portrait, of the Duchesse de Chaulnes, in these words: "The duchess is in décolleté, draped with a cloak edged with fur, regarding from on high we humble mortals, like a goddess with brown eyes. At the crown of her blonde hair she sports a star of sparkling diamonds analogous to the

70.

Eugene Carriers, c. 1880

Oil on canvas, 22 × 18½ (55.9 × 47)

Nebraska Art Association, Nelle Cochrane Woods Collection at the Sheldon Memorial Art Gallery, University of Nebraska, Lincoln

crescent on the head of Diana"; "Courrier de Paris," *L'Illustration*, 81 (February 24, 1883), p. 120.

The Diana motif abounded in the Salon art of the period, but Alexandre Falguière's sculpture of the goddess disdainfully regarding the most recent victim of her arrow (Fig. 56) was one of the most spectacular. She is crowned with a crescent tiara, and holds her bow in a position roughly approximating Gautreau's grip on her fan. Sargent surely knew the work since he had exhibited in the same Salon in which it appeared (1882), and Falguière was a close friend of both Carolus-Duran, whose bust he had executed for the Salon of 1876, and Pailleron; see Marie-Louise Pailleron, *Le paradis perdu* (Paris, 1947), p. 237.

Henry James surely had Diana in mind when he named the heroine of *Portrait of a Lady* (1880–81) Isabel Archer, referring here to the attribute of Diana the huntress. When she first appears in the novel, a dog leaps to her side for affection. Isabel takes up residence in the Villa Crescentini — another reference to Diana. She embodies the well-bred independence of the Diana ideal and, like Gautreau, is an American living abroad and participating in European high society.

36. De Fourcaud, "Le Salon de 1884," pp. 477–78, 482–84; see also Trevor J. Fairbrother, "The Shock of John Singer Sargent's 'Madame Gautreau,'" *Arts Magazine*, 55 (January 1981), p. 91. Fairbrother's essay has done much to stimulate my ideas on the subject.

37. It is possible that de Fourcaud here has in mind Baron Spitzer, one of the most spectacular *parvenus* of the period. He assembled a prodigious collection of over 4,000 objects — tapestries, ivories, enamels, faïences, furniture, marbles, bronzes, and glass — which required a team of specialists to analyze for the *Gazette des Beaux-Arts*. Not fortuitously, it was in Spitzer's mansion on 33, Rue de Villejuste, that Sargent held a pre-Salon "screening" of the portrait of Mme. Gautreau; see Perdican, "Courrier de Paris," *L'Illustration*, 83 (March 22, 1884), p. 182; Albert Boime, "Entrepreneurial Patronage in Nineteenth-Century France," in *Enterprise and Entrepreneurs in Nineteenth- and*

Twentieth-Century France, eds. Edward C. Carter II, Robert Forster, and Joseph N. Moody (Baltimore and London, 1976), p. 172.

38. The French, who had always perceived themselves as culturally superior, felt threatened by these new Americans. This is clearly seen in Perdican's articles immediately following the economic collapse: after earlier noting the impact of the crash on "le *high-life* parisien," within a month he was railing against "le yankeesme"; Perdican, "Courrier de Paris," *L'Illustration*, 79 (February 11, 1882), p. 86. The gossipy Philibert Audebrand noted with alarm: "How many beautiful residences the Almighty Dollar has built for herself from the Rue de Courcelles up to the Avenue Friedland!" He reflected on the passing carriages of the opulent U.S. citizens, accompanied by their women dressed in the height of fashion: "'These are no longer the old Yankees, the rail-splitters or the meat-packers of Chicago,' their harnesses are executed by the best coach-builder, their horses are frisky, their liveries are often fresher. Now in a period of fusion like the present it is not necessary to have more in order to walk side by side with the greatest names in Europe"; Audebrand, "Courrier de Paris," *L'Illustration*, 73 (February 15, 1879), p. 98.

39. In "Courrier de Paris," *L'Illustration*, 79 (May 27, 1882), pp. 342–43, Perdican viewed the coming summer invasion of 50,000 Yankees as catastrophic, even if they brought with them such "new inventions as the *surprise-party* that everyone here is talking about. . . ." The American presence was even having a deleterious impact on French culture; he regretted to see Sarah Bernhardt becoming "*américanisée*." By June 1883 his tone became even more strident, condemning Yankees for their two-faced position on France: complaining, on the one hand, about French colonial enterprises in Tunisia, Madagascar, and Tonkin because they were unable to share in the profits and, on the other, making an uproar in the life of Paris, crowding its theaters, the exhibitions, and substituting the tinsel for the real thing. He feared that France was in danger of losing its integrity, and he culminated with a tirade against the menacing commercial takeover by

71.
George Henschel, 1889
Oil on canvas, 25 × 21 (63.5 × 53.3)
Collection of Ira and Nancy Koger

American enterprise; "Courrier de Paris," *L'Illustration*, 81 (June 16, 1883), p. 371.

40. Perdican, "Courrier de Paris," *L'Illustration*, 77 (June 18, 1881), p. 412.

41. Gardner was Sargent's quintessential patron: she believed in using high society as a vehicle for creating a social renaissance. She had the rule of acquiring the best: "if she attended a polo game, she would be escorted to her seat by the best player of the day; the best tenor of the opera, the best painter, the best art critic, the best judge of horses . . . "; Morris Carter, *Isabella Stewart Gardner and Fenway Court* (Boston and New York, 1925), pp. 31–32, 90, 104.

42. Paul Bourget, *Outre-mer (Notes sur l'Amérique)*, 2 vols. (Paris, 1895), I, pp. 147–50.

43. Vernon Lee, "Imagination in Modern Art: Random Notes on Whistler, Sargent, and Besnard," *The Fortnightly Review*, 62 (October 1, 1897), pp. 515–17.

44. Allan Nevins, *Henry White: Thirty Years of American Diplomacy* (New York, 1930), pp. 82–85.

45. Nancy W. Ellenberger, "The Souls and London 'Society' at the End of the Nineteenth Century," *Victorian Studies*, 25 (1981–82), pp. 133–60. The Souls shared aesthetic and political positions, but these they articulated mainly in the form of parlor games. The women demonstrated their mental powers to an appreciative male audience, but did not threaten male dominance. Sargent's portraits of English women embody an interest in intelligent, vivacious types, but types whose nervous energy and tenseness nevertheless confine them to their niche in the basic social structure.

46. By the 1880s, too, half a decade of world depression had generated fear of foreign competition and imperialist rivalry. For the social and economic character of English society in these years, see Helen Merrell Lynd, *England in the Eighteen-Eighties* (London, 1945), pp. 3–4, 7–8, 10, 16, 25, 194–95; Lawrence Stone and Jeanne C. Fawtier Stone, *An Open Elite? England 1540–1880* (Oxford, 1984), pp. 421–26; F. M. L. Thompson, "Britain," in *European Landed Elites in the Nineteenth Century*, ed. David Spring (Baltimore and London, 1977), pp. 22–44.

47. T. H. S. Escott, *England: Its People, Polity and Pursuits* (London, 1881), pp. 291, 458.

48. For the quotations in this paragraph, see "The Salon, Paris," *The Athenaeum*, 88 (May 30, 1885), pp. 702–03; "Fine Arts: The Royal Academy," *The Athenaeum*, 88 (June 27, 1885), p. 828; "Fine Arts: The Royal Academy," *The Athenaeum*, 89 (June 12, 1886), p. 786.

49. See also Oscar Wilde's letter of 1883 to R. H. Sherard: "I think of you often, wandering in violet valleys with your honey-coloured hair"; quoted in Hart-Davis, ed., *The Letters of Oscar Wilde*, p. 147. Sargent's description of Ellen Terry's "magenta" hair is quoted in Charles Merrill Mount, *John Singer Sargent: A Biography* (New York, 1955), p. 142.

50. Consuelo Vanderbilt Balsan, *The Glitter and the Gold* (New York, 1952), p. 185.

51. "Fine Arts: The Royal Academy," *The Athenaeum*, 90 (June 23, 1888), p. 802.

52. Osbert Sitwell, *Left Hand, Right Hand!* (Boston, 1948), pp. 246–92; see also John Pearson, *Façades: Edith, Osbert, and Sacheverell Sitwell* (Essex, England, 1978), pp. 38–40.

53. Lord Ribblesdale, *Impressions and Memories* (London, 1927), p. xvii.

54. Charteris, *John Sargent*, pp. 119–20. This is one of the most telling incidents of Sargent's English career: Sargent not only destroyed the crop but also beat up the farmer because the latter insulted his "gentlemanly" honor.

55. George Henschel, *Musings and Memories of a Musician* (New York, 1919), p. 158; Adam, ed., *Mrs. J. Comyns Carr's Reminiscences*, pp. 39, 61, 243–44, 246–47, 249, 256; Robertson, *Life Was Worth Living*, pp. 244, 321. Dr. Playfair was the younger brother of Lyon Playfair, the husband of Edith, Lady Playfair, and was another middle-class servant of the elite: a brilliant obstetrician, he was the *accoucheur* to the royal family and most of the aristocracy.

56. Adam, ed., *Mrs. J. Comyns Carr's Reminiscences*, p. 86.

57. Anthony M. Ludovici, *A Defence of Aristocracy* (1915; ed. London, 1933), p. 420.

58. Graham Robertson recalled that Wilde's "serio-comic position as High Priest of Aestheticism was won in the drawing rooms by means of persistently making a fool of himself . . . "; *Life Was Worth Living*, p. 137; see also Jullian, *Prince of Aesthetes*, pp. 41–42, 68, 109.

The Arch-Apostle
of the Dab-and-Spot School:
John Singer Sargent
as an Impressionist

WILLIAM   H.   GERDTS

In May 1926, Evan Charteris made a pilgrimage to the home of Claude Monet in Giverny, France, in preparation for his biography of John Singer Sargent. Charteris wanted to question Monet about a letter Sargent had written to Frederick Jameson some fifteen years earlier in which Sargent had spelled out his understanding of the Impressionist aesthetic and of Monet's role in its development.[1] After a general discussion of the movement, Monet said of Sargent: "He wasn't an Impressionist as we used the term; he was always too influenced by Carolus-Duran."[2] Charteris concluded in his biography, "We must agree with Claude Monet, that Sargent was never an Impressionist in the Parisian sense of the word."[3]

Yet Charteris acknowledged that Sargent had made experiments in Impressionism, especially in 1888–89, even if they remained outside the main current of his art. During these years, Monet had noted Sargent's participation in Impressionist investigation: "Above all, I see that Sargent is engaged in this task and proceeds by imitating me."[4] Indeed, during the late 1880s, while Sargent was establishing his reputation as the most illustrious portrait painter on both sides of the Atlantic, his Impressionist experiments in non-portrait and "holiday" painting made him one of the most advanced artists in the English-speaking world. Charteris, though, was essentially correct: Sargent's Impressionist involvement lasted about five years and produced a small number of paintings, with only a few of these enjoying public exposure. But their exhibition placed Sargent in the artistic vanguard of both England and America and, given his rising reputation at the time, generated considerable critical impact.

Early in his career, Sargent had met Monet, most likely in Paris at Durand-Ruel's gallery in the spring of 1876 at the second Impressionist exhibition.[5] Yet Sargent's painting during most of the next decade can only be considered "impressionist" in the broadest sense of the term, that is, in the recording of momentary effects with a spontaneous, relatively "unfinished" brushwork. In the early 1880s, however, American critics associated him with the movement; not untypical were the remarks of a reviewer for *The Critic* in 1882: "if Mr. Sargent has joined the ranks of the French impressionists it is their gain and his loss."[6]

72.
Carnation, Lily, Lily, Rose, 1885–86
Oil on canvas, 68½ × 60½ (174 × 153.8)
The Tate Gallery, London; Chantrey Purchase
from the artist, 1887

111

Ironically, Sargent was then painting some of his most monochromatic, least colorful pictures, including the portrait of *The Daughters of Edward D. Boit* (Fig. 48) and many Venetian scenes. American writers on art were understandably confused about the meaning of Impressionism until the great French Impressionist display that Durand-Ruel brought over to New York in the spring of 1886. Until that time, sketchy, seemingly incomplete canvases were identified with the aesthetic, as was a palette dominated by the neutral tones.

Writing on Sargent in 1887, Henry James noted: "From the time of his first successes at the Salon he was hailed, I believe, as a recruit of high value to the camp of the Impressionists, and to-day he is for many people most conveniently pigeon-holed under that head."[7] But James was undoubtedly referring to the bravura brushwork and scintillating lights in Sargent's portraiture. By 1887, however, Sargent had in fact produced the first major display piece in England to be identified with the French avant-garde movement. Thus, Charles Merrill Mount is essentially correct in noting that Impressionism was brought to England by Sargent.[8] This work, *Carnation, Lily, Lily, Rose* (Fig. 72), was the most important picture that Sargent produced during his involvement with Impressionism and it was also one of the few non-portrait easel paintings that substantially enhanced his reputation.

The complex origins of *Carnation, Lily, Lily, Rose* lie, in part, in Sargent's earlier *Garden Study of the Vickers Children* (Fig. 74), painted in the early summer of 1884 on a visit to the home of Mr. and Mrs. Albert Vickers at Lavington Rectory near Petworth, Sussex. Sargent painted eleven members of the Vickers family in all; some of these are formal portraits, but in the present work, depicting Vincent and Dorothy Vickers, Sargent follows up on his celebrated outdoor portrait, *Madame Edouard Pailleron* of 1879 (Fig. 3). He depicts the Vickers children engulfed in a green garden setting amid tall-stalked lilies. Though painted directly and vigorously with spontaneous brushwork, the children appear to exist in an isolated, enchanted world of mystery where bright, white flowers seem to gesticulate with an inner life. With the absence of a horizon and with flat, unmodulated color areas, space is suggested only by the shadows of the lilies cast upon a green background. This outdoor painting is not yet Impressionist, since it has a minimal color range of white, black, and green, but the spontaneity of summer, holiday work, and the Pre-Raphaelite sentiment—here equating the tenderness of childhood with the lily, the flower of purity—would become an important prototype for *Carnation, Lily, Lily, Rose*, painted over the next two years.

Sargent painted the Vickers children in England, but he still resided in France, where he returned that winter of 1884–85. In contrast to his professional and social success in England, in Paris controversy greeted his portrait of *Madame X (Madame Pierre Gautreau)* (Fig. 47). The ensuing lack of portrait patronage in France, and the encouragement of such friends as Henry James, convinced Sargent to settle in England. Shortly after his arrival in the summer of 1885, he was brought by Edwin Austin Abbey to the artists' colony that had grown up at

Broadway in the Vale of Evesham, in the Cotswolds in Worcestershire. Here, Abbey shared the venerable Farnham House with another American painter, Frank Millet and his family. Sargent stayed at the Lygon Arms Inn, on the other side of the green from Farnham House.

Sargent began *Carnation, Lily, Lily, Rose* in late August at Farnham House. He transformed his portrait conception of the Vickers children in a garden into a subject picture, even though based on actual, identifiable models. With *Carnation, Lily, Lily, Rose*, Sargent was to resume his practice of creating, in addition to his staple of portraiture, major exhibition pieces such as he had done earlier with *The Oyster Gatherers of Cancale* (Fig. 9) and *El Jaleo* (Fig. 14)—but this time he actually painted outdoors.

Garden scenes were popular in the late nineteenth century in both Europe and America, uniting a renewed horticultural concern with the aesthetics of heightened coloration and the realist emphasis on actual appearances.[9] The elaborate conception of two children lighting Chinese lanterns in the midst of a flower garden came from a scene Sargent had noted earlier at Pangbourne. As Abbey recorded: "It was here that he saw the effect of the Chinese lanterns hung among the trees and the bed of lilies, and, when he took up his late summer residence in Broadway, he brought with him the sketch of these effects he had noted on the river."[10] In a letter to his sister, Sargent described the picture as a "fearful, difficult subject. Impossible brilliant colours of flowers, and lamps and brightest green lawn background. Paints are not bright enough, & then the effect only lasts ten minutes."[11]

Carnation, Lily, Lily, Rose occupied Sargent during two successive seasons, the late summer and autumn of 1885 and 1886. Initially, he painted in the garden at Farnham House because he lacked a studio. But this may have prompted him to expend his energies on outdoor works and to conceive of his chef d'oeuvre in this mode. Kate, his first model for *Carnation, Lily*, was the five-year-old daughter of the Millets. Sargent sketched her wearing a golden wig over her dark hair, in the act of lighting a Chinese lantern at evening time. But he found the Barnard children, Polly and Dorothy, more suitable in age (seven and eleven) and hair color; moreover, they seemed to promise more ease and stability as models (Figs. 220, 221). By late September, Abbey wrote of Sargent's progress to his friend and colleague, the American illustrator Charles Parsons:

. . . *Sargent has been painting a great big picture in the garden of the Barnards — two little girls in white, lighting Chinese lanterns hung about among rose trees and lilies. It is seven feet by five, and as the effect only lasts about twenty minutes a day — just after sunset — the picture does not get on very fast.*[12]

Sargent continued to work on the picture until the beginning of November, though the roses faded and dried, and artificial substitutes had to be found and fixed to the withered bushes. The picture remained unfinished and was stored in the Millet barn. Sargent returned to Broadway in the summer of 1886, where the

73.

Teresa Gosse, 1885
Oil on canvas, 25 × 19 (63.5 × 48.3)
Collection of Dr. and Mrs. John J. McDonough

Millets had taken the much larger and older Russell House, in which he could actually stay and also have a studio. Here Sargent resumed work on his canvas in the garden, after removing a large vertical strip at the left, which centered the figures and gave the picture a nearly square shape. Edmund Gosse described Sargent's method and the attention accorded the painting in Broadway:

The progress of the picture, when once it began to advance, was a matter of excited interest to the whole of our little artist-colony. Everything used to be placed in readiness, the easel, the canvas, the flowers, the demure little girls in their white dresses, before we began our daily afternoon lawn tennis, in which Sargent took his share. But at the exact moment, which of course came a minute or two earlier each evening, the game was stopped, and the painter was accompanied to the scene of his labours. Instantly, he took up his place at a distance from the canvas, and at a certain notation of the light ran forward over the lawn with the action of a wag-tail, planting at the same time rapid dabs of paint on the picture, and then retiring again,

only with equal suddenness to repeat the wag-tail action. All this occupied but two or three minutes, the light rapidly declining, and then while he left the young ladies to remove his machinery, Sargent would join us again, so long as the twilight permitted, in a last turn at lawn tennis.[13]

The fullest account of the painting of *Carnation, Lily* was recorded in several versions by the American painter Edwin Blashfield, who spent most of the summer of 1886 as a visitor in Broadway. His account is valuable, not only in regard to

Sargent's progress, but in correcting Gosse's report that Sargent's daily involvement with the picture lasted only several minutes. Blashfield recalled:

It was midsummer — each evening at twenty-five minutes to seven Sargent would drop his tennis racquet and, going into the seventy-foot long studio, would lug out the big canvas as if he were going to fly a huge kite. We would all leave our tennis for a time and watch the proceeding. Little Pollie and Dollie Barnard, daughters of the well-known English illustrator . . . would begin to light the Japanese lanterns among the tall stemmed lilies. For just twenty-five minutes, while the effect lasted, Sargent would paint away like mad, then would carry the canvas in, stand it against the studio wall and we would admire.

In the morning . . . we always found the canvas scraped down to the quick. This happened for many days, then the picture, daughter of repeated observation and reflection, suddenly came to stay. And it really did stay, and in staying grew more beautiful; the very slight crudity incidental to premier coup *method made the picture, when seen by me six months since, even more fascinating than it was when Sargent finished it and Pollie and Dollie put out the lanterns and took them down from the lilies that withered thirty-eight years ago.*[14]

The title Sargent chose for his canvas was of musical origin — a line from "The Wreath," a popular song by Joseph Mazzinghi that had been sung by the group at Russell House: "Have you seen my Flora pass this way? / Carnation, lily, lily, rose."[15] This line, like the picture itself, allies the age-old concept of feminine beauty with flowers, and with the specific flowers that bloomed in the Russell House garden, though Sargent almost surely was not inspired by the song for his original conception. He was, however, very much involved in the layout of the garden at Russell House and the choice of flowers to be planted as a setting for his picture. A flower bed was cut in a garden and the countryside ransacked for roses, carnations, and lilies. Sargent found a nursery of roses in Willersey, and bought them immediately. He also sent Lucia Millet fifty bulbs to plant in the garden.[16]

The literary title, the careful planning of the garden setting, and the choices and changes involving the youthful models fundamentally distinguish *Carnation, Lily, Lily, Rose* from orthodox Impressionism, specifically the recording of the momentary "impression." Yet the picture was seen as a revolutionary and avant-garde work because of its variegated chromatic range and its faithful recording of the momentary effects of light.

But even this limited relationship with Impressionism was a cautious one. While some sections of the picture — much of the background and the colored lanterns — are worked quite loosely and freely in somewhat broken color, the figures are carefully drawn and rather roundly modeled. Moreover, Sargent chose to record not the full light of day, but the tempered, lowered cast of evening light. This is consistent, of course, with the subject of the picture: the children are lighting their colored lanterns to provide an alternative light source to the fading sunlight. The lanterns match their own hues to those of the garden flowers and cast purple, pink, and yellow tones of colored light on the girls' white frocks.

Carnation, Lily, Lily, Rose is a calculated piece of work in another sense: it was

conceived and executed as a major exhibition entry for the Royal Academy, where it was shown in 1887. In the preceding years there had been a gradual expansion of Sargent's investigation of Impressionist methods, away from his lovely, modulated tonal recording of *In the Luxembourg Gardens* in 1879 (Fig. 17) and from the dramatic monochromes of his Venetian pictures of 1880–82. Impressionist color and verve begin to appear in his outdoor work done at Nice during visits in 1883–85, and reappear at Broadway in 1885 in such pictures as *Home Fields* (Fig. 75).[17] The strong chiaroscuro and the geometric structure of the emphatic fence posts and rails which dominate *Home Fields* give way the following year to the high coloration and sensuous painterly abandon of *Millet's Garden* (Fig. 76), which records the plethora of lilies at Russell House.[18] The background situation of the house, whose stark flat walls are partially shielded by the lush, leafy vegetation, also recalls that during his years of Impressionist experimentation Sargent avoided architecture, save as an occasional — and peripheral — reflective surface for light.

A feature of the actual garden which does not appear in Sargent's big exhibition picture is the field of poppies that grew there, often painted by artists of the colony, Sargent included. Blashfield noted that:

It was pleasant to see Abbey and Sargent together, working in the studio with Millet, or with all of us in the flower garden of the fourteenth century "Grange" in Worcestershire. One memory remains to me of an afternoon's sitting in the dazzling poppy path. Sargent's study was better than those of the rest of us, but he finally shut his sketching easel and carried it indoors remarking, "Well, I'm stumped." We all followed suit and very presently a shower approved our self-judgement.[19]

This concentration on the poppies at Russell House reflects, of course, the prominence that these vibrant flowers held at this time in the pictures of Claude Monet, to which American critics and viewers were especially attentive that very year in New York, in the great Durand-Ruel Impressionist exhibition of 1886. Abbey, surely referring to the same episode as Blashfield, wrote to his American colleague Charles S. Reinhart on October 2, 1886: "We grew a great bed of poppies on the purpose to paint, but it was too many for us, much the most intricate and puzzling affair I ever saw. I funked it entirely and gloated over the ineffectual struggles of Sargent, Millet, Alfred [Parsons] and Blashfield."[20] This unsuccessful joint pictorial assault on the poppy bed probably occurred in early August of that summer, for Lucia Millet wrote at the time to her parents concerning another of the Broadway colony, Emily Williams, the sister of Edmund Gosse, that "Mrs. Williams is at work on two pictures of the garden. It still flourishes but the poppies are on the wane. . . . "[21]

Carnation, Lily, Lily, Rose was the sensation of the Royal Academy exhibition in the spring of 1887. Some of the critics were slightly equivocal, others totally adulatory, but the triumph of painter and painting was unquestionable. Among those who stressed the picture's adherence to the tenets of the Impressionist school were Harry Quilter and the critic for *The Art Journal*. The latter reviewer, referring to a work by Frank Bramley, pointed out: "No. 350, 'Eyes and No Eyes,' Frank Bramley, is a good specimen of the 'dab and spot' school which has its arch-apostle in Mr. J. S. Sargent and its apotheosis in that artist's wonderful production, No. 359, 'Carnation, Lily, Lily, Rose.'"[22]

We may wonder today at this extreme characterization of the work as a prime example of "dab and spot" — surely a reference to orthodox Impressionism, of which *Carnation, Lily* is only an extremely modified example.[23] But perhaps that is just the point, given the still imperfect knowledge and understanding of French Impressionism in England at the time, and the extreme reluctance on both aesthetic and national terms to accept it. Sargent's picture was an artistic breakthrough, but still very palatable, charming and even beautiful, for it functioned on a variety of levels, apart from its quasi-radical aesthetic. It was a "modern life" picture, a recording of two pretty, contemporary young girls in a garden, with no further overt suggestions or symbolism to be read. It was also an exquisite piece of decoration on a monumental scale — its decorativeness enhanced by the nearly square shape and flattened composition. In this sense, Sargent's mastery could be seen to lie not in the picture's Impressionist light, color, and broken brushwork, but rather in its overall decorativeness and in the subtle expressivity of the figures. This critical emphasis corresponded with the reading of Impressionism that was developing in England and which, ultimately, found its way to America.[24]

By whatever criteria Sargent's involvement with Impressionism is judged, it clearly falls into two periods. The first, of 1885–86, centers around *Carnation, Lily,*

76.

Millet's Garden, 1886

Oil on canvas, 27 × 34 (68.6 × 86.4)

Collection of Mrs. John William Griffith

Lily, Rose, his major non-portrait opus of these years, although his less ambitious outdoor work was, in its way, more "impressionistic." Nevertheless, Sargent was himself moving closer to a commitment to Impressionism, and acknowledged this openly in 1886 when he helped to found the New English Art Club, an organization of fifty artists who championed the representation and exhibition of French-derived aesthetics in England. Indeed, Sargent had been one of those who endorsed the alternate name proposed for the organization — the Society of Anglo-French Painters.

The second period embraces the years when Sargent was most deeply involved with Monet. In September 1886, after the completion of *Carnation, Lily*, Sargent went to London, in March 1887 to Nice, and then back and forth between London and Paris. No complete documentation exists for his frequent intercourse during these years with Monet, but he certainly spent time with Monet both in Paris and in Giverny in 1887.[25] Sargent's well-known picture of *Claude Monet Painting at the Edge of a Wood* (Fig. 77) — a landscape outdoors, with a female

figure, presumably Suzanne Hoschedé, sitting on the grass at the right — was painted during one of these visits.

The picture is a key work in Sargent's growing affiliation with Impressionism, not only because it depicts the master French Impressionist, Sargent's closest colleague among the artists of the movement, but also because of its commitment to the momentary image transcribed out-of-doors. Although still far from Monet's broken brushwork, Sargent's technique is now closer to orthodox Impressionism than his work of the previous two years, in the recording of both the figures and the landscapes. Yet neutral tones of blacks and browns still figure liberally, particularly in the darker recesses of the woods. This may, in fact, have been the occasion recorded by the French art dealer René Gimpel, when Sargent, painting with Monet in Giverny, had borrowed Monet's colors and asked the Frenchman for black. To this Monet reported to Gimpel: "I gave him my colors and he wanted black, and I told him, 'But I haven't any.' 'Then I can't paint,' he cried, and added, 'How do you do it?'"[26]

This was not Sargent's first picture to depict an artist at work outdoors.[27] But *Claude Monet Painting at the Edge of a Wood* marks the beginning of a brilliantly colored series on the theme of outdoor painting and Sargent's commitment to a major aspect of the Impressionist enterprise. Thus, it is important to determine the date of the picture. Few works in Sargent's oeuvre, however, have generated as much controversy concerning dating, with the proposals ranging from 1887 to 1889.[28]

The date 1887 is more likely since Sargent's fullest commitment to Monet's aesthetic begins at just this time, the summer of 1887. The subject, moreover, is not just Monet, but Monet's aesthetic and his radical technique, which Sargent in this painting adopts by eliminating details, such as the features of Suzanne Hoschedé's face. On the same visit to Giverny in 1887, Sargent presumably painted the portrait of Monet which he showed the following May at the New Gallery in London, noted in *The Art Journal* as "Mr. Sargent's head of Claude Monet, the *impressioniste*."[29] It was at this time also that Sargent began to acquire paintings by Monet for his personal collection, works which almost certainly offered inspiration to him over the next several years when he was intensely occupied with the French master's methods.[30]

If Sargent was in France early in June 1887, he was back in London by the middle of the month, and then went on to the countryside for the Henley Regatta in July. One of the best descriptions of Sargent during this period is provided by the noted musician and conductor George Henschel (Fig. 71):

[I]n August, I first met Sargent. . . . He had built himself a little floating studio on a punt on the river, where it was a delight to see him, a splendid specimen of manly physique, clad — it was an exceptionally hot and dry summer, I remember — in a white flannel shirt and trousers, a silk scarf around the waist, and a small straw hat with coloured ribbon on his large head, sketching away all day, and once in a while skillfully manipulating the punt to some other coign of vantage."[31]

Although Sargent had adopted Monet's practice by working on the Thames itself, the better to record the casual and momentary impressions which he could seize in such an environment, he had difficulty with the limitations of a waterborne studio.[32] Perhaps this explains why so few paintings from the summer of 1887 have come to light, though these, such as *Under the Willows* (private collection) and *Lady and a Boy Asleep in a Punt under a Willow* (Gulbenkian Foundation, Lisbon), testify to Sargent's new understanding of, and commitment to, Monet-inspired Impressionism. They are loosely and freely painted, with a broad, chromatic range and little use of neutral tones. The light is rich and bright, reflecting the hotness of the summer Henschel described. Sargent did not adopt the more orthodox "comma-like" brushstroke, but opted for more irregular ones, often long, sometimes sword- or quill-like in shape. The vivacity of Sargent's technique consciously contrasts with the mood of summer somnolence which dominates these pictures. In *Under the Willows*, a single figure of a woman rests, totally relaxed, in a punt, and the deep red of her pillow or umbrella is broken and reflected in the gentle waves of the stream, mingling with the reflections of the sky and foliage.[33] Such pictures introduce the spirit of *dolce far niente* which is a basic characteristic of the paintings Sargent produced during the summers of 1887, 1888, and 1889.

Those summers in the west of England usually extended long into the autumn, and many of Sargent's finest holiday pictures were done in the early fall. Not in 1887, however, for on September 17, Sargent departed for America, to win new and significant glories, honors, and patronage in the art of portraiture. He returned to England in May 1888, and in July was back at the Henley Regatta, with Alfred Parsons as host at the Red House, Shiplake, and was a guest of the Robert Harrisons at Wargrave as he had been the previous summer.[34]

By June 1888, Sargent, with his family, had settled at Calcot Mill, a small village near Reading, on the Kennet, a branch of the Thames, not far from Pangbourne where he had first been inspired by the sight of children lighting Chinese lanterns. He was somewhat distanced from his old companions at Broadway, more than he had been at Henley or would be the following summer at Fladbury. But Sargent's summer at Calcot was significantly different from the several he had previously spent with the Broadway group for other reasons. Here, as head of a household, he had his own family present, including his sister Violet, who became his favorite model at the time, along with Vernon Lee and Flora Priestley.

Perhaps the fact that there were not the diversions of the Broadway colony, and there being no urgency to tackle a major exhibition piece conforming to Royal Academy strictures may account for the greater quantity of paintings Sargent produced this summer and also the greater degree of experimentation in outdoor painting more in the mainstream of avant-garde Impressionism. He concentrated not on garden pictures, as at Broadway, but on languid life on the quiet streams, continuing the themes he had begun to depict at Wargrave, and expanding upon the Impressionist techniques he had introduced in those works. For example, *A Backwater, Calcot Mill near Reading* (Fig. 78)* is even more sparkling than the few outdoor summer scenes of the previous year, and its animated brushwork contrasts with the sense of drowsy ease. The picture is a landscape, really, with a vague indication of a figure with a parasol in a punt at right, backed into a cove. The figure and boat, partially obscured by the tangle of tree leaves and underbush that dominate the composition, merge both scenically and aesthetically into the landscape. Purple and white tones sparkle through the foliage at the right, suggesting perhaps a light-colored structure obliterated, like the figure at the left, by the long green strokes of foliage.

The figure of a woman in a boat is much more clearly defined in Sargent's *By the River* (private collection).[35] She may be the same one who appears in *St. Martin's Summer* (Fig. 79), Sargent's most monumental treatment of the theme of women in a boat. Here two women are asleep in a boat on a stream, with a tree-filled landscape behind them. While this painting conveys a mood of *dolce far niente*, with the women in a state of total languor, the composition is as dynamic as his best portraits of the period. The women appear on a strong diagonal axis. Although they lie flat and still, they loom upward in the composition, from the lower left toward the massive trees, which bend back toward the right at top. Despite the

---

* As this essay was going to press, Warren Adelson suggested that the painting is not one of the works done in 1888 at Reading, but belongs to those executed at Henley in 1887; see *Sargent at Broadway: The Impressionist Years*, exhibition catalogue (New York, Coe Kerr Gallery, Inc., 1986), p. 45.

compositional "pull" exerted in order to carry the figures up and back, one woman holds a patterned parasol which plunges toward the lower right corner. Thus, a complex tension underlies this state of ostensible calm.

Sargent probably painted *St. Martin's Summer* after returning from an October visit to Bournemouth, where his father resided in increasingly poor health. The title refers to a mild, damp season which sometimes prevails in England from about November to Christmas, a kind of Indian summer, named after St. Martin's Day (November 11).[36] Indeed, the colors, sunlight, and parasol suggest the warmth of the weather, while the figures' voluminous clothing confirms the lateness of the season.

Perhaps Sargent's most fully Impressionist painting is *A Morning Walk* (Fig. 80), painted at Calcot that summer of 1888. It depicts his sister Violet standing on a path along the edge of a stream, dressed in sun-speckled white, and carrying a white parasol. Here Sargent has indeed eliminated all the neutral tones and adopted a rich, chromatic range; he uses loose and sometimes very broken brushwork, particularly in the landscape, and even dissolves the figural form to some degree. The inspiration for the work is almost certainly Monet's two paintings of 1886 depicting Suzanne Hoschedé, with a parasol, standing atop a hill. Sargent would most likely have seen them while visiting Monet in 1887 at Giverny, where the pictures remained. They were especially admired by Monet's American friends and colleagues.[37]

Yet *A Morning Walk* does not follow Monet's perspective. In the French master's two canvases, the spectator views Suzanne from below, so that she is silhouetted against the sky and almost dissolves in the bright, full midday sunlight. Sargent's light is far less intense, and he presents Violet as seen from above, silhouetted against the earth, with the blue of the sky as a mere reflected surface on the water.

Another of Sargent's paintings from his stay at Calcot, and a document of the passage of the Impressionist mode from Europe to America, is *Dennis Miller Bunker Painting at Calcot* (Fig. 81). Bunker was a very talented and very charming Boston artist, who had been academically trained in Paris before he returned to teach in Boston at the Cowles School. He was favored and patronized by the elite of Boston society. Bunker met Sargent in Boston in the winter of 1887–88, and was invited by the older artist to visit him the following summer. Though Bunker complained that he had difficulty working at Calcot,[38] Sargent records him standing in front of his easel in a landscape, with Violet at the right, sitting on the edge of a stream, and a tree-filled landscape in the rear.[39]

Bunker's inability to "get anything done" may have arisen from his exposure to Sargent's out-of-doors method and his attempts to emulate it. Certainly, for a young painter who had been trained in the studio of Jean-Léon Gérôme and mastered the academic approach, the spontaneity of outdoor painting must have been not only a revelation but a source of perturbation as well. While Violet Sargent occupies a similar function and position to that of Suzanne Hoschedé in

78.
A Backwater, Calcot Mill near Reading, 1888
Oil on canvas, 20³⁄₁₆ × 27 (51.3 × 68.6)
The Baltimore Museum of Art; Gift of
J. Gilman D'Arcy Paul

79.
St. Martin's Summer, 1888
Oil on canvas, 36 × 27 (91.4 × 68.6)
Collection of Mr. and Mrs. Peter Jay Solomon

Sargent's *Claude Monet Painting at the Edge of a Wood*, Bunker in the Calcot painting stands back from the easel to scrutinize the canvas, and the viewer sees only the back of it, with no indication of what Bunker has recorded or its state of completion. In contrast, Monet sits painting before his landscape in the Giverny picture, his palette in hand. There is thus, in *Dennis Miller Bunker Painting at Calcot*, a tentativeness which reflects Bunker's own dissatisfaction with his attempts at summer work.

Nevertheless, if Bunker was bewildered that summer by his confrontation with Sargent's newly developed Impressionism, the young Bostonian soon regained his confidence and adopted a similar method for his summer work during the remaining two years of his unfortunately abbreviated life. Given his high esteem among Boston collectors, Bunker's participation in exhibitions in Boston and New York with the fruit of these summer labors, and his impact on other young Boston artists just responding to the tenets of Impressionism in the United States, especially in Boston, were vital events in which Sargent, indirectly at least, played an important part.

Sargent's works of that summer of 1888 in Calcot had a direct impact, first in England and then in America. If their modernity did not suit the Royal Academy, they well represented the prevailing Francophile directions of the New English Art Club, where Sargent was an important member. In 1889 he exhibited two of his major pictures from the previous summer there: *St. Martin's Summer* and *A Morning Walk*. Fortuitously, the annual exhibition of the club coincided with "Impressions by Claude Monet," an exhibition of twenty works that opened at the London branch of the Goupil Gallery on April 13. The English critics immediately recognized the completeness of Sargent's new allegiance to Impressionism, though they did not entirely approve of it; nor did the American reviewers.[40]

It was a month before the London show, in April 1889, that Sargent's father passed away in Bournemouth. In March 1889, Sargent had taken a sublease on a property in Fladbury, seven miles from Broadway. He, his family and their friends spent much of the latter part of the summer there, after passing most of the spring in Paris, where he renewed his friendship with Monet.

The outdoor pictures Sargent painted in Fladbury continue the themes, mood, and techniques he had developed the previous summer in Calcot, with two modifications. First, a number of the works of that summer are larger than all of his earlier outdoor efforts with the exception of *Carnation, Lily, Lily, Rose*. Their size and scale suggest a new confidence and commitment to his modified Impressionist approach and the intention to create larger "exhibition paintings." Secondly, despite their aesthetic continuity, most of the summer paintings of 1889 appear less spontaneous and more structured. Sargent's Impressionist color and loose brushwork remains, but in some of these works there is a clear and visible geometric compositional framework. The greater structural sobriety, combined with a more introspective mood, may reflect Sargent's reaction to the death of his beloved parent. This more rigorous approach to composition also coincides with Sargent's revised form of brushstroke: instead of loading his brushes with several colors, as he had the summer before, he now allowed each stroke its prismatic distinction.

The painting that comes closest to the work of the previous summer, both in freedom of technique and theme, is *Two Girls with Parasols at Fladbury* (Fig. 82). It is something of a variation on *A Morning Walk*, with a second figure added behind the strolling woman with parasol, and without the meandering stream bordering the path. *Two Girls with Parasols* is even more loosely painted than *A Morning Walk*, and the figures are totally featureless. Despite the traditional identification with Fladbury, this may in fact be a variant of *A Morning Walk* and, like it, painted at Calcot.

In the summer work at Calcot and Fladbury, Sargent exploits the soft, feathery quality of the landscape and uses it as a background for his figural subjects, which are often absorbed in verdant growths. Although his figures are sometimes difficult to locate amid the mass of foliage, Sargent at this time seldom painted pure landscapes; he was an artist of the human condition, even when that condition was at its least dramatic.

Another of Sargent's unfinished works of that summer was his largest, the 6-foot-high *Lady Fishing — Mrs. Ormond* (Fig. 83), which depicts his sister Violet by the water's edge. It is difficult to gauge if the sketchiness of the picture in its present state would have been as noticeable had Sargent finished it. In some ways, one gets a fuller understanding of Sargent's conception in the smaller version known as *Violet Fishing* (Fig. 84), where Violet holds the fishing pole that is absent in the large picture. *Lady Fishing* and its variant are closest in form and format to *A Morning Walk* of the previous year. Violet is seen again in a glimmering white dress with mauve shadows, and refracted light emanates from the intense blue water, with brilliant greens and russets coloring the river bank. As in *A Morning Walk*, the lack of a horizon line accentuates the two-dimensionality of the design, following the aesthetics of Japanese art, which was exercising a profound influence on Western artistic sensibilities at the time. The abstract patterned design of the reflections in the water and the sharp profile of the figure also echo the insistent linearism of Oriental art.[41]

The painting's subject matter must also be considered here. Violet may well have "gone fishing" in the Avon, but such an activity was hardly consistent with

81.
Dennis Miller Bunker Painting at Calcot, 1888
Oil on canvas, 26¾ × 25 (67.9 × 63.5)
Terra Museum of American Art, Chicago;
Daniel J. Terra Collection

the traditional representation of women in Western art. Again, Sargent had an immediate precedent in Monet's *La Barque à Giverny* of c.1887 (Fig. 86), which he would have seen recently in Giverny. Again, however, Monet's painting is more spontaneous and real, while Sargent's is more posed and static. On the one hand, the theme of women fishing may be recognized as a subject taken from modern life, but on another level it adds a casual note of the unexpected and mysterious. A figure of refinement, clothed in an elegant garment of spotless white, is incongruous with the sport of fishing and the implications of all its activities.

The boating pictures which had preoccupied Sargent for the previous two summers found their ultimate expression in *A Boating Party* (Fig. 88), painted at Fladbury. Again, a large, almost 3-foot-square painting, it is the most complex, multifigured work of his Impressionist summers. Violet sits at the end of a punt at the right, warmly dressed with a fur stole, suggesting a cool summer day or possibly a September date for the painting. Lying in a canoe next to her boat is a new addition to the Fladbury summer party, Sargent's good friend Paul Helleu, the society portraitist and draftsman, who was visiting the Sargent family with his wife, Alice Louise Guérin, whom he had married in 1886. Alice herself has stepped

into another boat by the bank, at an angle to the first two and parallel to the picture plane, while an indistinct fourth figure hovers with a punting pole nearby. Balancing the structure of the boats, poles, and oars in the foreground is the plane of the old Fladbury rectory, which Sargent had rented, in the left distance.

The foliage along the bank, the tall trees partially screening the rectory, and the reflections in the water are rendered in Sargent's characteristic Impressionist manner. While the color is bright and fairly high-keyed, the figures are quite carefully drawn, so that the spectator is conscious of the pattern of varied shapes and splayed limbs. More important, the figures themselves betray individual identity by pose and definition: Helleu is jauntily relaxed, his long, tapering fingers suggesting his artistic sensitivity; Violet is a huddled mass, wan and inattentive; Alice Helleu is sprightly, thrusting forward in the punt, her arms slightly akimbo. Such a complex conception was probably completed in the studio, even if Sargent began it outdoors. And it has been suggested that the picture may have also been realized with the help of photographs.[42]

Paul and Alice Helleu appear by themselves in the best known of Sargent's Fladbury pictures, the work now entitled *Paul Helleu Sketching with His Wife* (Fig. 89).[43] Sargent's design here is bold and innovative. The figures are seen from above, sinking down in an embankment of reeds. The vessel and the paddles are pulled up beside them at the left. A fishing pole stands up in front against the top of Helleu's propped-up canvas, a reminder of the double purpose of their outing. Even more than the other Fladbury paintings, *Paul Helleu Sketching* exists on the picture plane itself. No horizon appears above the reeds and water, and the figures and boat tilt sharply upward. The canoe almost bisects the picture from lower left to upper right. Sharp geometric angles abound: the fishing pole intersecting with the canvas, the sharp-cornered palette and the angular poses of the figures themselves — Helleu leaning toward the right, Alice backing up against him in an opposing motion. The light-colored hats of both focus almost as flattened disks on the picture surface.

Although the scene is an outdoor picture, Sargent has drastically muted his Impressionism in a manner characteristic of many academy- and atelier-trained artists. His landscape does conform to the freedom and vivacity of outdoor painting. And the quill-like brushstrokes that are Sargent's signature technique appear *en masse* in the abundance of river reeds. Yet the lighting is even, outdoor illumination, reflecting more the tenets of Bastien-Lepage than of Monet. Moreover, the figures are painted quickly, but with sound, academic technique and careful definition. Helleu's pose even recalls the pose of his teacher, Carolus-Duran, in one of Sargent's first great portraits of a decade earlier (Fig. 4).

In the portrait of the Helleus, as in *A Boating Party* (but unlike the works of the previous summer, such as *A Morning Walk*), Sargent has concentrated more on the distinction between the individual figures and the creation of a sense of psychological mood, which is foreign to the Impressionist aesthetic. Helleu's face is obscured by the broad brim of his boater, but he nevertheless is concentrating upon his painting, as suggested by his somewhat awkward pose. The bored, unoccupied Alice stares off into space without interest or excitement. Her listless pose confirms her state of inertia. The evenness of the cool, bleak gray light, too, contrasts with the sparkling animation of Sargent's sunlit scenes of previous summers.

Finally, *Paul Helleu Sketching* must be seen as a further step in Sargent's development of the theme of outdoor painting. Helleu's canvas is turned away from the spectator, just as it had been in *Dennis Bunker Painting*. But whereas Bunker was shown ruminating, away from his easel, Helleu is busily at work, and presumably confidently so. The subject he paints is of no concern, nor does the spectator have a view of the scene which might be serving Helleu for his subject. What is certain is that it is an outdoor view, immediately recorded. Moreover, Helleu, like Sargent, was first and foremost a portrait painter, and by definition a portraitist of studio conceptions. Thus, Sargent presents Helleu as a convert to the new method, exploring new thematic interests. And it must be noted that Helleu is depicted doing exactly what Sargent was doing in his picture — painting out-of-doors. Helleu therefore becomes, in a sense, a surrogate Sargent himself, both men established artists in one tradition, sailing off into what was for them relatively uncharted waters.

By and large, most of Sargent's summer work done in the west of England in the later 1880s was a private affair. Little of it was seen publicly in English exhibitions, outside of *Carnation, Lily, Lily, Rose* at the Royal Academy in 1887, and the two Calcot paintings at the New English Art Club in 1889. The only Fladbury painting subsequently shown, *Paul Helleu Sketching*, appeared in the winter exhibition of the

84.
Violet Fishing, 1889
Oil on canvas, 28 × 21 (71.1 × 53.3)
Collection of the Ormond Family

85.
Autumn on the River (Miss Violet Sargent), 1889
Oil on canvas, 30 × 20 (76.2 × 50.8)
Private collection

New English Art Club in 1892 as *M. and Mme. Helleu* and elicited little attention. By then Sargent had turned his back upon his Impressionist experimentation. By October 1889 he had left Fladbury and was in London, and at the beginning of December he was on his way to New York to further his career as a portraitist and to begin his new involvement with mural painting.

   Traces of Sargent's interest in outdoor painting and Impressionist light and color effects surfaced only sporadically during his 1890 sojourn in America. A vivid *Garden Sketch* done in June, in Worcester, Massachusetts, survives,[44] and his fascinating portrait of *Sally Fairchild* (Fig. 95), painted that summer on Nahant, a peninsula north of Boston, testifies to the survival of some Impressionist concerns.

132

86.
Claude Monet, *La Barque à Giverny*, c. 1887
Oil on canvas, 35⅝ × 51½ (90.5 × 130.8)
Musée du Louvre, Paris

87.
Claude Monet, *In the Woods at Giverny—Blanche Hoschedé-Monet at Her Easel with Suzanne Hoschedé Reading*, c. 1885–90
Oil on canvas, 36 × 38½ (91.4 × 97.8)
Los Angeles County Museum of Art; Mr. and Mrs. George Gard De Sylva Collection

Ironically, just as Sargent was abandoning his role as a pioneer in avant-garde aesthetics, he chose to assert his modernity in America, to join the artistic tide of Impressionism just washing these shores, by bringing with him two works for exhibition: *A Morning Walk* and *Paul Helleu Sketching*, the latter never shown before.[45]

Appropriately enough, given Sargent's special connection and patronal favoritism in Boston, his Impressionist work had its first United States showing in that city, in the 1890 midwinter exhibition at the St. Botolph Club.[46] Boston had seen examples of French Impressionist painting as early as 1883, and some American Impressionist-related works had been shown during the decade by artists returning from Giverny.[47] But it was the post-Calcot summer landscapes by the local painter Dennis Bunker that best represented Impressionism to Bostonians. Since three such landscapes were also in the winter exhibition at the St. Botolph Club, it is not surprising that Sargent's *A Morning Walk* (retitled *Summer Morning* for the American showings) was critically compared to Bunker's work: "Mr. Sargent has had also a picture in the same scheme of color, but though brilliantly clever is almost too sketchy for exhibition walls."[48]

Sargent seems to have planned and timed the exhibition of his Impressionist work quite carefully. Less than a week after the show at the St. Botolph Club had closed in Boston, *Summer Morning*, along with the second outdoor picture, was on view in New York at the Union League Club. This exhibition was one of a series mounted at the Club which featured curious artistic combinations; in this case it consisted of "Pictures by American Figure Painters Together with an Exhibition of Persian and Indian Art." As was usual for these Union League Club shows, the exhibition was brief, from February 13 through 15, but for all its brevity, it did not lack for attendance or public notice.

Thanks principally to the efforts of Durand-Ruel and of the Society of American Artists, French and American Impressionism, respectively, were not unknown to New York audiences by February 1890, but American examples had only begun to be known, principally through the park scenes of Chase and the Giverny canvases that Theodore Wendel and, above all, Theodore Robinson, had exhibited at the Society in 1889. At the Union League Club show, however, Sargent was almost alone in showing Impressionist works, with only one example by Robinson, his *L'Arrosage*, also included. Sargent's entries, both noted as owned by the artist, were his *Summer Morning* (no. 35) and *An Out-of-Doors Study* (no. 36).

This latter was never identified as portraying Paul Helleu and his wife, but the compilation of descriptions from the critical reviews leaves no doubt that it was the same picture. Since this was the picture's earliest public exhibition, it is important to note its true and original title. It confirms that Sargent's purpose was not to identify an already well-known European artist, but to commemorate the act of outdoor painting. The term "Study" in the title refers not to Sargent's work, but to the painting being created by Paul Helleu. As Sargent had done in his depictions of Monet and Bunker, he here calls attention — more clearly and more specifically — to the validity of outdoor painting.

88.

A Boating Party, c. 1889
Oil on canvas, 34 × 36 (86.4 × 91.4)
Museum of Art, Rhode Island School of Design,
Providence; Gift of Mrs. Houghton P. Metcalf
in memory of her husband Houghton P.
Metcalf

As the paintings traveled across America — to New York, Chicago, and
Philadelphia — the critical reaction to them was often as equivocal as it had been
in Boston or, sometimes, simply disinterested.[49] Some critics allied the works
specifically to Impressionism, though again without wholehearted approval,
culminating with the writer for *The Philadelphia American*, who chose Sargent's two
outdoor paintings as the starting point for a diatribe against the advance of
Impressionism, against the replacement of academic values and standards with
what he viewed as the dangerous tendencies of modernism.[50]

In the fall of 1890, Sargent negotiated his participation in the great mural project
for the Boston Public Library, which marked a significant change in the direction
and emphases of his art. That November, he and his sister Violet left for England;
presumably the two outdoor pictures at the Philadelphia Art Club were later
returned separately to London. Thus ended both Sargent's exhibition of the works
he had painted following the principles of French Impressionism and also his direct
involvement with them.

Nevertheless, the impact of that aesthetic remained with him throughout his
career, both in formal strategies and in thematic concerns. These reflect the
influence of Monet's work of the mid-1880s as much as Sargent's adoption of
Impressionist techniques. We have noted how Sargent's women with parasols and

89.
Paul Helleu Sketching with His Wife, 1889
Oil on canvas, 26⅛ × 32⅛ (66.4 × 81.6)
The Brooklyn Museum, New York; Museum
Collection Fund

his women fishing derive from Monet, who painted such themes in 1886 and 1887. Likewise, the motif of women in boats coursing down a narrow stream, which was popular in Sargent's work at Henley, Calcot, and Fladbury, directly reflect such pictures by Monet as his *Jeune Filles en Barque* (1887; The National Museum of Western Art, Tokyo).

Even more central to Sargent's temporary involvement with the Impressionist aesthetic was his series of paintings of artists working at their easels, which had, in turn, been a significant motif for the French Impressionists from the late 1860s on. At first these artists painted each other at work indoors, but the Impressionists, naturally, moved outdoors in the early 1870s.[51]

Again, however, it was in 1887, at the same time that Sargent presumably painted Monet in Giverny, that the French master several times depicted Blanche Hoschedé-Monet painting outdoors, accompanied by her sister Suzanne, reading (Fig. 87). Almost certainly these pictures provided the inspiration for Sargent's series of paintings on a theme which so obviously fascinated him. And it continued

136

90.
Walter Osborne, *The Children's Party*, 1900
Oil on canvas, 21½ × 30 (54.6 × 76.2)
Pyms Gallery, London

91.
Frank Bramley, *Sleep*, 1895
Whereabouts unknown

to fascinate him: he depicted both professional and amateur artists painting, sketching, and etching, in both oils and watercolors, most notably perhaps in *The Sketchers* of 1914 (Fig. 161), a double record of Jane and Wilfrid von Glehn working outdoors.

The impact of Sargent's involvement with Impressionism is difficult to determine, in part because it was so relatively short-lived and so few of his productions were seen publicly. But although he was in the vanguard of Impressionist experimentation in the Anglo-American art world, his pictorial achievements in this regard became less conspicuous with the increasing participation of other American and British artists in French Impressionist aesthetics.

One must distinguish, too, the American from the British reaction to Sargent's Impressionism. In England, the impact lay almost totally with Sargent's initial contribution to the avant-garde — *Carnation, Lily, Lily, Rose*, first exhibited in 1887. We have seen the immediate reaction to the picture in the critical press, but equally effective were the recurrent homages paid to it, in such notable terms as the Chinese lanterns in *The Children's Party*, painted in 1900 by the leading Irish Impressionist, Walter Osborne (Fig. 90). The theme of children immersed in the tangle of a flower garden is reprised in Frank Bramley's *Sleep* (Fig. 91), shown at the Royal Academy in 1895, though the air of heavy narcosis indubitably assigns this painting to the last decade of the century, as a reflection of the Symbolist movement.[52]

Even Sargent's later critical archenemy, Roger Fry, while savagely castigating Sargent's achievements (conveniently posthumously!) nevertheless had to admit to the impact of *Carnation, Lily*, recollecting that it

seemed a new revelation of what colour could be and what painting might attempt, and of how it could be at once decorative and realistic. When I look now at the thin and tortured shapes those lily petals make on the lifeless green background, I realize that what thrilled us all then was the fact that this picture was the first feeble echo which came across the Channel of what Manet and his friends had been doing with a far different intensity for ten years or more. This new colour was only a vulgarisation of the new harmonies of the Impressionists; this new twilight effect only an emasculated version of their acceptance of hitherto rejected aspects of nature.[53]

In the spring of 1889, Sargent's Impressionism was being subsumed in the general English investigation of the aesthetic. It was the work of Philip Wilson Steer that has since been credited with initiating a sustained British interest in Impressionism; Steer's modern biographer, Bruce Laughton, has noted that Steer's *A Summer's Evening*, which occupied the artist through the winter of 1887–88, "is the earliest datable work in which the influence of Monet and Renoir can be clearly seen."[54] Laughton does note that Steer's opportunities for seeing French Impressionist work were limited to the four Monets shown in London that season at the Society of British Artists, but he ignores the possible impact of Sargent's contemporaneous experiments.

Yet Sargent's role in the development of Impressionism in England, especially through the agency of the New English Art Club, must be seriously

92.
Luther Van Gorder, *Japanese Lanterns*, 1895
Oil on canvas, 28¼ × 22½ (71.8 × 57.2)
Tweed Museum of Art, University of
Minnesota, Duluth; Gift of Mr. Howard W.
Lyon

93.
Childe Hassam, *July Night*, 1900
Oil on canvas, 37 × 31 (94 × 78.7)
Collection of Ira and Nancy Koger

considered. Years later, in recalling Sargent's participation in the exhibitions at the club, Walter Sickert observed:

The attitude of the Press was generally thus: "We know all about Impressionism, or whatever you like to call the beastly thing, that these people practise. It is an unpleasant and not very reputable thing, anyhow. But, of course, when Mr. Sargent condescends, in his moments of recreation, between the serious and respectable labours of painting proper expensive portraits, to dally with anything so trivial, it becomes supreme, etc."[55]

In the United States the pattern of Sargent's impact on Impressionist developments was necessarily different, since *Carnation, Lily, Lily, Rose* was not shown here during those crucial years. However, no English painting betrays such imitative homage to Sargent's masterwork as the 1895 *Japanese Lanterns* (Fig. 92) by the Ohio artist Luther Van Gorder. Childe Hassam's *July Night* (Fig. 93), an Easthampton scene of his wife in a garden, is also indebted to *Carnation, Lily*, though more distantly.[56]

Many of Sargent's favorite motifs during his Impressionist period were also adopted by his American colleagues, but this almost surely results from parallel influences of the work of Monet rather than from any direct influence by Sargent. Impressionist American art around 1890 and thereafter is rich in the iconography of women in boats, but these derive even more directly from Monet's works: Theodore Robinson's *Two in a Boat* of 1891 (The Phillips Collection, Washington, D.C.), Edmund Tarbell's *Mother and Child in a Boat* of 1892 (Fig. 94), and Frederick Frieseke's *Two Ladies in a Boat* of about 1905 (private collection).

Violet Fishing (Fig. 84), Sargent's monumental depiction of his sister, remained unfinished and unexhibited, but it found curious, almost contemporary, parallels in a number of American Impressionist pictures. Thomas Dewing painted Eleanor Pratt fishing at Cornish, New Hampshire, in his *Summer* of 1890 (National Museum of American Art, Washington, D.C.) and Philip Leslie Hale painted at least one and probably several pictures of ladies fishing on the banks of a stream in the 1890s, such as *At Water's Edge* (whereabouts unknown). In their long, flowing gowns, Dewing's and Hale's women seem even more incongruous in their preoccupation with the sport than does Violet Sargent.[57]

Sargent may not have been committed totally to Impressionism, but he was able to take its tenets and utilize those strategies to inform some of his most beautiful and most interesting paintings. If in England the recollection of this achievement centered especially around *Carnation, Lily, Lily, Rose*, the circulation of his Impressionist pictures in the United States was not forgotten, even if their impact was not so spectacular. In 1903, over a decade after Sargent's two Impressionist paintings had toured this country in 1890, the influential critic Royal Cortissoz recalled: "Not his most elaborate portrait of a gorgeous personage, set in the most luxurious surroundings has, if he has put nothing but mere workmanship into it, anything like the interest which attaches to some such sincere fragment as his sketch of the painter Helleu, working in the open air."[58]

94.
Edmund Charles Tarbell, *Mother and Child in a Boat*, 1892
Oil on canvas, 30 × 35 (76.2 × 88.9)
Museum of Fine Arts, Boston; Bequest of David P. Kimball in memory of his wife, Clara Bertram Kimball

NOTES

1. There are, presently, three studies devoted specifically to Sargent's Impressionist years: Charles Merrill Mount, "The English Sketches of J. S. Sargent," *Country Life*, 135 (April 16, 1964), pp. 931–34; Donelson F. Hoopes, "John S. Sargent: The Worcestershire Interlude, 1885–1889," *The Brooklyn Museum Annual*, 7 (1965-66), pp. 74-89; and *Sargent at Broadway: The Impressionist Years*, exhibition catalogue (New York, Coe Kerr Gallery, Inc., 1986). For their assistance in the writing of the present essay, the author would like particularly to thank Patricia Hills; Trevor J. Fairbrother; Kenneth McConkey; Maureen O'Brien; Stanley Olson; Donna Seldin, Warren Adelson and Odile Duff of the Coe Kerr Gallery, Inc.; and his graduate assistants, Carrie Rebora and Kathy O'Dell.

2. "Il n'était pas un Impressioniste, au sens où nous employons ce mot, il était trop sous l'influence de Carolus Duran"; Evan Charteris, *John Sargent* (New York, 1927), p. 130.

3. Ibid., p. 133.

4. "Je vois surtout que Sargent est très pris à partie et qu'il passe pour m'imiter"; letter to Alice Hoschedé in Giverny, written from Fresseline, April 21, 1889; quoted in Daniel Wildenstein, *Claude Monet: Biographie et catalogue raisonné*, 3 vols. (Lausanne and Paris, 1974–79), III, p. 959.

5. Sargent visited the exhibition with Helleu; see Charteris, *John Sargent*, p. 130, confirmed by Helleu's daughter, Mme. Paulette Howard-Johnston, to Stanley Olson, letter to the author, May 20, 1985.

6. "The Fine Arts. Mr. Sargent's 'El Jaleo,'" *The Critic*, 2 (October 21, 1882), p. 286.

7. Henry James, "John S. Sargent," *Harper's New Monthly Magazine*, 75 (October 1887), p. 684.

8. Mount, "The English Sketches of J. S. Sargent," p. 931.

9. See William H. Gerdts, *Down Garden Paths: The Floral Environment in American Art* (Rutherford, New Jersey, 1983).

10. E. V. Lucas, *Edwin Austin Abbey, Royal Academician: The Record of His Life and Work*, 2 vols. (London and New York, 1921), I, pp. 150–51, letter written by Abbey on September 28, 1885.

11. Charteris, *John Sargent*, reproduces this letter in facsimile between pp. 76–77; Richard Ormond, *John Singer Sargent: Paintings, Drawings, Watercolors* (New York, 1970), p. 39, states that it was written to Sargent's sister.

12. Quoted in William Howe Downes, *John S. Sargent: His Life and Work* (Boston, 1925), p. 24.

13. Quoted in Charteris, *John Sargent*, pp. 74–75.

14. See Edwin H. Blashfield, "John Singer Sargent: Recollections," *North American Review*, 221 (June 1925), pp. 643–44; a shorter variant of this account appears in Blashfield, "John Singer Sargent," *American Academy of Arts and Letters. Commemorative Tributes to Cable, Sargent, Pennell* (1927; reprinted in *Commemorative Tributes of the American Academy of Arts and Letters, 1905–1941*, New York, 1942), p. 187.

15. Sargent's interest in music was much noted at Broadway. On August 9, 1886, for example, Frank Millet's sister Lucia wrote to her parents that "Mr. Sargent is at Bayreuth wild over the music he is hearing . . ."; quoted and discussed by Kate Millet's daughter, Joyce A. Sharpey-Schafer, in correspondence with Donna Seldin of the Coe Kerr Gallery, Inc., New York, January 31, 1983. I am most grateful to Ms. Seldin for making this correspondence available to me.

16. Charteris, *John Sargent*, pp. 74–78, discusses the conception and progress of *Carnation, Lily, Lily, Rose* in detail.

17. Ormond, *John Singer Sargent*, p. 34, has described *Home Fields* as "squarely in an Impressionist context," with its "fleeting effects of light and highly keyed palette." As Ormond noted: "The fence in the foreground, treated in a series of jagged brush-strokes, leads the eye into a shimmering patchwork of greens, russets and blue-greys. Its sensuous response to the accidental and immediate is utterly alien to most contemporary English landscape painting."

18. There is some question as to whether the garden painting was done in 1885 or 1886, though earlier authorities generally agree with the 1886 date, as does the present author. On the other hand, if the garden depicted is that of Farnham House, rather than Russell House, it would, of course, more likely have been painted in 1885. Its advanced painterly treatment, high

coloration, and brilliant record of bright sunlight, however, would seem to suggest the later date.

19. Blashfield, "John Singer Sargent" (1927), p. 195.

20. Lucas, *Edwin Austin Abbey*, I, p. 159.

21. Quoted by Sharpey-Schafer, above n. 15. A study of *Poppies* remained in the Millet family and was sold from the collection of Mrs. Millet at Sotheby's, London, June 10, 1942, no. 88.

22. "The Royal Academy Exhibition," *The Art Journal*, 26 (June 1887), p. 248. Quilter published his remarks in *Preferences in Art, Life and Literature* (London, 1882), p. 358: "Honour to the young artist who has succeeded in combining, as we at least have never yet seen combined in a painting of this impressionist school, truth of effect and beauty of color." Maureen O'Brien of the Parrish Art Museum, Southampton, New York, and Barbara Gallati of The Brooklyn Museum both mentioned Quilter's comment on the painting to the author.

23. Mortimer Menpes, *Whistler as I Knew Him* (New York, 1904), p. 20, notes that at just this time, in the mid-1880s, a group of Whistler followers were experimenting in Impressionist methods and "began to paint more in spots and dots. . . . " In the spring of 1888, one of the group, Albert Ludovici, had an exhibition at Dowdeswell's gallery in London entitled "Dots, Notes, Spots," suggesting that the term used by *The Art Journal* critic was very much synonymous with avant-garde and Impressionist tendencies. I am indebted to my friend and colleague Dr. Kenneth McConkey, Head of the School of Art History at Newcastle upon Tyne Polytechnic, for this information.

24. For this emphasis on decorativeness and imaginative fantasy see, for example, "The Royal Academy," *The Saturday Review*, 63 (May 7, 1887), p. 650; Robert A. M. Stevenson, "J. S. Sargent," *The Art Journal*, 27 (March 1888), p. 69; A. Lys Baldry, "The Art of John S. Sargent, R.A.: Part II," *International Studio*, 10 (April 1900), pp. 111–12; T. Martin Wood, *Sargent* (London, n.d.), pp. 28–30; and Charles H. Caffin, *American Masters of Painting: Being Brief Appreciations of Some American Painters* (New York, 1902), pp. 65–66.

The most perceptive analysis of *Carnation, Lily, Lily, Rose* in recent years was offered by Martha Kingsbury, "John Singer Sargent: Aspects of His Works," Ph.D. dissertation (Harvard University, Cambridge, Massachusetts, 1969), pp. 41–76. For Kingsbury, the two-dimensionality of the space is not a decorative or an Impressionist device, but an effect which produces a sense of mystery in the "hiddenness" of the little girls, absorbed into the "special world" of childhood, neither communicating with each other nor with the spectator, who is kept out of the scene by the tangle of brush and the lack of a firm ground plane or three-dimensional recession.

25. A letter from Monet in Giverny to Auguste Rodin in Paris, written on June 5, 1887, notes that "Sargent n'est pas libre. Il est à la campagne jusqu'à demain. Je dois le voir et nous arrangerons cela probablement pour jeudi à déjeuner"; quoted in Wildenstein, *Claude Monet*, III, p. 223.

26. René Gimpel, *Diary of an Art Dealer* (New York, 1966), p. 75.

27. *In a Garden* (collection of the Ormond Family), for instance, a painting assigned to Sargent's visits to Nice, included a seated woman sketching in a landscape. This picture was published as painted in Nice in James Lomax and Richard Ormond, *John Singer Sargent and the Edwardian Age*, exhibition catalogue (Leeds, England, Leeds Art Galleries; London, National Portrait Gallery; and The Detroit Institute of Arts, 1979). However, Kate Millet's daughter, Joyce A. Sharpey-Schafer, dates the picture 1885–86, identifying it as a view in the Millet orchard at Russell House, Broadway, and the woman as Mrs. Emily Williams; letter to Donna Seldin of the Coe Kerr Gallery, Inc., January 31, 1983. *In a Garden*, or, better, *In an Orchard*, would thus be a significant precursor to the paintings of 1887–89 discussed above, pp. 121–31. though in this earlier painting the identification of the artist with the form of artistry is minimized, and the work produced is truly only a sketch, rather than a finished work of art.

28. Both Downes, *John S. Sargent*, p. 150, and Charteris, *John Sargent*, p. 133, date it to 1888, but Downes also identifies it with the portrait of Monet that Sargent exhibited at the New Gallery that year, which was certainly the picture now in the collection of the National Academy of Design, New York, and probably painted at the same

95.
Sally Fairchild, 1890
Oil on canvas, 30 × 25½ (76.2 × 64.8)
Terra Museum of American Art, Chicago;
Daniel J. Terra Collection

time as the Tate Gallery picture. (Charteris' dating is often incorrect; for instance, he states that *A Morning Walk* of 1888 was executed the following year.) Charles Merrill Mount, *John Singer Sargent: A Biography* (London, 1955), p. 356, lists the Tate painting of Monet as done in 1889.

More recently, attempts have been made to confirm the 1889 date by identifying the work on Monet's easel as one of two pictures Monet painted in Giverny during that year, *Les Saules* or *Les Saules au Soleil Couchant*; see Wildenstein, *Claude Monet*, III, pp. 128–29. It would seem, however, that such identification is somewhat specious, not only because Sargent's interest in his subject here is to associate himself with the great French master and his methodology, rather than to record specifics, but also because of the confusion in regard to the dates of the two *Les Saules* works. According to Wildenstein, the dates on both were painted on long after the completion of the works, the first *Les Saules* being dated in this way to 1886.

29. *The Art Journal*, 27 (June 1888), p. 249; the Sargent depiction of Monet is also referred to specifically as a "head" in "The New Gallery," *The Saturday Review*, 65 (May 12, 1888), p. 562.

30. In 1887, Sargent purchased Monet's *A Rock at Treport (Vaques à La Manepport)* of 1885 and wrote to the Frenchman: "C'est avec beaucoup de mal que je m'arrache de devant votre délicieux tableau pour lequel 'vous ne partagez pas mon admiration' (quelle blague!) pour vous redire combien je l'admire. Je resterais là devant pendant des heures entières dans un état d'abrutissement voluptueux ou d'enchantment si vous préférez. Je suis ravi d'avoir chez moi une telle source du plaisir"; quoted in Charteris, *John Sargent*, p. 97. Furthermore, Sargent was soon to own three more works by Monet: *Bennecourt* of 1887 was sold by Monet to Sargent in August 1887, and Sargent owned the French artist's *Paysage avec Figures, Giverny*, in 1889. In 1891, Sargent purchased Monet's 1884 *Maison de Jardinier*. For the complete list of Monet paintings owned by Sargent, see Wildenstein, *Claude Monet*, II, pp. 118 and 178; III, pp. 88, 114.

31. George Henschel, *Musings and Memories of a Musician* (New York, 1919), pp. 331–32.

32. As he wrote to Monet: "Quoique j'ai beaucoup travaillé dernièrement sur la Tamise je n'ai rien comme résultat. C'est un peu parceque ce sacré projet de voyage me rendait impossible l'achèvement de mon tableau, et puis les difficultés matérielles faire des gens en bateau sur l'eau, entre bateaux etc"; quoted in Charteris, *John Sargent*, p. 97.

33. The figure has been tentatively identified as Sargent's friend, the poet Alma Strettell, who would marry Robert Harrison's nephew, Lawrence A. "Peter" Harrison, in 1890.

34. During the summer of either 1887 or 1888 he painted *Wargrave, Backwater* (private collection), a somewhat dark and tonal landscape.

35. After Sargent's death, *By the River* was inscribed by a dealer with the date of 1885, probably because William Howe Downes, *John S. Sargent*, p. 141, stated that the picture was done at Broadway that year. Subsequent authorities, however, including Sargent's sister Emily, agree that the picture conforms to Sargent's work at Calcot in style and subject, and should be dated to 1888. The very attractive subject of the picture, perhaps Flora Priestley, is not identified.

36. Interestingly, Sargent's good friend Henry James introduced the simile of St. Martin's summer a few years later in his short story "Sir Edmund Orme," published first in *Black and White* in November 1891. In the story, Mrs. Marden encourages the nameless young hero in his pursuit of her daughter, Charlotte, in the hope of breaking the malevolent spell of a spirit which she herself had sent to his death; under the false illusion of a respite from her troubles, Mrs. Marden took comfort that "for herself she felt it to be a good time, a sort of St. Martin's summer of the soul."

37. See Lilla Cabot Perry, "Reminiscences of Claude Monet from 1889 to 1909," *The American Magazine of Art*, 18 (March 1927), p. 120.

38. See Bunker's letters to Joe Evans in the Dennis Miller Bunker Archives, Archives of American Art, Smithsonian Institution, Washington, D.C., especially those dated May 9, June 18, and September 11, 1888.

39. Bunker seems to have had romantic inclinations toward Sargent's sister. On June 25, 1888, he wrote to Isabella Stewart Gardner: "I expect to be off in the country [i.e., to Calcot] in a few days. Sargent has found a charming place near Reading . . . willows, boats — and I hope pretty girls. . . .

96.

The Old Chair, 1885
Oil on canvas, 26 × 22 (66 × 55.9)
Collection of the Ormond Family

The youngest Miss Sargent is awfully
pretty — charming. What if I should fall in
love with her? Dreadful thought, but I'm
sure to — I see it coming — It is at
moments like these that I feel most keenly
the absence of your restraining hand";
letter in the Isabella Stewart Gardner
Museum correspondence, Archives of
American Art, Smithsonian Institution,
Washington, D.C. The major studies of
Bunker's career are those by R. H. Ives
Gammell in: *Dennis Miller Bunker*,
exhibition catalogue (Museum of Fine Arts,
Boston, 1943); *Dennis Miller Bunker: A
Supplementary Group of Paintings and Water
Colors Including Some Early Works*, exhibition
catalogue (Museum of Fine Arts, Boston,
1945); and *Dennis Miller Bunker* (New York,
1953); see also Charles B. Ferguson, *Dennis
Miller Bunker (1861–1890) Rediscovered*,

exhibition catalogue (New Britain,
Connecticut, The New Britain Museum of
American Art, 1978). The present author
discusses Sargent and Bunker in *American
Impressionism* (New York, 1984), pp. 83–86.

40. The writer for the London *Times*, "English
and French 'Impressionists,'" April 18,
1889, p. 8, noted: "Claude Monet . . . is an
avowed 'Impressionist,' of a very
individual character indeed, and almost all
the members of the New English Art Club,
though they might only accept the title
with modifications, paint with pretty much
the same intention. It is true that only a
few are as marvellous in their choice of
colours as M. Monet is; perhaps, indeed,
Mr. P. W. Steer can alone claim that
distinction, though in his two curious
riverside sketches, 'St. Martin's Summer'
and 'A Morning Walk,' Mr. John Sargent
has for once gone rather far in this
direction." The critic for *The American
Magazine of Art*, "Exhibitions of the
Month" (May 1889), p. xix, generally
endorsed Sargent's Impressionism,
concurring that both *St. Martin's Summer*
and *A Morning Walk* were inspired by
Monet; however, the writer for *The
Spectator*, no less cognizant of Sargent's
radical aesthetics, voiced his objections,
finding the pictures "heavy in colour and
otherwise unpleasing . . . "; "Art: The
New English Art Club Exhibition of
Pictures," *The Spectator*, 174 (April 27,
1889), pp. 576–77.

In American publications, as in the
English ones, the reception of Sargent's
Impressionist work was qualified: "At the
recent charming little exhibition of the
New English Art Club in Piccadilly,
[Sargent] had two studies of landscape and
figures in the style of such Impressionists as
Monet and Pessaro [*sic*]. Marvellously
clever they were, as, indeed — I must
remark by the way — were scores of other
contributions to that little gallery of works
of the more promising of the younger men
in English painting, who now in revolt
against the conventionalism of the Royal
Academy, will one day make their
influence felt in that Philistine institution.
The trouble about these two pictures of
Mr. Sargent's is, that they were examples
of his cleverness and little more . . . "; *The
Art Amateur*, 21 (August 1889), p. 46.

41. See the particularly perceptive analysis of
Lady Fishing in Lomax and Ormond, *John*

Singer Sargent and the Edwardian Age, pp. 45–46.

42. For an excellent, perceptive discussion of this picture, see Maureen C. O'Brien, "Sargent, John Singer 1856–1925. A Boating Party," in *Museum of Art, Rhode Island School of Design, Selection VII: American Paintings from the Museum's Collection, c. 1800–1930* (Providence, 1977), pp. 179–82.

43. See Hoopes, "John S. Sargent," for a full discussion of this painting and its context within Sargent's Impressionist period.

44. For an excellent study of the work Sargent did in Worcester in 1890, see Susan E. Strickler, "John Singer Sargent and Worcester," *Worcester Art Museum Journal*, 6 (1982–83), pp. 18–39.

45. It is not known why Sargent chose these two works to exhibit in America. They may have offered a contrast between the more colorful and sunlit approach of 1888 (*A Morning Walk*) and the more structured and calculated painting of the following year; but it is more likely that he chose the two for their relative variety of outdoor subject matter — one a painting of casual beauty, the other concerned with the art of painting.

46. Only *A Morning Walk* was exhibited at the St. Botolph Club. *Paul Helleu Sketching*, which was exhibited with *A Morning Walk* in subsequent American showings, may not have arrived with the rest of Sargent's shipment, or may have been damaged in transit or otherwise in need of further work or retouching.

47. For a discussion of the gradual appearance of works by American Impressionist artists in public exhibitions and the critical reactions to them, see Gerdts, *American Impressionism, passim.*

48. "The Fine Arts. Exhibition of Oil Paintings at the St. Botolph Club," *The Boston Post*, February 8, 1890, p. 9. But see also the more positive review, "The Fine Arts: The Midwinter Exhibition of the St. Botolph Club," *The Boston Evening Transcript*, January 28, 1890, p. 6: "The skies are represented only by reflections in these interesting freaks of painting; and they may be classified as bold and original experimentations in the representations of the thermal phenomenon which possesses such a powerful fascination for all painters — sunlight." I am indebted to Liese Hilgeman for searching the Boston newspapers for me in order to locate the reviews of Sargent's pictures at the St. Botolph Club show. The writer in the *Transcript* was not alone in admiring Sargent's single entry, and the fullest enthusiasm was voiced by the critic for the *Boston Sunday Herald*, "The Fine Arts," February 2, 1890, p. 12: "brilliant impressions are more congenial to his temperament and of this order is a picture of a lady in white, carrying a white umbrella, and standing by a river's edge on summer morning. Here is a vision of sunniness and a dazzling blending of white, green and blue tints. If this rendering of dainty fashionable feminine grace is not true, nobody is hurt and the artist has given to the scene so much charm that we are sorry if it is not a veritable translation of his interviews with nature."

49. See, for example, Clarence Cook, "The Monthly Exhibition of the Union League Club," *The Studio*, 5 (February 22, 1890), p. 117: "Mr. John S. Sargent's 'Summer Morning' and 'An Out-of-Doors Study' are in this artist's clever off-hand manner with perhaps less than usual beneath the surface."

The two works were on view at the Union League Club in New York (February 13–15), and reappeared in the Twelfth Annual Exhibition of the Society of American Artists in that city on April 28. This show traveled to The Art Institute of Chicago (June 19–July 13) for its Third Annual Exhibition of Oil Paintings. In November, Sargent sent the two pictures to the Philadelphia Art Club. For reviews of the New York shows, see "The Union League Club Exhibition: American Figure Paintings," *New York Daily Tribune*, February 14, 1890, p. 7; "American Figure Painters in Line," *New York Herald*, February 14, 1890, p. 5; "Art at the Union League," *The New York Times*, February 14, 1890, p. 4; "American and European Art Notes," *Art Interchange*, 24 (May 24, 1890), p. 176; and "The Society of American Artists Exhibition," *The Art Amateur*, 23 (June 1890), p. 3.

For Chicago reviews, see *Chicago Tribune*, June 9, 1890, p. 4; *Chicago Evening Post*, June 11, 1890, p. 5. As with the critics in Boston and New York, *Summer Morning* was accorded the attention denied to the rendition of Paul Helleu painting outdoors. The critic for the *Chicago Tribune* noted that these two canvases "express less buoyant types [than *La Carmencita*], one a portrait of a lady whose elusive personality is expressed in changeable green and lavender, another an open air summer study of the artist's sister, who wanders white-robed along the banks of a stream vividly blue, a brilliant, sunny radiant bit of color." And in the *Chicago Evening Post* the writer pointed out that "In *A Summer Morning*, where a young lady is walking among the flowers, there are such high notes of pink and blue and such sunlight as is quite blinding, but still one feels the open air and the young woman is pretty and thoroughly alive, and the reflection of a fleecy cloud in the water is a dainty touch. The picture is also full of the opulent, full-grown green of summer and, when one has grown accustomed to the coloring, much that is pleasing is revealed."

I am extremely grateful to Wendy Greenhouse for locating and transcribing for me these Chicago reviews of Sargent's paintings. I am also indebted to Dr. Trevor J. Fairbrother, assistant curator at the Museum of Fine Arts, Boston, for disclosing to me the appearance of Sargent's Impressionist works at Chicago and, later, in Philadelphia, as well as for confirming the complete schedule of their exhibition, including the Boston and New York showings. His generosity in sharing and discussing this information has helped tremendously to clear up the confusion concerning the identification of the paintings that were shown and the obfuscation caused by contemporary and later writers.

For Philadelphia reviews, see "The Art Club Exhibition," *The Philadelphia Press*, November 3, 1890, p. 11; and the review cited below, n. 50. I am much indebted to Nina Purviance for locating and transcribing these two reviews for me.

The relative lack of interest in Sargent's two outdoor paintings at some of the exhibitions may be due to several factors. In the April exhibition in New York, the paintings were already familiar works, having been exhibited in February. In addition, there were also many other American Impressionist pictures on exhibition. More significantly, here and in Chicago, Sargent's Impressionist works were only two among seven examples of his art. Among the other five, *La Carmencita* became the star of the exhibitions.

50. "2nd Exhibition of the Art Club," *The Philadelphia American*, November 8, 1890, p. 71:

Unfortunately, for Mr. Sargent, however, the impression which he produces here will not be associated very closely with this beautiful and masterly work [Portrait of a Boy, Fig. 108] for he has seen fit to exhibit along with it a couple of so-called "plein air" studies, large enough and loud enough in their crude way to attract a great deal of attention, and childish enough to neutralize to a great extent the effect produced by a more serious work.

To painters largely occupied as they necessarily are with the discussion of purely technical matters, any new "fad" possesses a certain interest of course, and these studies of Mr. Sargent will doubtlessly excite, as on this ground they may well do, a lively interest among those whose minds are mainly occupied with means and methods. But, in their essential foolishness, their inherent trivialness is none the less obvious for all that.

The everlasting verities with which art seriously concerns itself, although their complexion changes somewhat with the altered habits and varying tastes of the generations that come and go, still preserve in the main the lineaments that they have always worn; their characters were found and fixed long years ago, and they have certainly not much in common with such nonsense as this. The idea that possibly the academical scheme does not exhaust the possibilities of art is well enough. The feeling that instead of always trying to paint what we see with half-closed eyes, there is no harm trying to render the impressions which nature makes on eyes wide open, — nobody can fault with this, — but it is hard to see how self styled "impressionists" with whose work these studies of Mr. Sargent are to be classed, have contributed much to the advance for which emancipation stands. They claim to have done it all I know, but I do not see that their claim is established, for men who do not make such a parade of detestable drawing, and who do not find it beneath them to treat subjects which possess some little dignity and interest in the estimate of thoughtful people, have carried the color key quite as high, and reproduced as distinctly the effect of intense illumination, and so in spite of the prominence that is given to this kind of discussion in the talk of those who affect this phase of art, the animus of the movement must be sought elsewhere.

Among the less strident, but nonetheless critical reviews of Sargent's Impressionist works is that in the *New York Daily Tribune* (cited above, n. 49): "It is clear that Mr. Sargent has been sitting at the feet of Claude Monet, but his impressions of outdoor light and air bear the mark of his own individuality. Both pictures are luminous, brilliantly painted and audacious. . . . Much may be claimed from the rendering of grasses and boat in [*Paul Helleu Sketching*], and the coloring seems a little forced, save in the absolutely colorless faces, which are the faces of the dead." For other associations with Impressionism, see "The Monthly Exhibition of the Union League Club," *The Studio*, 5 (February 22, 1890), p. 117; "Art Notes," *Art Interchange*, 24 (March 1, 1890), p. 68; "My Note Book," *The Art Amateur*, 22 (March 1890), p. 72. I am indebted to my students Gerald Bolas, Carol Lowery, and Diane Fischer, who analyzed these respective art periodicals for my course in nineteenth-century American art criticism in the spring of 1985, and located the references pertinent to Sargent's canvases.

On the whole, Chicago critics were surprisingly receptive to Impressionist work, which had not been extensively known there before. Philadelphia, on the other hand, though it had as little familiarity with Impressionism, was to accept it only reluctantly during the 1890s.

51. Renoir portrayed Frédéric Bazille at his easel in 1867; Fantin-Latour paid tribute to Manet in his *Studio in the Batignolles* of 1870, and Bazille painted *Artist's Studio* in that same year. Renoir portrayed *Monet Working in His Garden at Argenteuil* the following year, and Manet, reciprocating, painted *Monet Working on His Boat* in 1874.

52. I am extremely grateful to Dr. Kenneth McConkey for bringing the paintings by Osborne and Bramley to my attention, and for discussing with me, generally, the possible impact of Sargent's Impressionist work on British artists of the period.

53. Roger Fry, "J. S. Sargent as Seen at the Royal Academy Exhibition of His Works, 1926, and in the National Gallery," in *Transformations: Critical and Speculative Essays on Art* (New York, 1926; reprint, Freeport, New York, 1968), pp. 125–26.

54. Bruce Laughton, "Steer and French Painting," *Apollo*, 91 (March 1970), p. 212; see also Laughton, *Phillip Wilson Steer 1860–1940* (Oxford, 1971), pp. 16, 72, 76, 78.

55. Walter Sickert, "Sargentolatry," *The New Age*, 7 (May 19, 1910), pp. 56–57; reprinted in Carter Ratcliff, *John Singer Sargent* (New York, 1982), pp. 233–34.

56. *Carnation, Lily, Lily, Rose* was on public display after its acquisition by the Tate Gallery in 1887. It was also reproduced in *The Art Journal*, 40 (March 1888), p. 65; *Harper's New Monthly Magazine*, 79 (September 1889), p. 496; and in Theodore Child, *Art and Criticism* (New York, 1892), p. 105.

57. See R. E. Wilson, "Trout Fishing in California," *The Overland Monthly*, 18 (September 1891), pp. 240–43, in which the illustrations specifically depict women "fishermen." The description of the proper garb for this activity is given on p. 242. I am most grateful to L. Bailey Van Hook for bringing this article to my attention.

58. Royal Cortissoz, "John S. Sargent," *Scribner's Magazine*, 34 (November 1903), p. 532.

Sargent's Late Portraits

GARY A. REYNOLDS

Although he painted almost every kind of picture, from still life to religious allegory, John Singer Sargent's reputation has always rested upon his career as a portrait painter. In 1908, Christian Brinton wrote in *Modern Artists*:

Beyond all question he is the most conspicuous of living portrait painters. Before his eyes pass in continuous procession the world of art, science, and letters, the world financial, diplomatic, or military, and the world frankly social. To-day comes a savant, a captain of industry, or a slender, troubled child. To-morrow it will be an insinuating Semitic Plutus; next week may bring some fresh-tinted Diana, radiant with vernal bloom. Everyone, from poet to general, from duchess to dark-eyed dancer, finds a place in this shifting throng.[1]

For his own part, Sargent often seemed uncomfortable or ambiguous about this emphasis on his portraits. In 1907, after more than a decade as the English-speaking world's most sought-after portraitist, he declared: "I have long been sick and tired of portrait painting, and when I was painting my own 'mug,' I firmly decided to devote myself to other branches of art as soon as possible."[2]

Sargent may have eventually tired of the demands placed upon him as society's favorite portraitist, but it is clear that from the start of his career he aimed at this goal. During his years in Paris he studied with Carolus-Duran, an artist particularly known for his portraits. The younger artist eagerly sought commissions to paint members of French and expatriate American society; and his portraits of them comprise the majority of the works Sargent sent to the annual Salon exhibitions. In 1886, when his portrait business in Paris was foundering, particularly after the hostile reception given to *Madame X* two years earlier (Fig. 47), Sargent moved permanently to London. Between 1882 and 1904, he exhibited seventy-five portraits at the Royal Academy, as opposed to only a handful of landscapes and subject pictures.[3] The other places in the city where Sargent frequently exhibited, such as the Grosvenor Gallery or the New Gallery, also received mostly portraits.

Only in the United States, and prior to about 1890, does Sargent's reputation appear to have rested equally upon landscapes, subject pictures, and portraits. However, as a result of the numerous commissions received during his trips to

97.
Mrs. Edward L. Davis and Her Son Livingston, 1890
Oil on canvas, 86 × 48 (218.4 × 121.9)
Los Angeles County Museum of Art; Frances and Armand Hammer Foundation Purchase Fund

98.
Lady with the Rose
(Charlotte Louise Burckhardt), 1882
Oil on canvas, 84 × 44¾ (213.4 × 113.7)
The Metropolitan Museum of Art, New York;
Bequest of Valerie B. Hadden, 1932

America between 1887 and 1903, his portraits became predominant in exhibitions at Boston, New York, Philadelphia, and Chicago. Sargent rarely sent works to the annual exhibitions of the National Academy of Design in New York, but other artistic events made his portraits a conspicuous presence in the city.

Chief among these were the charity portrait shows sponsored by prominent members of New York society and held in the galleries of the National Academy of Design during the late 1890s for the benefit of St. John's Hospital. As much social as artistic events, these exhibitions were composed primarily of paintings loaned from New York's social elite and were opened with great fanfare in the press. Important for Sargent's growing reputation as a society portraitist was the opportunity such shows gave the public and critics to compare his work to that of European and American contemporaries. In 1895, *The New York Times* reported that over six hundred portraits were hanging in the benefit exhibition, including examples by Carolus-Duran, Bonnat, Madrazo, Zorn, and Manet. Sargent was represented by five works, among them *Ada Rehan* (1894; The Metropolitan Museum of Art, New York) and *Beatrice Goelet* (1890; private collection). The latter received lavish praise from a critic who found the Goelet child's portrait "a veritable gem and a delicious piece of technical work."[4] At the 1898 exhibition, Sargent's portrait of *Asher Wertheimer* (Fig. 116) was placed facing Whistler's *Symphony in White, No. 1: The White Girl*.[5]

During the early 1900s, Sargent began declining portrait commissions in favor of subject pictures and landscapes, painted in both oil and watercolor. However, his reputation had already been established as a portrait painter among critics and the public. He was the "Van Dyck," the "Velázquez," the "Reynolds" of modern times. When writers such as Christian Brinton, Charles H. Caffin, or John C. Van Dyke included him in their histories of art published early in the century, they discussed him primarily as a portraitist.

These books were published late in Sargent's career, and by writers with perspectives and critical skills far more sophisticated than most who wrote on Sargent's work during the 1880s and 1890s. And yet, they addressed many of the same questions: should Sargent really be considered an American painter; was the bravura of his style brilliant or simply facile; could he convey character in his portraits; did his work represent a new, distinctly modern, type of portrait; and was he, indeed, the greatest painter of his age. These are still the questions we most often ask about Sargent.

Perhaps because John Singer Sargent was such a success at the end of his career, it is often forgotten that he struggled long and hard to develop a personal style and to gain acceptance for it. During his Paris years, he enjoyed moderate success as a promising young portrait painter. As the prize pupil of Carolus-Duran, he could take pride in a growing number of large, full-length portraits, such as *Madame Edouard Pailleron* (Fig. 3), *Dr. Pozzi at Home* (Fig. 55), *Lady with the Rose (Charlotte Louise Burckhardt)* (Fig. 98), and *Mrs. Henry White* (Fig. 64), all of which attracted the attention, if not the unanimous approval, of the critics. Indeed, had it

99.
James Jacques Joseph Tissot, *October*, 1877
Oil on canvas, 85¼ × 43⅛ (216.5 × 109.5)
The Montreal Museum of Fine Arts

not been for the great scandal that erupted over *Madame X* in the Salon of 1884, Sargent might well have remained in Paris.

Among Sargent's earliest essays in the field of portrait painting, *Frances Sherburne Ridley Watts* (Fig. 1), *Carolus-Duran* (Fig. 4), and *The Pailleron Children (Edouard and Marie-Louise)* (Fig. 6), are masterfully handled, yet not essentially different in composition, rendering, and mood from portraits by contemporary academic painters such as Bonnat, Cabanel, or even Bouguereau. They show an artist experimenting with new effects of dramatic composition and color, but still working within the popular style of French academic portraiture learned from his teacher. The *Carolus-Duran* portrait received an Honorable Mention in the Salon of 1879 and favorable criticism when shown the following year at the Society of American Artists. The critic Mariana Griswold Van Rensselaer later recalled it as "the picture of the year in New York where it was the first of his works to be shown."[6] Typical of Sargent's work of the late 1870s is the controlled modeling of the figure, the subdued light, the carefully balanced color scheme, and the austere background.

Very soon, however, Sargent began to break away from the methods of his teacher and to work with the more innovative ideas that became current in French art of the 1880s. *Madame Edouard Pailleron* employs an artificially high viewpoint, with the noticeable effect of elongating the figure and flattening the background. The contrast between the impressionistic landscape and the more solidly rendered Mme. Pailleron creates an ambiguity between the figure and the space it occupies not unlike that found in the contemporary outdoor peasant subjects of Jules Bastien-Lepage. Although *Madame Edouard Pailleron* can also be compared to the eighteenth-century out-of-doors portraits of Sir Joshua Reynolds or Thomas Gainsborough, the flattened, tapestrylike background and strongly silhouetted figure are more like those in contemporary figure paintings by James Jacques Joseph Tissot (Fig. 99), Manet (*Autumn [Mery Laureat]*, 1881) or Monet (*Madame Monet in Japanese Guise*, 1876).

Sargent painted Mme. Pailleron during the summer of 1879, and in the fall left for Spain to study the work of Velázquez. Much has been written about the impact of the Spanish painter's work on Sargent.[7] On the most superficial level, Velázquez's portraits provided a compositional vocabulary from which Sargent drew throughout his career. Perhaps more important were the lessons he learned about the use of tonal values, fluid paint surfaces, and carefully constructed interior spaces. Sargent was led to Velázquez by Carolus-Duran, who encouraged his students to practice a style of direct painting derived from the Spanish master. Portraits such as *Lady with the Rose* and *The Daughters of Edward D. Boit* (Fig. 48) are skillfully conceived and executed homages to Velázquez, as filtered through Sargent's nineteenth-century eye.

The boldly painted canvases of the seventeenth-century Dutch painter Frans Hals also attracted the young Sargent. In August 1880, he traveled to Haarlem to study Hals' expressive, yet economical, brushwork. Eager to learn from the great

100.

Madame Paul Poirson, 1885
Oil on canvas, 59 × 33½ (149.9 × 85.1)
The Detroit Institute of Arts; Founders
Society Purchase with funds from Mr. and Mrs.
Richard A. Manoogian and Beatrice Rogers
Bequest Fund, Gibbs-Williams Fund and
Ralph Harman Booth Bequest Fund

artists of the past, Sargent also copied the paintings of Titian, Tintoretto, El
Greco, and Rubens. Writing in 1907 of Sargent's relationship to the style of
painterly realism that grew from these influences, the American critic Charles H.
Caffin noted:

*These discoveries effected the emancipation of painting from the thraldom of Academic
draughtsmanship. It restored the actual craftsmanship of the brush to an honourable standing,
and gave the painter thereby an opportunity of developing and exhibiting his individuality.*[8]

Sargent's use of fluid strokes of paint to render form and light grew in
boldness and authority during the 1880s and, in essence, became the "signature" of
his mature style. It is this freedom of execution that separates portraits such as
Madame Paul Poirson (Fig. 100) and *Edith, Lady Playfair* (Fig. 65) from their more
staid academic counterparts, to which they are so closely allied in mood and
composition. As might be expected, the growing bravura of Sargent's style put
him at odds with more conservative critics. When shown in Brussels at the
exhibition "Les XX" in 1884, the magnificent *Dr. Pozzi at Home* was attacked by a
writer for *La Libre Revue* as too theatrical and arresting, "comme un verre à
champagne trop précipitamment rempli, plus de mousse que de vin d'or."[9] Even
the more sedate *Mrs. Henry White*, with its carefully modulated color scheme of
silvery whites and golds, offended the critic for *The Athenaeum* when exhibited at
the Royal Academy in 1884. He considered the colors "raw" and the execution
unrefined.[10]

In the fall of 1885, Sargent had written to an English friend, John Russell,
about the possibility of moving to London, but with the reservation that "it might
be a long struggle for my painting to be accepted. It is thought beastly French."[11]
This criticism obviously concerned the artist and is one that forms a leitmotif in
virtually all of the contemporary writing about him, whether positive or negative.
Even the French critic Arthur Baignères, writing for the *Gazette des Beaux-Arts* in
1883, questioned: "Must one count M. Sargent among the foreigners? He was born
in America [*sic*], but he learned to paint in Paris, under the tutelage of M. Carolus-
Duran. He does an honor to our city and to his teacher."[12] When *The Misses Vickers*
(Fig. 61) was shown in the Salon of 1885, it received a favorable reception from the
French critics. However, when it debuted in England the following year at the
Royal Academy, the English press was relentless in its criticism of the contrived
gestures and dramatic light effects. *The Spectator* declared it "the *ne plus ultra* of
French painting, or rather, the French method as learned by a clever foreigner, in
which everything is sacrificed to technical considerations."[13]

What was this French influence that so concerned the critics of Sargent's
work during the 1880s and 1890s? Although few writers could adequately define a
single "French style," for most it had to do with a perceived emphasis on technical
fluency. *The Athenaeum*, for example, emphasized the technical skill and refinement
of the more conservative French portrait painters in reviewing the Salon of 1888.

Several of the best artists in France are devoting themselves to portraiture, and unlike the majority of our artists of the same class, they expend all the resources of their learning, taste, and skill upon them. In Paris no painter of reputation is content with the merest indication of an eye or ear; no accomplished master lets the hands resemble the flappers of seals, nor does he descend to the vulgar tricks some of our popular likeness-takers permit themselves. Fine taste prevails, and solid, graceful, accomplished workmanship is the usual rule.[14]

Two years earlier, the periodical had criticized Sargent's portrait of *Mrs. Robert Harrison* (1886; private collection) for its "rawness and crudity of an uncompromising treatment of the features, forms and expression."[15]

Malcolm Bell briefly addressed the subject of French influence in a review of the 1891 Society of American Artists exhibition, which included Sargent's *Beatrice Goelet*. On the whole, he felt that French training had led to a "lack of imagination and poetry" in the work of many of the artists. Furthermore, too many younger American artists were inclined to imitate what they saw abroad without any deeper understanding of the styles. Bell exempted Sargent from this criticism, however, praising the *Goelet* portrait for the "brilliant reality" of the image and "the audacity of the direct challenge to a comparison with Velasquez" in the arrangement and color scheme. For him, Sargent's work at the exhibition represented "the difference between a man repeating with inconsiderate glibness the words of a fine speaker and a man pouring out burning eloquence from his own heart — the difference between saying something and meaning something."[16]

Clearly, the "French style" could have very different meanings for early critics and could be used to either praise or damn an artist's work. By the time of Sargent's death in 1925, enough historical perspective had been gained for writers such as Mariana Van Rensselaer to successfully argue that the essence of his style was cosmopolitan, "for the France that taught him was teaching half the world."[17] Brinton gave this argument a unique twist when he wrote in 1908:

His adaptability and his very lack of bias bespeak the native complexity of his origin. It cannot for a moment be maintained that the French paint themselves as Sargent paints them, or the English either. His art is neither Gallic nor British, it is American, and the chief reason why it is so different from most Anglo-Saxon art is because it is so superior, not because it is unAmerican.[18]

Writers such as Brinton were not only eager to claim Sargent as an *American* artist, but also to express the growing national chauvinism of American culture prior to World War I.

By late 1887, Sargent's career was approaching something of a crisis. He had hoped to rebuild his reputation as a portrait painter in London, but found his circumstances there little improved. As Henry James had confided to Vernon Lee in 1885, most women were "afraid of him lest he should make them too eccentric looking."[19] In addition, the relative austerity of portraits such as *Lady with the Rose* and *Madame X* was beginning to give way to more complex compositions and

heavily impastoed surfaces, probably influenced by his experiments with
Impressionism.

At this crucial moment, Sargent decided to accept a commission to paint
Mrs. Henry G. Marquand, the wife of the future president of The Metropolitan
Museum of Art, New York, at their home in Newport, Rhode Island. Initially the
artist had been reluctant to make this trip, quoting triple his normal fee in hopes
of discouraging their interest. He could not foresee the great success that the
1887–88 painting excursion would produce, nor that he would remain in America
for eight months, painting more than twenty portraits in Newport, Boston, and
New York — a vast improvement over his dwindling portrait business in both
Paris and London.[20]

Prior to this visit, Sargent's figure and landscape subjects had fared well in
America.[21] His portraits, however, were not well known to the public nor entirely
successful with the critics. Henry James' article on Sargent for the October issue of
Harper's New Monthly Magazine — in which he described Sargent's portraits as
offering "the slightly 'uncanny' spectacle of a talent which on the very threshold of
its career has nothing more to learn" — served as a well-timed piece of propa-
ganda for potential American sitters.[22] When the artist arrived in Boston later that
year, the *Evening Transcript* enthusiastically joined in welcoming Sargent to his
ancestral city by assuring its citizens that his "unusual success as a portrait painter
in Paris and London has been fully merited and the patent of European approval
which he brings hither has been legitimately won by him."[23] Although Sargent
was considered a rising young talent, the majority of his portraits were still too
unconventional to have won the patent of European, or even American, approval.

The portraits that Sargent painted during the 1887–88 American trip were
remarkably diverse and in many cases reflect a rethinking of earlier works. His
seated portrait of *Elizabeth Allen Marquand (Mrs. Henry G. Marquand)* (Fig. 102) is
restrained in both composition and technique. When exhibited at the Royal
Academy in 1888, it was praised by *The Athenaeum* for its harmonious tone, color
and disposition, indications that the artist was finally "bent upon refining his
painting in every way." The more extravagant *Mrs. Edward D. Boit* (Fig. 103) was
found by the writer to be more "ambitious and masterly," but less pleasing.

*It is painted in a broad, large style, the treatment of the flesh is firm and robust, but the face
itself is disfigured by a coarse and rough dash of dark color, placed for mere effect, and in
contempt of nature, by the side of the nose. Abounding in "go", it is a Velazquez vulgarized.
The hands, unlike those of No. 365 [Elizabeth Allen Marquand], are worse than indifferent.[24]*

In Boston, Sargent also painted a full-length portrait of the wealthy collector
Isabella Stewart Gardner (Fig. 59), who had visited the artist's London studio in 1886
at the suggestion of Henry James. Unlike most sitters, Mrs. Gardner appears to
have wanted a flamboyant portrait to match her self-image. Yet after eight false
starts, Sargent painted her in a simple, almost severe, pose that focuses attention
on her face and elegantly flowing arms. The gently rounded shapes of the folded

hands, the strands of pearls at the waist and neck, the sloping shoulders and the patterned Renaissance fabric of the background all reinforce the softness of the sitter's face. As in the earlier portrait of *Madame X*, Mrs. Gardner reveals a daring décolletage and her pale skin contrasts sharply with the dark dress and background. Sargent must have been pleased with the effect of a patterned fabric background, because he used similar devices in later portraits such as *Ada Rehan*, *Lady Agnew of Lochnaw* (Fig. 110), and *Mrs. Charles Thursby* (Fig. 119).

Despite the devastating effect of *Madame X* on his early career, Sargent now seemed intent upon continuing to use it as a prototype for other works, but with modifications in some of its more strident characteristics. In New York, he painted *Mrs. Adrian Iselin* (Fig. 104) standing beside a small Neoclassical table, upon which she rests her right hand in the manner of *Madame X*. Dressed in black, she is strongly silhouetted against the neutral background. The intensity and directness of Mrs. Iselin's gaze is as arresting as Mme. Gautreau's haughty profile. The same

arrangement of figure and accessories was also used for a portrait of *Mrs. Elliott Fitch Shepard* (1888; San Antonio Museum of Art), a member of New York's Vanderbilt family.

Near the end of this trip, in January 1888, an exhibition of Sargent's work opened at the St. Botolph Club in Boston. The mixed reception that greeted his recent portraits was humorously summed up by a writer for *The Art Amateur*:

Boston propriety has not yet got over the start Mr. John D. [sic] Sargent's exhibition of portraits at the St. Botolph Club gave it; it fairly jumped at the first sight, and on second thoughts did not know whether it ought to feel really shocked or only amused. It is still undecided, I think, if it was insulted or delighted. . . . Not, of course, that there were any nudities or any such improprieties in the collection, but the spirit and style of the painter were so audacious, reckless and unconventional! He actually presented people in attitudes and costumes that were never seen in serious, costly portraits before, and the painting was done in an irreverently rapid, off-hand, dashing manner of clever brush-work.[25]

LATE PORTRAITS

104.
Mrs. Adrian Iselin, 1888
Oil on canvas, 60½ × 36⅝ (153.7 × 93)
National Gallery of Art, Washington, D.C.;
Gift of Ernest Iselin

105.
Miss Elsie Palmer, 1889–90
Oil on canvas, 75 × 45 (190.5 × 114.3)
Colorado Springs Fine Arts Center

106.
La Carmencita, 1890
Oil on canvas, 90 × 54½ (228.6 × 138.4)
Musée d'Orsay, Paris

The writer ended the notice by remarking that Bostonians usually preferred "more painstaking efforts," a nod no doubt to the academic craftsmanship of Frederick Porter Vinton, Boston's most popular portraitist of the time. Regardless of such reservations, by the time Sargent left for London in the spring of 1888, he had developed a new and successful style of portrait, one that retained the freshness and mood of elegant informality of his most inventive early work, but was tempered by a less "eccentric" look.

Sargent's father died the following year, and in December 1889 the artist returned with his sister Violet to America, where she was to spend the year with family friends. This trip turned into another highly profitable portrait-painting excursion. During the ten-month sojourn, Sargent almost doubled the number of commissions received in 1887–88, in addition to receiving one of the mural commissions for the Boston Public Library.[26] After returning to Europe, Sargent spent much of the next five years working on these murals and painting fewer

107.
Mr. and Mrs. John W. Field, 1882
Oil on canvas, 44 × 33 (111.8 × 83.8)
Pennsylvania Academy of the Fine Arts,
Philadelphia; Presented by Mrs. John W. Field,
1891

108.
*Portrait of a Boy (Homer Saint-Gaudens and His
Mother)*, 1890
Oil on canvas, 59¾ × 56 (151.8 × 142.2)
Museum of Art, Carnegie Institute, Pittsburgh

portraits. Thus, his American commissions of 1889–90 represent the artist's most prolific period of portrait painting for several years.

The portraits Sargent completed during this trip range in mood from the arch theatricality of *La Carmencita* (Fig. 106) to the tenderness of *Mrs. Edward L. Davis and Her Son Livingston* (Fig. 97). The latter, painted in Worcester, Massachusetts, depicts the subjects in a simple shallow space with no accessories, much like the earlier Velázquez-inspired manner of *Lady with the Rose*. Previously, Sargent had attempted relatively few double or group portraits. Rather than repeating the complicated gestures of *The Misses Vickers* (Fig. 61), which had been so denounced by the English critics, he now chose to bring the mother and child together in an informal clinging gesture that recalls the close familial bond of *Mr. and Mrs. John W. Field* (Fig. 107). This mood of tenderness is characteristic of several portraits of children painted during his trip, such as *Beatrice Goelet, Gordon Fairchild* (private collection), and *Portrait of a Boy (Homer Saint-Gaudens and His Mother)* (Fig. 108). Sargent must have been especially pleased with the portrait of Mrs. Davis and her son, for it was exhibited frequently.

Although some writers of the period attempted to read more into the faces than Sargent intended, most agreed that the artist was little interested in

109.
Miss Helen Dunham, 1892
Oil on canvas, 48 × 32
(121.9 × 81.3)
Private collection

110.

Lady Agnew of Lochnaw, c. 1892–93

Oil on canvas, 49 × 39¼ (124.5 × 99.7)

The National Galleries of Scotland, Edinburgh

III.
Giovanni Boldini, *Lady Colin Campbell*, c. 1897
Oil on canvas, 71¾ × 46¼ (182.2 × 117.5)
National Portrait Gallery, London

capturing the deeper nuances of his sitters' characters. In 1888, a reviewer for *The New York Times* remarked:

It is all surface and no soul with most of Mr. Sargent's portraits, and the fault must lie with him, not with his sitters, for it can hardly be that all of them are as flinty and impudent in character as they appear.[27]

Sargent himself maintained that he could paint only what appeared before him, and routinely declined the kind of social intimacy with his sitters that might lead to a better understanding of their personalities. However, when Mariana Van Rensselaer published a highly sympathetic article on Sargent for the December 1891 issue of *Harper's New Monthly Magazine*, in which she defended him against the charge of being only a "master of the brush," the artist sent her a warm note of thanks for having given him credit "for insides, so to speak."[28]

It is possible, at least at this point in his career, that Sargent was more concerned with capturing the personality of some of his sitters than he was willing to admit. The portrait of *Miss Elsie Palmer* (Fig. 105), begun during the summer of 1889 but not completed until the following year, depicts the young girl with an intensely solemn expression that seems to demand a response from the viewer. That this response stems as much from the highly subjective eye of the beholder as from the visual facts as Sargent recorded them, is indicated by the reaction of the various critics. While *The Athenaeum* found Miss Palmer's face "mask-like," a writer for the *Magazine of Art* thought it full of "an extraordinary, almost crazy, intensity of life."[29] This complex relationship of artist, sitter, and viewer was best expressed by later writers on Sargent, such as John C. Van Dyke, who felt that his portraits did give clues to the personalities of the sitters simply through the careful recording of visual facts. According to Van Dyke, Sargent did not care to see below the surface because "he thinks the surface in itself, if rightly handled, is sufficient."[30]

Perhaps the first portrait to convince the majority of critics and the public that Sargent could combine both character and technical virtuosity was *Lady Agnew of Lochnaw* (Fig. 110), begun in 1892 and publicly exhibited the following year at the Royal Academy. By most accounts, it was not only a success but a "masterpiece." The London *Times* saw in it "not only a triumph of *technique* [emphasis original] but the finest example of portraiture in the literal sense of the word, that has been seen here for a long while."[31]

The critical reception that greeted *Lady Agnew* marks a change in the public perception of Sargent's work which, during the mid-1890s, grew into what the painter Walter Sickert termed "Sargentolatry." Although a masterpiece of the kind of effortless-seeming painting that Henry James eloquently described as "pure tact of vision,"[32] *Lady Agnew* is not radically different from much of Sargent's earlier work. The informal pose, the fluid brushwork and the direct, easy gaze of the sitter — the qualities most often singled out for praise — had all been used before. Sargent had certainly refined and expanded his talents during the previous

112.

The Wyndham Sisters: Lady Elcho, Mrs. Adeane,
and Mrs. Tennant, 1899
Oil on canvas, 115 × 84⅛ (292.1 × 213.7)
The Metropolitan Museum of Art, New York;
Catherine Lorillard Wolfe Collection,
Purchase, 1927, Wolfe Fund

decade and a half. Perhaps the real change had occurred not on his canvases but in the minds of the critics. For example, by 1894, it was possible for *The Art Amateur* to reconsider the merits of *Madame X* and to prefer it to Gustave Courtois' more conventional portrait of Mme. Gautreau (1891; Musée du Louvre, Paris).

Mr. Courtois had a manner of painting a fair and delicate complexion that comes near [sic] nature's handiwork than Mr. Sargent's, marred by a willful exaggeration of the accessories of the toilette. Still we do not doubt that Mr. Sargent's portrait will be the more admired by posterity, concerning which this artist cares more probably than he does for his subject. He has, indeed a marvellous talent for bringing out the faults, or it may be, only the less desirable possibilities of his model, yet so as to make a splendid picture. . . . This is a sort of talent which,

113.
Catherine Vlasto, 1897
Oil on canvas, 58½ × 33⅝ (148.6 × 85.4)
Hirshhorn Museum and Sculpture Garden,
Smithsonian Institution, Washington, D.C.

114.
Mrs. Carl Meyer and Her Children, 1896
Oil on canvas, 79 × 53 (200.7 × 134.6)
Private collection

115.
Mr. and Mrs. I. N. Phelps Stokes, 1897
Oil on canvas, 84¼ × 39¾ (214 × 101)
The Metropolitan Museum of Art, New York;
Bequest of Edith Phelps Stokes, 1938

116.
Asher Wertheimer, 1898
Oil on canvas, 58 × 38½ (147.3 × 97.8)
The Tate Gallery, London

117.
*Ena and Betty, Daughters of Mr. and Mrs. Asher
Wertheimer*, 1901
Oil on canvas, 73 × 51½ (185.4 × 130.8)
The Tate Gallery, London

*we believe, has been quite unknown in serious painting hitherto, and, taken together with his
splendid brushwork and his subtle sense of color and values, makes Mr. Sargent's fame assured,
however little satisfaction his sitters and their friends may get out of his work.*[33]

This change in attitude on the part of the public and press — the willingness
to accept portraiture on the artist's terms, as pure painting — and the maturation
of Sargent's personal style of bravura paint handling, propelled the artist to the
forefront of international society portraiture at the end of the nineteenth century.
He became not only a success, but also a tremendous influence on American and
European painters working in the field. When, for example, *Mrs. Carl Meyer and Her
Children* (Fig. 114) and *Mrs. George Swinton* (Fig. 118) were publicly exhibited in
London in 1897, they were not attacked but praised by the press for their
expressive brushwork, daring compositions and worldly characterizations. *The
Spectator* went so far as to ask if anyone else could have painted Mrs. Swinton's left
arm "— or rather left it out — with such complete feeling of the solid structure
beneath the loose scarf," adding that it is "by these resources of the art of
suggestion that the painter has made his canvas seem alive."[34]

118.
Mrs. George Swinton, 1897
Oil on canvas, 90 × 49 (228.6 × 124.5)
The Art Institute of Chicago; Wirt D. Walker
Collection

119.
Mrs. Charles Thursby, c. 1897–98
Oil on canvas, 78 × 39¾ (198.1 × 101)
The Newark Museum, New Jersey

120.

The Marlborough Family, 1905
Oil on canvas, 131 × 94 (332.7 × 238.8)
The Duke of Marlborough, Blenheim Palace,
Oxfordshire

121.

The Four Doctors, 1906
Oil on canvas, 129 × 107 (327.7 × 271.8)
The Welch Medical Library of The Johns
Hopkins Institutions, Baltimore

The artificially high viewpoint and flattened perspective of the Meyer family portrait was repeated the following year in *Mrs. Charles Thursby* (Fig. 119). The Belgian Symbolist painter Fernand Khnopff, writing for the *Magazine of Art*, discussed the portrait at length in his review of the New Gallery exhibition of 1898. He pointed to three artists whose works that year best expressed the ideals of contemporary English art: Burne-Jones was representative of art-for-art's-sake; Watts, of moral art ("art as a means of utterance"); Sargent, of pure impressionism ("genuinely the outcome of an impression").

Mr. Sargent is beyond comparison the greatest master of brush-work and of color-material now living. Though the placing of a touch may sometimes seem a little forced, a little too artificially instantaneous, and though the attitude of his figures very often is one of unstable equilibrium, we cannot, on the other hand, too highly praise certain "condensed effects," if I may say so, which are really quite marvellous.[35]

The lack of equilibrium noted by Khnopff in the portrait of Mrs. Thursby characterizes many of Sargent's late portraits and was often commented upon by other writers. Brinton found this quality — "the scattered arrangement, the violent foreshortenings, and the various lines forced into relation" — the chief failing of Sargent's large group portraits, such as *The Wyndham Sisters: Lady Elcho,*

170

122.
Sir Frank Swettenham, 1904
Oil on canvas, 67½ × 42½
(171.5 × 108)
National Museum, Singapore

123.
Millicent, Duchess of Sutherland, 1904
Oil on canvas, 100 × 57½ (254 × 146.1)
Thyssen-Bornemisza Collection, Lugano,
Switzerland

124.
Charles Stewart, Sixth Marquess of Londonderry,
Carrying the Great Sword of State at the Coronation
of King Edward VII, August, 1902, and Mr. W.
C. Beaumont, His Page on That Occasion, 1904
Oil on canvas, 113 × 77 (287 × 195.6)
Collection of Henry R. Kravis

125.
Anthony Van Dyck, *James Stuart, Duke of Richmond and Lennox*
Oil on canvas, 85 × 50¼ (215.9 × 127.6)
The Metropolitan Museum of Art; Gift of Henry G. Marquand, 1889

126.
Thomas Gainsborough, *Mary, Countess Howe*,
c. 1763–64
Oil on canvas, 96 × 60 (243.8 × 152.4)
The Iveagh Bequest, Kenwood, England

Mrs. Adeane, and Mrs. Tennant (Fig. 112). But still he had to admit that "these creatures vibrate with the nervous tension of the age. Other artists have given us calm, or momentarily arrested motion. Sargent gives us motion itself."[36]

This sense of the sitter in motion can be traced back in Sargent's work to *Mrs. Kate A. Moore* (Fig. 101) of 1884. Sargent portrayed the ebullient Mrs. Moore, an American expatriate in Paris known for her malapropisms and social climbing, in the slightly awkward pose of being half-seated on the edge of a large pillow-strewn chaise and almost engulfed by her surroundings. Her body seems propelled both forward and backward, as she starts to rise from her seated position. Although Sargent progressively stripped away the clutter of objects, later paintings such as *Mrs. Edward D. Boit, Mrs. Carl Meyer and Her Children*, and *Mrs. Charles Thursby* retain the high viewpoint, the tilted perspective, and the precarious pose of Mrs. Moore's portrait. Even the less extreme compositions of *Miss Helen Dunham* (Fig. 109) and *Sir Frank Swettenham* (Fig. 122) have a slightly nervous, active edge to them.

In order to keep his numerous portraits from becoming stale, Sargent continuously experimented during the 1890s with new poses and compositions. *Catherine Vlasto* (Fig. 113) casually leans against a piano, her fingers absentmindedly depressing the keys as she stares off into space. *Mr. and Mrs. I. N. Phelps Stokes* (Fig. 115) pause after having just walked off the street into the artist's studio (which is how Sargent chose the striking daytime attire of the sitters).[37] *Ena and Betty, Daughters of Mr. and Mrs. Asher Wertheimer* (Fig. 117) stroll arm-in-arm into the drawing room of their father's house on Connaught Place. All of these portraits have a tremendous sense of immediacy and spontaneity that allies them to the informal portraits of Lautrec, Monet or Renoir, none of whom depended so completely on commissioned portraits for their livelihood.

However, the informality of Sargent's late portraits was tempered by his respect for the tradition of Grand Manner portraiture, as passed down by Velázquez and, more especially, Van Dyck. The latter's full-length portraits (Fig. 125) are the compositional antecedents for Sargent's stately portrait of *Charles Stewart, Sixth Marquess of Londonderry* (Fig. 124). And similarly, *Millicent, Duchess of Sutherland* (Fig. 123) makes a veiled reference to Gainsborough's outdoor portraits, such as *Mary, Countess Howe* (Fig. 126). Sargent did not simply mimic the poses and props of Grand Manner portraiture, but reinvented the style for the late nineteenth century. *The Marlborough Family* (Fig. 120) and *The Four Doctors* (Fig. 121) exemplify this approach at its grandest. This is why a portrait such as *Asher Wertheimer* (Fig. 116), regardless of its informal pose and restless modernity, could strike one of Sargent's contemporaries as "surely one of the greatest portraits of the world, the only modern picture which challenges the Doria Velázquez at Rome — Innocent X."[38]

It was what Charles Caffin termed Sargent's "instinctive refinement" that finally made the artist acceptable to wealthy society and launched his career as their most sought-after portraitist. In *American Masters of Painting* (1902), he

127.
Mrs. Hugh Hammersley, 1893
Oil on canvas, 81 × 45¼
(205.7 × 114.9)
Private collection;
on loan to The Brooklyn
Museum, New York

128.
François Flameng and Paul Helleu, c. 1882–85
Oil on canvas, 21 × 17 (53.3 × 43.2)
Private collection

129.
Charles Stuart Forbes, c. 1889
Oil on canvas, 29 × 24 (73.7 × 61)
Henry E. Huntington Library and Art Gallery,
San Marino, California

explains this quality by comparing Sargent's work to that of his popular contemporary Giovanni Boldini:

It would be quite impossible for him to have any feelings toward his [Sargent's] subjects other than those of a true gentleman; and, though he may represent in a lady a full flavour of the modern spirit, he never allows the modernity to exceed the limits of good taste. For the same reason Sargent's pictures, though many of them have a restlessness of their own, seem quiet alongside Boldini's. The latter makes a motive of nervous tenuosity, and his pictures, if seen frequently, become wiry in suggestion, and defeat their own purpose of being vibrative; but Sargent's, controlled by a fine sobriety of feeling, another phase of his unfailing taste and tact, retain their suppleness. Their actuality is all the more convincing because it is not the motive, but an incident.[39]

Although there were numerous portraitists working in Europe and America at the end of the nineteenth century, Sargent had no serious competition in the field from the mid-1890s until he painted almost the last of his portraits in oil in 1908. During those years he sent an average of six to eight new portraits to the annual Royal Academy exhibitions, and is thought to have painted over eight hundred portraits during his entire career. Giovanni Boldini, James McNeill

130.
Alberto Falchetti, c. 1905–08
Oil on canvas, 29½ × 21½ (74.9 × 54.6)
Collection of Mr. and Mrs. Richard M. Thune

131.
Carl Maldoner, 1914
Oil on canvas, 25¼ × 20 (64.1 × 50.8)
Collection of Mr. and Mrs. William F.
Reighley

Whistler, Paul Helleu, William Merritt Chase — all friends whose work relates to Sargent's — were never as prolific. And in almost all cases, the lines of stylistic influence emanate from Sargent. The informality and restless energy of Boldini's *Lady Colin Campbell* (Fig. 111) can be found in Sargent's *Mrs. Edward D. Boit* (Fig. 103), *Mrs. Carl Meyer and Her Children* (Fig. 114) or *Mrs. Hugh Hammersley* (Fig. 127). Perhaps more revealing is Sargent's influence on the slightly younger generation of American and European painters who learned to paint portraits in variations of his style: Anders Zorn, Philip de Laszlo, Luke Fildes, Sir John Lavery, Irving Wiles, Cecilia Beaux, or Harper Pennington. While greatly admiring Sargent's work, Charles Caffin worried about its influence on lesser talents:

Sargent's eminence has had a great influence upon American painting. On the one hand, it has helped to popularise the new method of painting, and on the other, to foster the idea that masterfulness of technique may justify a lack of ability or inclination to penetrate the character of the sitter.[40]

In the years following Sargent's death, it became increasingly prevalent for critics and historians to see his portraits as little more than frothy evocations of Edwardian society. Writers such as Roger Fry and Clive Bell, whose interests lay

132.
Self-Portrait, 1907
Oil on canvas, 30 × 25 (76.2 × 63.5)
Galleria degli Uffizi, Florence

133.
Henry James, 1913
Oil on canvas, 33 × 26 (83.8 × 66)
National Portrait Gallery, London

in promoting Post-Impressionism and the abstract styles that grew from it, chided Sargent for not being more attuned to the new modern art. Few remembered that the artist had fought for many years to bring late Victorian portraiture out of the realm of flattering likenesses and to base it on the more abstract considerations of pure painting. Especially in his informal portrait sketches, usually done for family or friends, Sargent let the paint and brushwork carry the picture. This is one of the reasons that modern taste so often opts for portraits such as *Charles Stuart Forbes* (Fig. 129) or *Alberto Falchetti* (Fig. 130). But Sargent's most important contributions to painting were his large formal portraits. They were the bridges between nineteenth- and twentieth-century concepts of what a portrait should be, and they set a standard that lasted well beyond Sargent's lifetime.

1. Christian Brinton, *Modern Artists* (New York, 1908), pp. 155–56.

2. Quoted in Carter Ratcliff, *John Singer Sargent* (New York, 1982), p. 191.

3. See Algernon Graves, *The Royal Academy of Arts: A Complete Dictionary of Contributors and Their Work from Its Foundation in 1769 to 1904*, 8 vols. (New York, 1972), VII.

4. "Portraits at the Academy," *The New York Times*, October 30, 1895, p. 4.

5. "Art Topics of the Week," *The New York Times Saturday Review of Books and Art*, December 17, 1898, p. 850.

6. Mariana Van Rensselaer in *Memorial Exhibition of the Work of John Singer Sargent*, exhibition catalogue (New York, The Metropolitan Museum of Art, 1926), p. xiii.

7. See, for example, Evan Charteris, *John Sargent* (New York, 1927), pp. 27–28, 35.

8. Charles H. Caffin, *The Story of American Painting: The Evolution of Painting in America* (1907; ed. Garden City, New York, 1937), p. 242.

9. As quoted by Trevor J. Fairbrother in Theodore E. Stebbins, Jr., Carol Troyen, and Trevor J. Fairbrother, *A New World: Masterpieces of American Painting 1760–1910*, exhibition catalogue (Museum of Fine Arts, Boston, 1983), p. 300 n. 5.

10. "Fine Arts: The Royal Academy," *The Athenaeum*, 87 (June 21, 1884), p. 798.

11. Quoted in Richard Ormond, *John Singer Sargent: Paintings, Drawings, Watercolors* (New York, 1970), p. 39.

12. Arthur Baignères, "Première exposition de la Société des Peintres et Sculpteurs," *Gazette des Beaux-Arts*, 26 (1883), pp. 187–92.

13. "Art: Royal Academy," *The Spectator*, 60 (May 1, 1886), p. 580.

14. "The Salon, Paris," *The Athenaeum*, 90 (May 26, 1888), p. 670.

15. "Fine Arts: The Royal Academy," *The Athenaeum*, 89 (June 12, 1886), p. 786.

16. Malcolm Bell, "The Society of American Artists," *The Art Amateur*, 25 (June 1891), pp. 5–6.

17. Van Rensselaer in *Memorial Exhibition*, p. xviii.

18. Brinton, *Modern Artists*, p. 157.

19. Quoted in Ratcliff, *John Singer Sargent*, p. 101.

20. Trevor J. Fairbrother, "Notes on John Singer Sargent in New York, 1888–1890," *Archives of American Art Journal*, 22, no. 4 (1982), pp. 27–32.

21. Meg Robertson, "John Singer Sargent: His Early Success in America, 1878–1879," *Archives of American Art Journal*, 22, no. 4 (1982), pp. 20–26.

22. Henry James, "John S. Sargent," *Harper's New Monthly Magazine*, 75 (October 1887), pp. 684–91.

23. Quoted in Fairbrother, "Notes on John Singer Sargent in New York," p. 29.

24. "Fine Arts: The Royal Academy," *The Athenaeum*, 90 (June 23, 1888), p. 802.

25. Greta, "Art in Boston: The Sargent Portrait Exhibition," *The Art Amateur*, 18 (April 1888), p. 110.

26. Susan E. Strickler, "John Singer Sargent and Worcester," *Worcester Art Museum Journal*, 6 (1982–83), pp. 19–39.

27. Quoted in Fairbrother, "Notes on John Singer Sargent," p. 32.

28. See Mariana Griswold Van Rensselaer, "Another Portrait by Sargent," *Harper's New Monthly Magazine*, 35 (December 19, 1891), p. 1012; Sargent's letter is quoted in Charteris, *John Sargent*, pp. 109–10.

29. See "The New Gallery," *The Athenaeum*, 97 (May 9, 1891), p. 609, and "The New Gallery," *Magazine of Art*, 14 (May 1891), p. 261.

30. John C. Van Dyke, *American Painting and Its Tradition* (New York, 1919), p. 255.

31. Quoted in James Lomax and Richard Ormond, *John Singer Sargent and the Edwardian Age*, exhibition catalogue (Leeds, England, Leeds Art Galleries; London, National Portrait Gallery; and The Detroit Institute of Arts, 1979), p. 56.

32. James, "John S. Sargent," p. 684.

33. "Two Portraits of a Lady," *The Art Amateur*, 30 (January 1894), p. 45.

34. H.S., "Art: The New Gallery," *The Spectator*, 78 (May 1, 1897), p. 625.

35. Fernand Khnopff, "The New Gallery," *Magazine of Art* (1898), pp. 429–30.

36. Brinton, *Modern Artists*, p. 160.

37. See Doreen Bolger Burke, *American Paintings in the Metropolitan Museum of Art, III: A Catalogue of Works by Artists Born Between 1846 and 1864* (New York, 1980), pp. 247–50.

38. Robert Ross, "The Wertheimer Sargents," *The Art Journal* (January 1911), p. 7.

39. Charles H. Caffin, *American Masters of Painting: Being Brief Appreciations of Some American Painters* (New York, 1902), pp. 61–62.

40. Caffin, *The Story of American Painting*, p. 253.

"Painted Diaries": Sargent's Late Subject Pictures

PATRICIA HILLS

In the subject pictures Sargent painted after the summers in Broadway, Calcot, and Fladbury, that is, after 1889, he continued to explore some of his earlier preoccupations with technique and with holiday subject matter. The previous four years of Impressionist experimentation had been valuable, for they had opened up the possibilities of perceptual, Impressionist vision. This new way of seeing went beyond the ocular, camera vision that seized on light as the prime conveyor of empirical information about the world, as exemplified in Sargent's Venetian scenes and in *El Jaleo* (Fig. 14). It was, rather, an Impressionist "retinal" vision that absorbed the *color* reflected from surfaces in full sunlight. To the painter this meant a broadening of the range of subject matter and site as well as a search for sunshine.

The catalyst for this expansion was the commission Sargent received to paint a major mural for the third-floor vault of the new Boston Public Library.[1] This commission was to give a new focus to his life and provide him the opportunity to travel to lands of almost unrelenting brightness and color. Thus when Sargent and Violet returned to Europe in November 1890, meeting their sister Emily and their mother at Marseilles, they immediately made preparations to travel to Egypt. They reached Alexandria by Christmas, and continued on to Cairo. Here Sargent rented a studio, and they briefly settled in, before embarking on a steamer which took them to the cities of Luxor and Philae on the upper Nile. Later in the spring, the Sargent party traveled to Athens and then on to Constantinople before returning to Paris.[2]

Although Sargent had first proposed that the theme for the Public Library focus on medieval Spanish imagery, he abandoned that idea for the more ambitious one of *The History of Religion*. At what point he made the decision is unknown, but it seems clear that the trip to the Middle East confirmed his awareness of the pictorial possibilities of Middle Eastern subject matter for his religious theme, which was to begin with the pagans and Egyptians, and move on to the Old Testament and the New Testament.

During the months spent in the Middle East, Sargent painted scenes of Egyptian life, such as *Egyptians Raising Water from the Nile* (Fig. 138), studies of

134.
A Hotel Room, after 1900
Oil on canvas, 24 × 17½ (61 × 44.5)
Collection of the Ormond Family

181

135.
Study from Life, 1891
Oil on canvas, 73 × 23 (185.4 × 58.4).
Private collection; on loan to
The Art Institute of Chicago

ancient sculpture, and interiors of mosques — all subjects which an artist on holiday might paint. However, the Library commission lent new urgency to a return to painting large-size figures, which he had learned to do in 1877 when working with Carolus-Duran on the Luxembourg ceiling. Furthermore, he would need studies covering a range of physiognomic types and poses. During this trip, Sargent painted a number of figures and heads, including the nude *Study from Life* (Fig. 135), *Egyptian Woman with Earrings* (The Metropolitan Museum of Art, New York), and *A Bedouin Arab* (Fig. 137), the latter a handsome study of physiognomy and character.[3]

Painting a female nude was a new challenge for Sargent, although he had discussed the possibility with his friend Edwin Austin Abbey before he left for America in 1890. At that time Abbey was taking lessons in oil from Sargent, and he wrote to his fiancée about the novelty of painting nudes: "[Sargent] may paint a nude in New York, if he can find any good figure, and thinks I ought to do the same — that it would widen me out to paint — rather over life size — a large, pale, fattish, nude woman with no particular drawing in her. I never painted from the nude at all — *think of that!*"[4] Sargent was apparently too busy to turn his attention to the subject during his 1890 American sojourn — at least no nudes in oil have come to light. However, he did begin drawing from the male nude, and when in Egypt — with a studio and available models — he tried his hand at more ambitious undertakings. Instead of a Rubensian "large, pale, fattish, nude woman with no particular drawing in her," for *Study from Life* he selected a slim, lithe, golden-skinned maiden, and painted her seen from the back, in the process of plaiting her long hair. Sargent was satisfied with the results and he submitted the painting to the 1891 exhibition of the New English Art Club and to the Columbian Exposition held in Chicago in 1893.[5] During the next fifteen years, however, he seems only to have painted an occasional subject picture in oil, his time being divided between a prodigious output of portraits and his murals.

In 1905, Sargent began planning a second trip to the Middle East, this time to Syria and Palestine. He must have felt a need to do more research for his next set of murals for the Boston Public Library: the six lunettes connecting the Pagan and Christian ends of the Library hall, which were installed in 1916. Since a "Sermon on the Mount" was to be included in the pictorial scheme, he perhaps wanted to see firsthand the topography of the Holy Land.[6] He asked the Austrian artist Wilfrid von Glehn, who had been assisting him on his murals, to accompany him and even offered to pay all expenses, according to von Glehn's young wife, the American painter Jane Emmet von Glehn, whose voluminous letters to her family provide insights into Sargent's life from 1904 to about 1907.[7] Von Glehn rejected the offer; and Sargent, who preferred to travel with friends, made a similar proposition to Albert de Belleroche, who also declined.

In a letter to Lady Lewis from Palestine, Sargent reported on the mixed results of his research:

136.

The Plains of Esdraelon, 1905–06

Oil on canvas, 28 × 43½ (71.1 × 110.5)

The Tate Gallery, London; Presented by the
heirs of Mrs. Ormond, 1957

*Some new material I have secured but it is different from what I had in view and not
abundant — no miraculous draught but I shall still fish here for a while and try to bring back
some weightier stuff than lots of impossible sketches and perhaps useless studies.*[8]

It was on this trip that Sargent painted a number of watercolors as well as many
landscapes, including *The Mountains of Moab* (1905–06; The Tate Gallery, London),
one of the first landscapes he exhibited at the Royal Academy. *The Plains of
Esdraelon* (Fig. 136) and *Near the Mount of Olives* (Fig. 139) differ from almost all of
Sargent's previous outdoor scenes in that they present to the eye landscapes which
sweep back into the distance. But Sargent's trip to the Holy Land was cut short by
news of his mother's death on January 21, 1906. He returned to London ten days
later to supervise the funeral service.[9]

Musical evenings provided some diversion from mourning in early 1906,[10]
but during that spring Sargent also finished up a number of portraits, including the
major group portrait *The Four Doctors* (Fig. 121), representing the heads of the
departments at the Johns Hopkins Medical School.[11] During the next year he
attempted to wind down his portrait commissions — persuading potential
customers to sit for charcoal drawings instead (see p. 269). According to Jane von
Glehn, Sargent had then vowed that he "was going to absolutely stop painting
portraits. Wasn't going to do one after this year. He is going to paint what he has a
mind to. East and scenes and any old thing."[12]

Not only did Sargent cut back on his portrait commissions, but he seems also
to have vowed to spend more time with his unmarried sister, Emily, and with
Violet's growing family, which included six children. Charteris noted the
connection between Sargent's travels after 1906 and his mother's death:

137.
A Bedouin Arab, c. 1891
Oil on canvas, 26 × 20¼ (66 × 51.4)
Private collection

Every autumn after his mother's death . . . would see him crossing the Channel, always with his sister Emily, and either with the de Glehns or Miss Eliza Wedgwood, or the Misses Barnard, or Mrs. Ormond and her children, bound for some sketching centre in Italy or Corfu, Majorca or Spain, or in the Val d'Aosta.[13]

During August 1907 the von Glehns were in Purtud in the Swiss Alps with the Sargent party, and Jane von Glehn's letters chronicle the daily activities as well as the series of pictures Sargent painted of the women in the party, often dressed in costumes he had brought along expressly for that purpose:

138.
Egyptians Raising Water from the Nile, 1890–91
Oil on canvas, 25 × 21 (63.5 × 53.3)
The Metropolitan Museum of Art, New York;
Gift of Mrs. Francis Ormond, 1950

139.
Near the Mount of Olives, 1905–06
Oil on canvas, 25½ × 38 (64.8 × 96.5)
Syndics of the Fitzwilliam Museum,
Cambridge, England

140.

Val d'Aosta: A Man Fishing, c. 1910
Oil on canvas, 22 × 28 (55.9 × 71.1)
Addison Gallery of American Art, Phillips
Academy, Andover, Massachusetts

Yesterday I spent all day posing in the morning in Turkish costume for Sargent on the mossy banks of the Brook. I and Rose-Marie, one of the little Ormondes [sic]. He is doing a harem disporting itself on the banks of the stream. He has stacks of lovely Oriental clothes and dresses anyone he can set in them. It is marvellous to watch him paint.... Every morning Wil [Wilfrid von Glehn] and the little boys, Jean-Louis, Guillaume, and Conrad, go in bathing in the icy brook.... The children look so jolly rushing around the sunny meadow, naked and rolling in the crystal water. They are the nicest kids I ever saw almost.... They never squabble or fight or are boring in any way. As we sit in the woods every few minutes we hear the roar of an avalanche. The hot sun makes lots of them. The people are all cutting the hay in the high pastures and are living in the chalets up here.... [14]

The Brook (Fig. 144) appears to be the painting described in Jane von Glehn's letter as the one for which she and Sargent's niece Rose-Marie Ormond posed in 1907.[15] Polly and Dorothy Barnard, who had some twenty years earlier modeled for *Carnation, Lily, Lily, Rose* (Fig. 72), also took part in the Turkish masquerade in the Alpine setting. Sometimes the sitters got out a chessboard and played while Sargent painted; such is the activity in *Dolce Far Niente* (c. 1908–09; The Brooklyn Museum) and *The Chess Game* (Fig. 143). These works are broadly painted with bright yellow and eggshell white paint, matching the effects of strong sunlight on the forms.

Sargent also focused his eye and brush on the Alpine streams and ponds with their moving waters and reflections. Sometimes these corners of nature include parts of a figure — cut off, as in a snapshot; *Val d'Aosta: A Man Fishing* (Fig. 140) is one such picture, where figure and surroundings are given equal focus and density.

141.

A Turkish Woman by a Stream, c. 1907

Watercolor and gouache on paper, $14\frac{1}{8} \times 20$ (35.9 × 50.8)

Victoria and Albert Museum, London

142.

Breakfast in the Loggia, 1910

Oil on canvas, $20\frac{1}{2} \times 28$ (52.1 × 71.1)

Freer Gallery of Art, Smithsonian Institution, Washington, D.C.

143.
The Chess Game, c. 1907
Oil on canvas, 28 × 21¾ (71.1 × 55.2)
The Harvard Club of New York City

144.
The Brook, 1907
Oil on canvas, 21 × 27½ (53.3 × 69.9)
Collection of the Ormond Family

145.
Alpine Pool, 1909
Oil on canvas, 27½ × 38 (69.9 × 96.5)
The Metropolitan Museum of Art, New York;
Gift of Mrs. Francis Ormond, 1950

146.
The Hermit (Il Solitario), 1908
Oil on canvas, 37¾ × 38 (95.9 × 96.5)
The Metropolitan Museum of Art, New York;
Rogers Fund, 1911

147.
Muleteria, c. 1910
Oil on canvas, 22 × 28 (55.9 × 71.1)
The Warner Collection of Gulf States Paper
Corporation, Tuscaloosa, Alabama

In other compositions, such as *Alpine Pool* (Fig. 145), Sargent focused his brush on the reflections in the limpid water.

In September 1907, Sargent met the von Glehns in Italy. The three painted together in the garden of the Villa Torlonia and Sargent chose to render Jane herself painting at her easel. Jane described Sargent's painting, entitled *The Fountain, Villa Torlonia, Frascati, Italy* (Fig. 149), in a letter to her sister Lydia:

Sargent is doing a most amusing and killingly funny picture in oils of me perched on a balustrade painting. It is the very "spit" of me. He has stuck Wilfrid in looking at my sketch with rather a contemptuous expression as much to say "Can you do plain sewing any better than that?" He made Wilfrid put on this expression to avoid the danger of the picture looking like an "idyl in a P. & O. steamer" as he expressed it. We tried to go on with it this morning but too much rain. When we are headed off from painting, Sargent suggests we all take strychnine. This morning he said there was nothing left but hari-kari. I am all in white with a white painting blouse and a pale blue veil around my hat. I look rather like a pierrot, but have rather a worried expression as every painter should have who isn't a perfect fool, says Sargent. Wilfrid is in short sleeves, very idle and good for nothing, and our heads come against the great "panache" of the fountain. It is in the Torlonia. Our heads are about 3 inches long. It is awfully good and I hope I will get it for a Xmas present. Poor Wilfrid can't pose for more than a few minutes at a time as the position is torture after a while.[16]

Sargent did not give *The Fountain* to the von Glehns. He did, however, submit it to the New English Art Club later in the year, and sent it to an exhibition at The Art

148.
Jane de Glehn in Corfu (*In the Garden, Corfu*),
1909
Oil on canvas, 36 × 28⅛ (91.4 × 71.4)
Terra Museum of American Art, Chicago;
Daniel J. Terra Collection

149.
The Fountain, Villa Torlonia, Frascati, Italy, 1907
Oil on canvas, 28½ × 22 (72.4 × 55.9)
The Art Institute of Chicago; Friends of
American Art Gift

Institute of Chicago in 1912, where it was purchased and donated to the museum.
Two years later he painted the comely Jane in Corfu (Fig. 148).

In addition to Oriental garments, Sargent also brought along a stuffed gazelle
on trips to the Alps. This prop was incorporated twice in his painting *The Hermit*
(*Il Solitario*) (Fig. 146), which depicts an old man seated on the forest floor while
two "gazelles" move by him into the interior of the forest. As in some other
contemporaneous works, Sargent reduced tonal variations to a middle range so
that most of the information we receive to identify the subject is based on color
alone. When the painting was shown at the New English Art Club in 1909, one
reviewer described it as

*a piece of extraordinarily brilliant execution. The first impression is that of actual blinding
sunlight and shadow among the eucalyptus stems of a southern forest; one is there in the hot*

150.
Albanian Olive Gatherers, 1909
Oil on canvas, 37 × 44 (94 × 111.8)
Manchester City Art Galleries, England

atmosphere; the dazing effect on the brain, the coming headache, are admirably suggested. It is only after some time that you make out in the tangle of lights the forms of two deer and of a naked hermit reclining among rocks. If to represent the sensations of the eye with the utmost possible vividness and completeness be the master aim of art, then this is among the final masterpieces; but what is the effect on our minds? Beyond admiration of miraculous skill it is quite null.[17]

Like the critics in the early 1880s who had praised *El Jaleo* for its dramatization of the pyrotechnics of lighting on the dancers (see p. 40), this writer, almost thirty years later, hails *The Hermit* for its representation of the flecked intensity of colored light on the retina.[18]

Whatever Sargent's contemporaries might have thought about this as a literal transcription of nature, the inclusion of the stuffed gazelle marks it as elaborately contrived, as concocted as the scenes with women in Turkish costume. But although Sargent obviously fudged nature with his contrived props, he did not fudge his perceptions either of light or color.

Just as Sargent believed that "modern painters made a mistake in showing that they know too much about the substances they paint" (see p. 39), he resisted over-interpretation of his works on the part of the spectator. *The Hermit* is a case in point. When The Metropolitan Museum of Art acquired the painting, Sargent wrote to the director, Edward Robinson. The artist approved of the museum's translation of the original title, *Il Solitario*, into *The Hermit*, but added: "I wish

151.

Bringing Down Marble from the Quarries to
Carrara, 1911
Oil on canvas, 28⅛ × 36⅛ (71.4 × 91.8)
The Metropolitan Museum of Art, New York;
Harris Brisbane Dick Fund, 1917

there were another simple word that did not bring with it any Christian association, and that rather suggested quietness or pantheism."[19] With the exception of his mural paintings, allegorical allusion was not part of Sargent's materialist endeavor. Moreover, this painting, as so many of his subject pictures, avoids having to deal with sky — with the literally immaterial. He admitted to his friend Henry Tonks in 1920: "As you know enormous views and huge skies do not tempt me." It was the materiality of things that interested him rather than the nebulous ether of the sky with its changeable clouds.[20]

In a ten-year period, from 1906 to about 1916, Sargent painted the greatest number of his subject pictures in oil, with sites ranging from Corfu to Florida and the Canadian Rockies. He seems to have been accompanied by other artists almost continually, as well as by his valet, Nicola d'Inverno, who handled the props and painting gear. Mary Newbold Patterson Hale, Sargent's second cousin, called his pictures of these sites his "painted diaries":

Other travellers wrote their diaries; he painted his, and his sisters, his nieces and nephews, Miss Wedgewood [sic], the Misses Barnard, Mr. and Mrs. de Glehn, Mr. Harrison are all on its pages. Palestine, the Dolomites, Corfu, Italy, Spain, Portugal, Turkey, Norway, Greece, Egypt, France, and the Balearic Islands are on record.[21]

Sargent painted not just his friends, but also enclosed landscapes and scenes of the local people. He would paint a grove of olive trees with the pickers enjoying

152.
Olive Trees at Corfu, 1909
Oil on canvas, 28⅛ × 36¼ (71.4 × 92.1)
Collection of Mr. and Mrs. Marshall Field

153.
Gypsy Encampment, c. 1913
Oil on canvas, 28⅛ × 36⅛ (71.4 × 91.8)
Addison Gallery of American Art, Phillips
Academy, Andover, Massachusetts

154.
Oxen Resting, 1907
Oil on canvas, 22 × 28 (55.9 × 71.1)
Private collection

a moment of shade (Fig. 150) or a family of gypsies doing odd tasks during the heat of the day (Fig. 153). Charteris recounts an anecdote Jane von Glehn told him about Sargent's ability to find picturesque subject matter on any occasion:

Mrs. de Glehn recalls how on a hot day in Italy, having missed a connection at a junction, the party had to wait a considerable time. The rest of them had no thought but how to keep cool, but Sargent at once unpacked his easel and in the great heat he brought off one of his most brilliant studies of white oxen outside the station. This is a typical instance of his zeal, which coined even the accidents of life into opportunity.[22]

Sargent's choice of subjects was odd and personal, quite unlike the usual picturesque views painted by American and European artists who swarmed over Etretat, Brittany, and Dutch hamlets during the summers. In the autumn of 1911 he went to the marble quarries at Carrara, known for the beautiful and flawless white marble which Michelangelo himself had employed. Since the trip was

155.
Yoho Falls, 1916
Oil on canvas, 36 × 44½ (91.4 × 113)
Isabella Stewart Gardner Museum, Boston

arduous, Sargent apparently visited Carrara without his family; he allegedly withstood the rigors of the undertaking even better than his workmen companions.[23] Although he made individual sketches of the marble cutters, those workmen serve as mere staffage figures in most of the completed watercolors and in the major oil produced from the trip, *Bringing Down Marble from the Quarries to Carrara* (Fig. 151), a painting which picks up the peach tints reflected by the marble in the late afternoon.

On other trips, Sargent went back to Venice, employing a gondolier to ferry him and his friends around the canals. From the vantage point of the gondola, he painted the narrow canals, corners of churches, tops of libraries, and, on occasion, broader views of famous Baroque monuments. Usually he waited for the full sunlight, staying indoors on rainy days to play chess or piano duets with his friends.[24] Sargent structured some of the paintings, such as *Church of St. Stäe, Venice*

156.
Lake O'Hara, 1916
Oil on canvas, 37¼ × 44 (94.6 × 111.8)
Harvard University Art Museums, Fogg Art
Museum, Cambridge, Massachusetts; Louise
G. Bettens Fund

(Fig. 157), with strong architectural lines enclosing the planes. He painted other
works, such as *Palazzo Labia and San Geremia, Venice* (Fig. 159), with an open vista
of sky, clouds, and water. This last painting is one of the few in which Sargent
includes an expanse of sky.

    In America during July 1916, when the work on his Boston Public Library
murals no longer needed immediate supervision, Sargent set out for the Canadian
Rockies with Nicola d'Inverno. He had been tempted to visit Canada's Yoho
National Park by a postcard he received of the Twin Falls. Further encouragement
came from Mrs. Isabella Gardner, who commissioned him to paint the waterfall;
Edward W. Forbes, then director of the Fogg Art Museum, requested a landscape
in oil as well.[25] The trip was exhilarating for the sixty-year-old artist who quickly,
if reluctantly, adjusted to tinned food, rain, and snow. He painted a number of
watercolors, including *Camping at Lake O'Hara* (Fig. 205) and two large oils roughly

157.
Church of St. Stäe, Venice, 1913
Oil on canvas, 28 × 22 (71.1 × 55.9)
Private collection

158.
A Marble Fountain at Aranjuez, Spain, 1912
Oil on canvas, 22 × 28 (55.9 × 71.1)
Collection of Mr. and Mrs. Isaac Arnold, Jr.

159.
Palazzo Labia and San Geremia, Venice, 1913
Oil on canvas, 21½ × 27½ (54.6 × 69.9)
Private collection

160.

Simplon Pass: At the Top, c. 1910
Watercolor on paper, 15¾ × 20½ (40 × 52.1)
Museum of Fine Arts, Boston; The Hayden
Collection

the same size, *Yoho Falls* (Fig. 155), done for Mrs. Gardner, and *Lake O'Hara*
(Fig. 156), the painting which Forbes secured for the Fogg. Whereas the Gardner
painting forcefully suggests the energy of the plunging falls and the tall spray
billowing upward in reaction to that energy, *Lake O'Hara* is a serene panoramic
view of clear green lake water with a solid embankment of mountains behind. The
painting seems to have been conceived as a grand vista, appropriate as a museum
piece. On the same trip he made other oil paintings of camp life in and around Lake
O'Hara that were more typical of his sunny "slice-of-life" subject matter. Sargent's
letters from the West to friends and relatives reveal a painter who could not paint
on cloudy or rainy days, but who had a sense of humor about it. To his cousin
Mary on August 30, 1916, he wrote:

*As I told you in my first or my last it was raining and snowing, my tent flooded, mushrooms
sprouting in my boots, porcupines taking shelter in my clothes, canned food always fried in a
black frying pan getting on my nerves, and a fine waterfall which was the attraction to the place
pounding and thundering all night. I stood it for three weeks and yesterday came away with a
repulsive picture. Now the weather has changed for the better and I am off again to try the
simple life (ach pfui) in tents at the top of another valley, this time with a gridiron instead of a
frying pan and a perforated India rubber mat to stand on. It takes time to learn how to be really
happy.*[26]

Being at the tops of mountains with friends, having a measure of creature comforts
and the sun were what seemed to make Sargent "really happy." The Simplon Pass
oils and watercolors chronicle those times: his nieces, with their skirts spread out
on the grass and parasols shielding their faces from the glare of the sun (Fig. 199),

161.

The Sketchers, 1914

Oil on canvas, 22 × 28 (55.9 × 71.1)

Virginia Museum of Fine Arts, Richmond;

The Arthur and Margaret Glasgow

Endowment Fund

his artist friends with their paint boxes in their laps as they study the terrain (Fig. 164), and other assorted friends lolling about (Figs. 160, 162). These pictures are the *fêtes galantes* of the era.[27] No raucous gaiety asserts itself; no melancholy affects our appreciation. We have no clues of time passing. Instead, we have the sweet life, the *dolce far niente*, where emotions are restrained and unengaged. The bright sunlight creates a sensuousness of surface, and the ensuing spectacle deflects any concern for what might be a deeper, intrinsic meaning.

It is not surprising that the repeating theme in these paintings is art itself, the artist painting in a world deliberately removed from the urban centers of power and struggle (Fig. 161). In fact, one of Sargent's last recorded subject pictures (Fig. 165) is of his friend Dwight Blaney painting in the woods, looking like Sargent himself, the detached artist enclosed within a secure world, painting just what he wants to see. And what Sargent wanted to see was not reality, but the holiday, aestheticized world of the late nineteenth and the early twentieth centuries.

162.
Group with Parasols (*A Siesta*), c. 1908–11
Oil on canvas, 21¾ × 27⅞ (55.2 × 70.8)
Collection of Rita and Daniel Fraad

163.
Simplon Pass, 1910
Oil on canvas, 28 × 36 (71.1 × 91.4)
Corcoran Gallery of Art, Washington, D.C.;
Bequest of James Parmelee

164.
Simplon Pass: Mountain Brook, c. 1911
Watercolor on paper, 14 × 19⅞ (35.6 × 50.5)
Museum of Fine Arts, Boston; The Hayden
Collection

165.
The Artist Sketching, 1922
Oil on canvas, 22 × 28 (55.9 × 71.1)
Private collection; on loan to the Museum of
Art, Rhode Island School of Design, Providence

166.
Tyrolese Crucifix, 1914
Oil on canvas, 36 × 28 (91.4 × 71.1)
Private collection

NOTES

1. For a discussion of Sargent's Library murals, see Martha Kingsbury, "Sargent's Murals in the Boston Public Library," *Winterthur Portfolio*, 11 (1976), pp. 153–72.

2. Evan Charteris, *John Sargent* (New York, 1927), p. 114.

3. The Sargent catalogue raisonné being prepared by the Coe Kerr Gallery, Inc. should reveal the full extent of Sargent's subject pictures. In 1986, Odile Duff, who is researching pictures for the catalogue, estimated that there are about 1,800 to 2,000 subject pictures and landscapes, including watercolors; see "Sargent's Works in Oil" in Charles Merrill Mount, *John Singer Sargent: A Biography* (New York, 1955), pp. 427–53.

4. Quoted in E. V. Lucas, *Edwin Austin Abbey, Royal Academician: The Record of His Life and Work*, 2 vols. (London and New York, 1921), I, p. 210.

5. A critic for the *Magazine of Art* pronounced *Study from Life* to be: "A superb studio study of the nude, masterly alike in strength, truth, and grace of drawing, and exhaustive painting of the golden flesh"; quoted in William Howe Downes, *John S. Sargent: His Life and Work* (Boston, 1925), p. 166.

6. See Trevor J. Fairbrother, *John Singer Sargent and America* (New York, 1986), p. 351 n. 1.

7. For Sargent's offer to pay all expenses, see the letter from Jane Emmet von Glehn (later de Glehn) to her mother, postmarked December 9, 1905, in the collection of Rosamond Sherwood (niece of Jane von Glehn). I am grateful to Rosamond Sherwood for granting me permission to read these letters and publish the excerpts quoted in the text of this essay. For the other letters, see below, nn. 9, 10, 12, 14, 16, 23, and 24. I also want to thank Liese Hilgeman and Kevin Whitfield for helping me transcribe the letters.

8. Quoted in Charteris, *John Sargent*, p. 172.

9. Jane von Glehn to her mother, letter postmarked February 7, 1906. On February 10, 1906, she wrote: "[Wilfrid] saw poor Sargent today. He is more cut up and more jerky and powerless to express himself than ever."

10. Letters written that spring by Jane von Glehn to her family document the musical evenings.

11. For a discussion of Sargent's *The Four Doctors* (Fig. 121) (Drs. William Henry Welch, William Stewart Halsted, William Osler, and Howard Atwood Kelly), see Patricia Hills, "Thomas Eakins's *Agnew Clinic* and John S. Sargent's *Four Doctors*: Sublimity, Decorum, and Professionalism," *Prospects: A Journal of American Cultural Studies*, 11 (1986), in press.

12. Jane von Glehn to her sister Rosina Emmet Sherwood, July 17, 1907.

13. Charteris, *John Sargent*, p. 170.

14. Letter from Jane von Glehn to her mother, Mrs. W. J. Emmet, August 13, 1907.

15. The dating problems of these Alpine pictures are discussed in James Lomax and

167.
View from a Window at Genoa, after 1900
Pencil, watercolor, and oil on paper,
$15\frac{3}{4} \times 20\frac{3}{4}$ (40 × 52.7)
Trustees of the British Museum, London;
Presented by Mrs. Ormond

Richard Ormond, *John Singer Sargent and the Edwardian Age*, exhibition catalogue (Leeds, England, Leeds Art Galleries; London, National Portrait Gallery; and The Detroit Institute of Arts, 1979), pp. 96–100.

16. Jane von Glehn to Lydia Emmet, October 6, 1907.

17. Lawrence Binyon, "The New English Art Club," *The Saturday Review*, 107 (May 29, 1909), p. 684. The stuffed gazelle story is related in Charteris, *John Sargent*, p. 170.

18. Kenyon Cox, writing in 1911, called *The Hermit* "the most successful piece of pure impressionism I have ever seen. . . . It is amazingly like nature, and the hermit is as inconspicuous a part of nature as if the picture were intended for an illustration of protective coloring! . . . Sargent . . . convinced me . . . that I did not want to paint nature as it really looks"; quoted in Doreen Bolger Burke, *American Paintings in the Metropolitan Museum of Art, III: A Catalogue of Works by Artists Born Between 1846 and 1864* (New York, 1980), p. 264.

19. Quoted in ibid.

20. Quoted in Richard Ormond, *John Singer Sargent: Paintings, Drawings, Watercolors* (New York, 1970), p. 69.

21. Mary Newbold Patterson Hale, "The Sargent I Knew," *World Today*, 50 (November 1927); reprinted in Carter Ratcliff, *John Singer Sargent* (New York, 1982), p. 237.

22. Charteris, *John Sargent*, pp. 95–96.

23. Burke, *American Paintings in the Metropolitan Museum*, p. 267.

24. Jane von Glehn's letters to her family between 1904 and 1907 discuss their pastimes while waiting out the rainy days.

25. See Rebecca W. Karo, "Ah Wilderness! Sargent in the Rockies, 1916," in *Fenway Court: Isabella Stewart Gardner Museum, 1976* (Boston, 1977), p. 21.

26. Quoted in Charteris, *John Sargent*, pp. 204–05.

27. Charles H. Caffin, "Some American Portrait Painters," *The Critic*, 44 (January 1904), p. 31, was the first to suggest a possible connection between Sargent's works and those of Watteau, although Caffin was then discussing Sargent's portraits: "Now, one of the characteristics of Sargent, obvious to all who can read between the lines, is that, like Watteau in his era, he is immeasurably indifferent to the class of people whom he represents; that with him the artistic interest in the picture is a *parti pris* so complete as to exclude almost every other consideration." I am grateful to William H. Gerdts for bringing this source to my attention.

"Sunshine Captured": The Development and Dispersement of Sargent's Watercolors

ANNETTE BLAUGRUND

Although watercolor was used to advantage by many late nineteenth-century European and American artists, the versatility and range of John Singer Sargent's technique, the singularity of his highly personal vision, and the dazzling bravura of his brushstrokes clearly distinguish his work. Around 1900, as his focus shifted from portraits to landscapes, he increasingly used watercolor, and ultimately painted many more watercolors than oils. Freed from the conventions of portraiture, he profited from the immediacy and portability of this medium, especially during his extended travels.

Sargent's increased production in watercolor after 1900 probably derived from a series of experiences, particularly during the 1880s, which formed his taste for the medium and his knowledge of its possibilities. These influences, which will be traced below, seem to have come to the fore not only, as has been said, when he needed a release from the demands of portrait painting, but also as a reprieve from the carefully structured, clearly outlined mural paintings he began in the 1890s.

Sargent's valuation of his work in watercolor has often been questioned. Some biographers and art critics have claimed that he denigrated them and was reluctant to sell them, while others have referred to them as a vacation pastime.[1] Since he devoted a good part of the last twenty-five years of his life to painting in this medium, one could infer that he was often on holiday; but this, of course, was not the case, for even while traveling he was a prodigious worker. These notions must be reevaluated by examining Sargent's use of the medium throughout his career, the crucial role it played in his total oeuvre, and his involvement with the exhibition and placement of his watercolors in American museums.

Watercolor was a primary medium for Sargent early in his life, beginning with childhood sketches made under the tutelage of his mother. Vernon Lee (Violet Paget), Sargent's friend, remembers Mrs. Sargent as an avid watercolorist, "painting, painting, painting away, always with an open paint-box in front of her."[2] During the winter of 1868–69 in Rome, Sargent became further acquainted with the medium through his lessons with the German-American landscape

168.
Villa di Marlia, Lucca, c. 1910
Watercolor on paper, 15¾ × 20¾ (40 × 52.7)
Museum of Fine Arts, Boston; The Hayden Collection

169.
Figure in Costume, c. 1875–76 (inscribed 1869)
Watercolor on paper, 14 × 19⅞ (35.6 × 50.5)
The Metropolitan Museum of Art, New York;
Gift of Mrs. Francis Ormond, 1950

170.
The Model, c. 1876
Watercolor and pencil on paper, 11¹¹⁄₁₆ × 9⁹⁄₁₆
(29.7 × 23)
Museum of Fine Arts, Houston; Gift of Miss
Ima Hogg

painter Carl Welsch. Sketchbooks of this period reveal Sargent's precocious talent as well as his interest in subject matter that appears in mature works — oxen, chalets, water, boats, rocks, and crucifixes; some thematic similarities, however, were a function of his return to the same locales. These early watercolors — amateurish, traditional landscape views, somber in color, tightly painted, and conventionally composed — do not foretell future innovative techniques, including fragmentation of objects, high-keyed palette, and broken brushstrokes.[3]

When Sargent applied to enter Carolus-Duran's atelier in 1874, his portfolio included watercolors as well as oils, museum copies, and pencil sketches.[4] Even Whistler is said to have been impressed with Sargent's watercolors and drawings.[5] Nevertheless, Sargent more or less abandoned watercolor painting, concentrating on the prescribed, finished oils and oil sketches during his years with Carolus-Duran.

In the mid-1870s watercolor was not as popular a medium as pastel in France. It had its advocates, however, in artists such as Paul Huet and Henri-Joseph Harpignies, and three years after Sargent settled in Paris, the Beaux-Arts administration devoted a small room to watercolors at the Salon of 1877.[6] The following year the Exposition Universelle featured works by English water-

171.
Young Woman with Black Skirt, c. 1876–82
Watercolor on paper, 14 × 9⅞ (35.6 × 25.1)
The Metropolitan Museum of Art, New York;
Gift of Mrs. Francis Ormond, 1950

172.
Bedroom, c. 1880–82
Watercolor on paper, $11\frac{1}{8} \times 8$ (28.3 × 20.3)
Private collection

colorists.[7] By 1879, possibly encouraged by the frequency and success of watercolor exhibitions in England and America, sufficient gains had been made by French watercolorists to form the Société d'Aquarellistes Français.[8] Sargent was friends with two members, Ernest-Ange Duez and Joseph Roger-Jourdain, and their inspiration may have prompted the portrait of Roger-Jourdain's wife that Sargent painted in watercolor (collection of John Hay Whitney) and fostered his limited return to the medium in the eighties.[9]

Sargent's interest in watercolor was not entirely dormant in the seventies, however, for there exist a few academic works like *The Model* (Fig. 170) and *Young Woman with Black Skirt* (Fig. 171), probably painted at about the same time since they share a dark palette, a linear style, and a lack of figure-ground integration. During this period Sargent did not exploit watercolor for its intrinsic transparent properties. Instead, he used it conventionally for studies and preparatory sketches, as in the one for *El Jaleo* (Fig. 175), which supplemented his multiple oil and pencil studies.[10]

Another work, *Figure in Costume* (Fig. 169), bears the questionable date of 1869, but its style is more consistent with watercolors of the mid-seventies. If the

173.
A Moorish Patio, c. 1880
Watercolor and pencil on paper, 9¾ × 13½
(24.8 × 34.3)
Trustees of the British Museum, London;
Presented by Mrs. Ormond

174.
Campo dei Frari, Venice, c. 1880
Watercolor and pencil with gouache on paper,
9⅞ × 14 (25.1 × 35.6)
Corcoran Gallery of Art, Washington, D.C.;
Bequest of Mrs. Mabel Stevens Smithers

date were accurate, it would mean that Sargent painted this when he was only
thirteen. Interestingly, it was at one time attributed to Giovanni Boldini, the
Italian painter whose early landscapes derive from his association with the
Macchiaioli, and whose later portraits demonstrate a vitality similar to Sargent's.
Boldini and his compatriot Antonio Mancini are both claimed to have had a
"liberating influence . . . that captured John Sargent. . . ."[11] A kinship in freedom
of handling exists between Sargent's watercolors and those of Boldini and Mancini,

but there seems to be no specific relationship, except for his familiarity with their work. His admiration for these men is evidenced by the presence of their paintings in his collection.[12]

On trips to Venice in 1880 and 1882, Sargent painted in watercolor and oil to record sites, just as he had done during his childhood. *A Venetian Interior* (c. 1880; collection of the Ormond Family) is characterized by somber tonalities and punctuated by dramatic light effects which parallel those in his oil paintings of the same period, such as *Venetian Bead Stringers* (Fig. 23). *Campo dei Frari, Venice* (Fig. 174), on the other hand, exhibits looser paint application and brighter colors, probably the result of painting outdoors. While both of these watercolors share with each other, and with Sargent's oils, the conceit of an empty foreground, the interior scene presents the diagonal recession into the picture space common to the nineteenth-century French paintings of Monet, Manet, and particularly of Degas and Caillebotte, which Sargent probably saw on exhibition in Paris. He submitted two watercolors of Venetian views from his 1880 trip to the Salon of 1881, one of which may have been *Campo dei Frari, Venice*.[13]

Watercolor portraits, such as a sketch for *Madame X* (Fogg Art Museum, Cambridge, Massachusetts) and others not directly related to oils, appear at this time. Many of them were of Sargent's friends and family, such as Fanny Watts, Judith Gautier, and his two sisters. These watercolors, complete works which stand on their own, do not yet break through traditional watercolor practices. The summarily painted *Judith Gautier* (Fig. 176), however, is more dramatic in lighting and format and differs from others of the period in its bolder presentation of the figure and its broader application of paint; in this way, it prefigures such later watercolor portraits as *Alice Runnels James (Mrs. William James)* (Fig. 212) and *Isabella Stewart Gardner* (1922; Isabella Stewart Gardner Museum, Boston).

Sargent began to summer in Broadway, a village in the Cotswolds, in 1885, and his permanent move to England the following year brought him into contact with such artist-illustrators as Edwin Austin Abbey, Alfred Parsons, and Frank Millet, all of whom painted in watercolor. Many of them used the medium extensively and exhibited their work at watercolor society exhibitions both in England and America, some producing large, highly finished exhibition pieces like Abbey's *Stony Ground* of 1886 (The Brooklyn Museum).[14] Although in technique and subject, Abbey's tightly painted literary work, utilizing the opacity of gouache, did not influence Sargent per se, the close working relationship between the two artists during the second half of the eighties and early nineties must have served to keep watercolor in Sargent's mind. Even more important was Abbey's connection with the American watercolor movement and with the Tile Club, many of whose members were active watercolorists, which provided Sargent with a link to American activities.[15]

Hercules Brabazon is frequently mentioned as an influence on Sargent's watercolors. Brabazon, a wealthy English amateur painter who shared with

179.
A Tramp, after 1900
Watercolor on paper, 19¹¹⁄₁₆ × 13³⁄₁₆ (50 × 33.5)
The Brooklyn Museum, New York; Purchased
by Special Subscription

Sargent an interest in music and travel, devoted himself to watercolor by way of documenting his frequent travels.[16] His paintings were widely admired by many artists for their harmonious sense of color, freedom of handling, and seemingly transparent technique, so different from contemporaneous works like Abbey's; these qualities may have awakened in Sargent the possibilities watercolor had for painting out-of-doors. But broadly painted, wet, amorphous works such as Brabazon's were not the rule in Sargent's oeuvre; indeed, few pictures painted at the turn of the century have the freedom of Brabazon's work.

Sargent articulated the aspects of watercolor painting that appealed to him in a laudatory preface to the catalogue of Brabazon's first one-man show at the Goupil Gallery in London in 1892. He extolled "the gift of colour, together with an exquisite sensitiveness of impressions of Nature" and "the immunity from

180.

Bedouins, c. 1905–06

Watercolor on paper, 18 × 12 (45.7 × 30.5)

The Brooklyn Museum, New York;

Purchased by Special Subscription

181.

Arab Gypsies in a Tent, c. 1905–06

Watercolor heightened with white on paper,

12 × 18 (30.5 × 45.7)

The Brooklyn Museum, New York;

Purchased by Special Subscription

'picture' making" which kept Brabazon's "perception delicate and execution convincing." Using a musical analogy, appropriate for both of them, he continued, "Each sketch is a new delight of harmony and the harmonies are innumerable and unexpected, taken from Nature, or, rather, imposed by her. . . . Only after years of the contemplation of Nature can the process of selection become so sure an instinct; and a handling so spontaneous and so freed from the commonplaces of expression is final mastery, the result of long artistic training."[17]

Since Sargent rarely verbalized his thoughts, this introduction provides a rare opportunity to learn what he valued in watercolor: the unusual point of view, lack of artifice, and spontaneity of expression.[18] His adoption of some of these characteristics begins to appear in the few watercolors produced in the nineties. Thus the gradual increase in Sargent's watercolor output in the last two decades of the nineteenth century was probably due in part to his constant exposure to the medium through a network of friends and colleagues, while the broadening of his technique may indeed derive from Brabazon's example.

In the twentieth century, watercolor began to play a more dominant role in Sargent's oeuvre. The marked rise in his production has often been explained as a release from the burden of portraiture and as a private endeavor indulged in during vacations. Some even have said that his sister Emily's interest in watercolor led to his predilection for this medium.[19] More important, as Hardie observed, was the fact that "in water-colour he found endless scope for his driving need of unhampered personal expression."[20] Watercolors of this period no longer are preparatory studies linked to oil paintings nor slight works to be distributed as gifts. By the early 1900s, the watercolor medium, familiar to him from childhood, best suited his artistic needs as well as his way of life.

As Sargent's travels increased, the portability of watercolors became even more appealing. "He would arrive at the station loaded with canvases and sketch-books, bristling with the equipment for *plein air* sketching, and with these piled up round him in a fly he would draw up at his destination dominant and smiling."[21] Adrian Stokes, the artist who accompanied him on some of his vacations to the Simplon Pass in Switzerland between 1911 and 1914, observed him firsthand and recalled:

Though he most likely considered himself to be on a holiday his industry was constant. Whatever the weather was he came down early — not extravagantly early — and I think the time was 8:30 when, if fine, he started out accompanied by his, often heavily laden, Italian manservant, for one of the landscape subjects he had in progress, or to find a new one. . . . When once settled, and protected maybe by as many as three painting umbrellas — one to keep off a cold wind, another the sun, and a third some tiresome reflection — the rapidity and directness with which he worked was amazing. . . . [illustration, p. 22] His hand seemed to move with the same agility as when playing over the keys of a piano. . . . It was — if you will — a kind of shorthand, but it was magical. . . . After lunch he retired for a siesta, and then went out to work again until dinner time.[22]

182.
La Riva, c. 1903–08
Watercolor on paper, 14 × 20⅟₁₆ (35.6 × 51)
The Brooklyn Museum, New York; Purchased
by Special Subscription

183.
From the Gondola, c. 1905–08
Watercolor and pencil on paper, 10 × 14
(25.4 × 35.6)
The Brooklyn Museum, New York; Purchased
by Special Subscription

Although umbrellas and easels were part of his paraphernalia, "his water-color equipment was an ordinary folding tin box of colours in pans, with dabs of dirty colour all around," wrote Martin Birnbaum.[23] With this simple equipment he could "make the best of an emergency," which is what Sargent, according to Charteris, called "the painting of a watercolour."[24] While many artists carried tubes of color, Sargent, possibly because his palette was restricted to six or seven colors, found "'box colour' very useful," and he added, "I use a great many different brushes, keeping my fist full when I work. . . . "[25] Hardie specified that as

184.
Doorway of a Venetian Palace, c. 1906–10
Watercolor on paper, 23 × 18 (58.4 × 45.7)
Westmoreland Museum of Art, Greensburg,
Pennsylvania

185.
The Library in Venice, c. 1906–10
Watercolor and pencil with gouache on paper,
22⅛ × 17¾ (56.2 × 45.1)
National Gallery of Art, Washington, D.C.;
Ailsa Mellon Bruce Collection

a general rule he worked on damp paper, applied a layer of pure color wash to the paper that spread to the edges, and then worked rapidly, using Chinese white (also referred to as gouache or body color) when it was expedient. Hardie felt that Sargent, probably more than other contemporary watercolorists, "knew the value of high lights obtained by leaving the white of the paper."[26] Such techniques, generally recommended in nineteenth-century watercolor manuals, took on new dimensions in Sargent's hands. Sometimes he left the edges of the paper unfinished or vague with watery washes, concentrating on some central point or feature. He almost always used white paper for its light-reflecting qualities, but the paper texture varied from smooth to lightly grained. The rougher surface was most visible when he pulled a dry brush charged with undiluted pigment across the grain and the paint rested on the peaks, leaving the lower areas white, as if light were seeping through the color. His paper, probably torn from sketchbooks, does not seem to have watermarks, and fractional variations in size suggest that he trimmed the edges to suit his composition.[27]

That Sargent considered his work in watercolor a serious endeavor, not one to be used only when he was making "the best of an emergency," is demonstrated by his advance planning of watercolor subjects as well as by his systematic placement of them in American museums. He even chose to decorate his studio with them.[28] *A Turkish Woman by a Stream* (Fig. 141), a picture of Polly Barnard in "Oriental clothes, which he took with him from London," bespeaks a preconceived

186.
Santa Maria della Salute, 1904
Watercolor and pencil heightened with
white on paper, 18⅛ × 23 (46 × 58.4)
The Brooklyn Museum, New York;
Purchased by Special Subscription

187.
Sketching on the Giudecca, Venice, c. 1904
Watercolor and gouache on paper,
14 × 20¾ (35.6 × 52.7)
Private collection

188.
Piazza Navona, Rome, 1907
Watercolor and sepia ink on paper, 20¾ × 16½
(52.7 × 41.9)
Collection of Erving and Joyce Wolf

189.
In a Levantine Port, c. 1905–06
Watercolor and pencil on paper, 12¹⁄₁₆ × 18⅛
(30.6 × 46)
The Brooklyn Museum, New York;
Purchased by Special Subscription

rather than a spontaneous watercolor.[29] He dressed Polly in other clothes in *Zuleika* (c. 1908; The Brooklyn Museum), and did a series of related oils and watercolors of languid figures in richly patterned garb by a brook in Purtud (Val d'Aosta) (Figs. 141, 143, 144). For Sargent, these robes had no narrative content; they were simply used for their visual qualities. Here Sargent's approach recalls the decorative tendencies of artists of the Aesthetic Movement who often focused their attention on the play of light on drapery folds. Such contrived figural arrangements in Sargent's work most likely grew out of and continued his own Impressionist investigations in the eighties, as in *Garden Study of the Vickers Children* (Fig. 74) and *Carnation, Lily, Lily, Rose* (Fig. 72), where figures and flowers are decoratively juxtaposed.

Although Sargent's use of watercolor after 1900 may have been initiated as a respite from serious portraiture and mural painting, by the end of the first decade he held his watercolors in high enough regard to exhibit them regularly. He exhibited his wash portrait of *Judith Gautier* (Fig. 176) in 1899 at Copley Hall in Boston, along with a large number of oil portraits, sketches, and charcoal drawings.[30] After the turn of the century, however, he showed his works on paper constantly, first at the Carfax Gallery, London, from May to June 1903, and then the following year at the Royal Water Colour Society, where he had just been elected an associate member (he became a full member in 1908). He sent pictures to Society exhibitions almost every year until his death, with the exception of 1909, 1917, and 1921–23.[31]

In 1905, the Carfax Gallery exhibited forty-seven of Sargent's watercolors, six from private collections, the rest belonging to the artist; in 1908, they showed fifty, including some that had been previously exhibited.[32] Sargent also gave some as gifts, others he probably sold, but many remained in his hands until they were exhibited at Knoedler's in New York in 1909, when eighty-three were acquired by The Brooklyn Museum.[33] Although Sargent was by then exhibiting his watercolors on a regular basis, his own appreciation of their value seemed to increase with the growing demand for them in America. After 1909 his watercolors were frequently shown in the United States. Another set was exhibited at Knoedler's again in 1912, and thereafter they appeared regularly on the walls of the museums that owned them and in loan shows.[34]

The acquisition of eighty-three watercolors by The Brooklyn Museum in 1909 was part of what seems to have been Sargent's premeditated plan to place his pictures in American institutions, an effort which extended into the next decade.[35] His persistence in selling large groups of watercolors to museums every two or three years, or as soon as he had finished enough of them to give a representative sampling, serves the dual purpose of providing a key to his development as a watercolorist and an important chronological record of his watercolor production from just before 1909 (when he substantially cut down his commissioned oil portraiture).[36]

The Brooklyn Museum was not the only institution to vie for the watercolors exhibited at Knoedler's. Boston's Museum of Fine Arts "hoped that the Museum would get possession of a remarkable collection of eighty-three watercolors by Mr. Sargent, but before the difficulties could be surmounted these paintings went to The Brooklyn Museum."[37] The contest to procure Sargent watercolors by the end of the first decade of this century confirms that they were by then recognized as exceptional works of art, as worthy of inclusion in museums as were his oil paintings. In addition, Sargent took special interest in developing the art collections of the institutions that bought his work, thus becoming adviser as well as contributor.[38] This dual role, not uncommon in those years, was perhaps part of his nationalistic leanings, but it can also be explained as a function of the innate generosity and affability which manifested itself in the help he gave to friends as well as institutions.

Brooklyn's watercolors date from the beginning of the century to 1908 and constitute the first and largest set Sargent sold. Their great diversity in subject and technique merits some detailed discussion. *Spanish Soldiers* (Fig. 178) shows the hallmarks of Sargent's earlier style, seen in the Venetian compositions of the 1880s — limited palette, somber colors, receding perspective, and relatively empty foreground. Nonetheless, in an attempt to capture outdoor light, it reveals a new, looser handling and lighter palette which differentiates it and other works in this group from the watercolors of the eighties and nineties.

It is, however, in the eleven Bedouin subjects (1905–06), part of a series he painted on his second trip to Palestine in search of material for the Boston Public Library mural decorations, that Sargent clearly demonstrates a change in his watercolor style.[39] Shimmering with desert light, they are predominantly highlighted by what seems to be ultramarine blue and sienna brown, colors found increasingly and consistently in these and almost all of Sargent's twentieth-century watercolors. So varied is the artist's handling that the ubiquity of these two colors is not always noticeable. As early as the 1880s, ultramarine and sienna appear in the *Bedroom* (Fig. 172), in muted form, wiped out, and manipulated to simulate interior light. The colors are also found in reduced strength in the group painted in Spain in 1902–03 (Fig. 178). But they are the dominant hues in the Bedouin series, and they are frequently undiluted, modified by gouache, or varied by Sargent's alternation of wet and dry brush techniques. In some cases they are so altered by blending that it is difficult to identify them. Blue Bedouin robes are outlined in brown and sometimes in a darker shade of blue; figures are juxtaposed against backgrounds that expand this duo of colors into broad washes (Figs. 180, 181). By varying the intensity of the two hues Sargent used them tonally, without regard for specific local color, to render light and shadow, as well as to contrast warm and cool sensations. In this synthetic system, which he modified as time went on, he established a singular method of capturing the effects of outdoor light.

The recurrence of blue and brown in so many watercolors, even in landscapes where other colors predominate, is noteworthy because it reveals that Sargent's

palette was not really naturalistic, but rather interpretive. Instead of closely adhering to nature, he fabricated what Henry James called "a comprehensive impression."[40] This treatment differs from actual Impressionist handling of outdoor light and color, and from the theories of optical mixture of Michel Eugène Chevreul, who advocated placing complementary colors side by side so that the retina itself could mix them for greater intensity.[41]

Like so many American artists, Sargent incorporated some of the concepts of the Impressionists. He adopted the *plein-air* approach wholeheartedly, but apparently was not interested in the Impressionist technique of applying dabs of broken color uniformly to his paper; rather he varied the surface, alternating flickering movements with broad washes. Given his experimentation in oil with Impressionism in the eighties, it is surprising that Sargent did not begin to utilize watercolor, which seems ideal for describing ephemeral and atmospheric effects, until after 1900. More than a decade elapsed before he reactivated the high-keyed colors and broken brushstroke he had applied to oils in the eighties.

In a Levantine Port (Fig. 189), with its contrast of strokes and bright colors, is a prime example of Sargent's modification of Impressionist ideas. In handling the areas around the water, Sargent comes closest to some aspects of Impressionism; stroke and color — short dabs of orange, yellow, blue, and red — are used to suggest the reflections of sunlight. Color, freed from its descriptive role, creates instead of defines form. Ships are white with blue definitions, and paler shades of the same hue serve as shadows, sponged out while wet, thus allowing the white of the paper to gleam through. In addition to ultramarine blue and sienna brown, Sargent often used burnt umber, cadmium orange, permanent violet, madder

191.

Pomegranates, 1908

Watercolor and pencil on paper, $21\frac{3}{16} \times 14\frac{7}{16}$

(53.8×36.7)

The Brooklyn Museum, New York; Purchased

by Special Subscription

192.

Gourds, c. 1905–08

Watercolor on paper, 14×20 (35.6×50.8)

The Brooklyn Museum, New York; Purchased

by Special Subscription

carmen, Prussian green, and Prussian blue, colors typical of a nineteenth-century palette.[42] He frequently alternated unadulterated Chinese white with the white of the paper for highlights, infusing the entire picture with light as in Fig. 189. By expanding the virtuoso brushwork which distinguished his oil portraits, and by repeating favored hues which did not routinely define local color, Sargent achieved a semblance of Impressionism in his watercolors by largely different means.

Such suggestive and energetic brushwork is evident in *Mountain Fire* (Fig. 213) where, uncharacteristically, form is diffused by color and stroke to virtual abstraction. Hardie, writing with admiration for Sargent's versatility, said, "he knew exactly how his free blots and dashes of colour . . . would fuse and coalesce into form and meaning when seen from a few feet away."[43] Although in many of his works there are areas akin to abstraction, as in later Impressionist works, Sargent comes closest to obliterating his subject in this rendition of smoke and fire in the mountains.

Venetian architecture, gardens, sculpture, and figures both indoor and out make up the rest of Brooklyn's cache. Venice, a constant and favored subject, which Sargent painted more than any other, gave him the opportunity to explore his predilection for oddly cropped fragments of buildings. These were not just accidental occurrences, but rather the result of a practiced eye seeking the eccentric and the unusual, abstracting forms from the context of the whole while concentrating on the play of light on isolated details.[44] Technique varied from painting to painting: *From the Gondola* (Fig. 183) and *All' Ave Maria* (1907) are rapid sketches probably executed from his boat and painted almost entirely in wet

194.
Carrara, Lizzatori I, c. 1911
Watercolor on paper, 20⅞ × 15¹³⁄₁₆ (53 × 40.2)
Museum of Fine Arts, Boston; The Hayden
Collection

washes, while *La Riva* (Fig. 182) is painted with a dryer brush, suggesting a firmer hand that probably worked on solid ground.[45]

Santa Maria della Salute (Fig. 186), a church Sargent painted from various angles, displays a combination of methods.[46] The foreground, rendered in wet brushwork, is blurred and out of focus like a photograph; the bow of his gondola, like a *repoussoir*, looms large and low on the picture plane. It is clear that the artist's attention is centered on the Baroque architecture in the middle ground because in addition to the visible pencil underdrawing, such architectural details as columns and steps are delineated with ruled lines applied over the paint; these were possibly added in the studio. Contrasting techniques differentiate the activity on the water from the stillness of the monumental building, and achieve perceptual accuracy from a distance which partially dissolves upon close observation. Here, as

195.
Workmen at Carrara, c. 1911
Watercolor and pencil on paper, 15½ × 20½
(39.4 × 52.1)
The Art Institute of Chicago; Olivia Shaler
Swan Collection

in the Bedouin series, blue and brown predominate; thus this watercolor is not a
topographical record, but, like so many of Sargent's Venetian scenes, an impression of a place, snapshotlike in its effect but not in its specificity.[47]

After The Brooklyn Museum succeeded in capturing the first group of
Sargent watercolors to enter an American institution, Boston's museum was
apparently anxious to follow suit. "As soon as it became known that a new series of
water-colors was to be exhibited in New York in March 1912, the Boston Museum
determined to examine them before they left the studio of the artist, and to
purchase them immediately if that were possible. Mr. Sargent's kindness and
generosity were only rivaled by the modesty with which he questioned the merit
of certain of the paintings, which he hesitated to leave with the rest; it required
not a little persuasion before he would consent to keep the collection intact."[48]
Sargent's dissatisfaction with some of his watercolors was probably part of his
innate modesty, just as the comic names he gave them, such as "Intertwingles,"
were part of his sense of humor.[49] Initially he may not have recognized their value
or their appeal, but his willingness to have them purchased by American museums
seems to negate Charteris' notion that he was reluctant to sell them.

Boston acquired forty-five watercolors painted during a three-year period in
Venice, Genoa, Florence, Switzerland, Corfu, and at Carrara.[50] An expansion of
techniques, including an increase in the use of wax crayon as a masking agent, is
particularly noticeable in the Corfu pictures of 1908.[51] Subjects similar to those in
Brooklyn's cache — gardens, sculpture, architecture, and figures painted
outdoors — formed Boston's collection. Special to this group, as the Bedouins were
to Brooklyn's trove, was the series of pictures painted at the marble quarries of

230

196.
Blind Musicians, 1912
Watercolor and pencil on paper, 15½ × 21
(39.4 × 53.3)
Aberdeen Art Gallery and Museums, Scotland

Carrara in 1911. Sargent was intrigued by the angular shapes of the stone and by the laborers straining at their various activities or at rest against the setting of the mountainous terrain. It provided an exotic subject, different from his usual studies of the upper class at leisure, and a chance to indulge a lifelong interest in rocks. In this fascination, Sargent recalls Cézanne, whose late watercolors also played a crucial role in his oeuvre, and who manifested a preoccupation with cubelike rock formations in works such as *Bibemus Quarry* (c. 1895; Museum Folkwang, Essen).[52]

A lone worker humanizes the rockscape called *Carrara: Trajan's Quarry* (Fig. 193). Background cliffs on a diagonal axis pull back into the picture space, but the texture of the fractured stone and lack of horizon line counteract the diagonal, attenuating the space and abstracting the highlighted marble blocks into geometric surface patterns. In this series Sargent's chromatic scale, which often contrasts dark and light, becomes more muted, reflecting local color in shades of brown and ocher, with blue mainly reserved for shadows. In *Workmen at Carrara* (Fig. 195), he focuses on the laborers; it is they, not the terrain, who fill the foreground. Sargent was not interested in their faces, nor in making a social comment, but in using them as vehicles for other visual interests, such as the plasticity and decorative arrangement of the rope they carry. These works are a compendium of watercolor methods, demonstrating such reductive techniques as scraping, wiping out, and waxing, used in combination with gouache and transparent layering to achieve the glistening effects of sunlight on stone.

The Metropolitan Museum of Art was next in line, purchasing its main group in 1915, although it had actually agreed to buy its first Sargent watercolor as early as 1913, just one year after the Boston acquisition. Edward Robinson, director of the museum from 1910 to 1931, wrote to his old friend Sargent on December 17, 1912, requesting "eight or ten" watercolors, no more because of limited space. "We should naturally be guided largely by your own selection. . . . "[53] Ten handpicked watercolors and an oil, *Tyrolese Interior*, were accessioned by the spring of 1915.[54] Included among the ten was the one bought in 1913 — *Granada Fountain*, now called *Spanish Fountain* (similar to Fig. 177), which Sargent apparently held back to send with the other nine: *Giudecca*, *Venetian Canal*, *Idle Sails*, *In the Generalife*, *Escutcheon of Charles V*, *Mountain Stream*, *Sirmione*, *Boats*, and *Tyrolese Crucifix*.[55] These works constitute a sampling of Sargent's favorite subjects and locations painted between 1912 and 1914. Although one or two, such as *Sirmione*, lack his usual vitality, the others, for the most part, demonstrate that he was at the height of his watercolor career. His technical versatility is made clear from the wet washes of *Idle Sails*, a *tour de force* of handling, especially in the white of the crumpled sail cloth, in the range from suggestive to more meticulous likenesses of his sister Emily, Jane von Glehn, and a Spanish friend named Dolores in *In the Generalife*, and in the ephemeral impressions of architectural wall decorations in *The Escutcheon of Charles V*. Heavy dashes of Chinese white highlights are no longer visible here and gouache is mixed directly with the pigments in a dilute form, closely approximating pure watercolor but still retaining some of the opacity of oil. New, too, are Granada motifs from his trip in 1912, and a subject seen in early sketchbooks as well as in the Boston Public Library murals — the crucifix. Unusual croppings, as in the *Tyrolese Crucifix*, appear to be accidental approaches, but are in reality as carefully planned as the fragmented Venetian buildings. These strongly colored, striking compositions differ greatly from the centrally focused, tightly brushed, subdued works of his early years and from the diagonal emphasis and diluted, somber colors of the end of the century.

One sees a continuation of Sargent's close focus and variety of techniques in the several watercolors resulting from a trip to Lake O'Hara in the Rocky Mountains of British Columbia in 1916. Plagued with bad weather, which reduced his output considerably, he focused mainly on the area around the camp site, as in *Camping at Lake O'Hara* (Fig. 205), and not on the panoramic view. He was not compelled by the magnitude of the landscape as were Albert Bierstadt and Thomas Moran, American painters who glorified these majestic mountains. Here, an economy of strokes reveals Sargent's facility in painting figures, while the handling of the tents illustrates his ability to render the texture and substance of textiles by juxtaposing the white of the paper with pale buff washes which delineate folds and shadows. The deep tones of the woods are subtly shaded, not at all murky as in the wooded background of *In the Generalife* and some of the Boboli Gardens series. Thus by the second decade of the century, Sargent, committed to the use of watercolor, divided his time between painting *plein-air* oils and watercolors on his frequent trips (except on rainy days when he painted interiors), and working on his mural commissions. By then he had all but given up oil portraiture, although he continued to do charcoal portraits that took only a few hours.[56]

The Worcester Art Museum was the last American museum to obtain a series of watercolors, the product of Sargent's trip to Miami, Florida, in 1917. Sargent's friend Frederick S. Pratt, a businessman turned artist, had inquired about the availability of some watercolors for the museum as early as 1913.[57] Having the Metropolitan's request to fill, and having been relatively unproductive on his trip to the Rockies in 1916, Sargent was not able to accommodate Pratt's request for quite a while, which indicates the continued demand for his watercolors. Sargent went to Florida to paint a portrait of John D. Rockefeller, one of the very few in those years. Inspired by a combination of the tropical light and fantastic architectural views of "Villa Vizcaya," the ornate Italian Renaissance home belonging to the brother of his friend Charles Deering, Sargent produced a series of about seventeen dramatic watercolors, eleven of which were purchased by Worcester.[58] "It combines Venice and Frascati and Aranjuez, and all that one is never likely to see again," Sargent wrote of the villa.[59] Ironically, he associated one of the few American subjects he painted with European locales.

Not only the architecture and gardens of the villa, but also more typical Floridian subjects interested Sargent. His depiction of the bright tropical light, the activities of some of the native population, and the splendor of tropical vegetation parallel watercolors by Winslow Homer painted between 1886 and 1904. It is

198.

Simplon Pass: The Tease, 1911
Watercolor on paper, 15¾ × 20¾ (40 × 52.7)
Museum of Fine Arts, Boston; The Hayden
Collection

interesting to compare the "clarity" and "rude strength" that art critic Royal
Cortissoz said made Homer American and saved him from "the hardness of
sophistication," with the "flashing celerity" that made Sargent seem cosmopolitan.[60] In *Bathers* (Fig. 201), Sargent summarily dealt with the movement and
musculature of nude black bodies highlighted by sun-dappling light, and broke up
his space into small components by using short, darting strokes that produced a
dazzling picture surface. Relying more than ever on the transparent qualities of
the paint to provide the luminosity he sought, Sargent nevertheless continued to
use gouache and other techniques to achieve variety and contrast. Homer,
confronting a similar theme in *Rum Cay* (Fig. 202), reduced his picture to essentials
by sweeping large areas of wash across broad compositional planes. His figure,
running on a sunlit beach, maintains solidity under close scrutiny; light and color
are synonymous, arrived at solely with transparent layers of pigment and no
visible use of reductive methods. Sargent's more complex composition, painterly
brushwork and fragmented views, on the other hand, need distance to remain
visually intact. Even in their pictures of Florida palms, which at first glance seem

234

199.
Reading, 1911
Watercolor and gouache on paper, 20 × 14
(50.8 × 35.6)
Museum of Fine Arts, Boston ; The Hayden
Collection

200.
Simplon Pass: The Lesson, 1911
Watercolor on paper, 15 × 18¼ (38.1 × 46.4)
Museum of Fine Arts, Boston ; The Hayden
Collection

201.

Bathers, 1917

Watercolor on paper, 15¾ × 20⅞ (40 × 53)

Worcester Art Museum, Massachusetts

202.

Winslow Homer, *Rum Cay*, 1898 or 1899

Watercolor on paper, 38 × 54⁵⁄₁₆ (96.5 × 137.9)

Worcester Art Museum, Massachusetts

similar, Sargent's attention to form-flattening surface patterns in his numerous renditions of *Palmettos* (Fig. 203) sets his work apart from Homer's unwavering interest in realistic recording. Yet, although their goals and methods were different, both artists were, as Cortissoz observed, "dedicated to material things, tangible things, closely apprehended."[61]

The high proportion of watercolors placed in American institutions testifies to Sargent's definite intention to locate his work in this country, perhaps in

203.
Palmettos, 1917
Watercolor on paper, 13½ × 18 (34.3 × 45.7)
Collection of the Ormond Family

204.
Muddy Alligators, 1917
Watercolor on paper, 13½ × 20½ (34.3 × 52.1)
Worcester Art Museum, Massachusetts

205.

Camping at Lake O'Hara, 1916
Watercolor on paper, 15¾ × 20⅞ (40 × 53)
The Newark Museum, New Jersey

response to his expatriate status. Charteris reiterates: "America, indeed, was a much more constant motive for his actions than was generally supposed. His decorative work at Boston . . . was prompted by this national allegiance, and to this has to be added his constant desire that America should be the home of so large a share of his best work . . . . the idea of his country and of his obligations as an American citizen never left him."[62]

Ten watercolors executed at the front in 1918 were, however, donated by Sargent to the Imperial War Museum in London a year later.[63] He advised that museum: "I think my watercolours gain by being seen together in a certain quantity, and I would be glad to add to the four you have selected by giving some more. But I would like to have your assurance that they would all be hung and hung together."[64] This sheds light on another possible reason for Sargent selling watercolors to museums in clusters — the desire to have them exhibited together, which they were.

Asked by the British government to commemorate the combined efforts of the American and British soldiers during World War I, a commission which

238

206.
Thou Shalt Not Steal, 1918
Watercolor on paper, 20¾ × 13¼ (52.7 × 33.6)
The Trustees of the Imperial War Museum,
London

207.
The Interior of a Hospital Tent, 1918
Watercolor on paper, 15³⁄₁₆ × 20⁷⁄₁₆
(38.5 × 51.9)
The Trustees of the Imperial War Museum,
London

208.
A Street in Arras, 1918
Watercolor on paper, 15⅜ × 20¹¹⁄₁₆
(38.5 × 52.5)
The Trustees of the Imperial War Museum,
London

resulted in the painting *Gassed* (Fig. 256), Sargent recorded the war zone in watercolor — the troops, the barracks, the tents, soldiers resting — with a greater looseness and directness than before. Fewer pencil notations are visible, revealing that he worked more *alla prima* than usual; those that are perceptible are rudimentary and, as with pentimenti, indicate that he often changed initial concepts as he worked. His expertise allowed him to limit his customary repertoire of reductive techniques and exploit the inherent qualities of watercolor, as in *The Interior of a Hospital Tent* (Fig. 207), or *Thou Shalt Not Steal* (Fig. 206), where two soldiers pluck the fruit of enveloping pomegranate trees. Painted with a wetter brush than his earlier *Pomegranates* (Fig. 191), it consists almost entirely of transparent washes, with gouache used sparingly to lighten and modify color.[65]

From the set bought by The Brooklyn Museum in 1909 to the war pictures presented to the Imperial War Museum in 1919, and even in later watercolors painted in Ironbound, Maine, in 1922, continual refinement rather than overt dramatic change is evident in Sargent's technical development. This gradual

209.

Highlanders Resting at the Front, 1918
Watercolor and pencil on paper, 13½ × 21¼
(34.3 × 54)
Syndics of the Fitzwilliam Museum,
Cambridge, England

210.

Camouflaged Tanks, Berles-au-Bois, 1918
Watercolor on paper, 13⅜ × 20⁹⁄₁₆ (34 × 52.3)
The Trustees of the Imperial War Museum,
London

211.
Figure with Red Drapery, n.d.
Watercolor on paper, $14\frac{1}{2} \times 21\frac{13}{16}$
(36.8×55.4)
The Metropolitan Museum of Art, New York;
Gift of Mrs. Francis Ormond, 1950

evolution, with certain exceptions, shows itself in Sargent's progressively lighter and broader touch, his diminished use of gouache and strong color contrasts, his increased dependence on the white of the paper, and his expanded use of color to define form. These changes imply an ever more masterful exploitation of the essential qualities of the medium — immediacy and transparency. Although in his persistent quest to capture direct and reflected light and color, Sargent sometimes displayed an abstract aesthetic akin to the work of some early modernists, his art, firmly rooted in nineteenth-century traditions, never sacrificed the integrity of the objects he painted. In the choice of subjects and colors that delighted his eye, he created a body of work that has enduring appeal; a school of followers established in his lifetime abides today.[66] As an international figure, he left a singular artistic legacy to the world which Charteris aptly expressed: "To live with Sargent's water-colours is to live with sunshine captured and held."[67]

242

212.
Alice Runnels James (Mrs. William James), 1921
Watercolor on paper, 21⅛ × 13½ (53.7 × 34.3)
Museum of Fine Arts, Boston; Gift of William
James, 1977

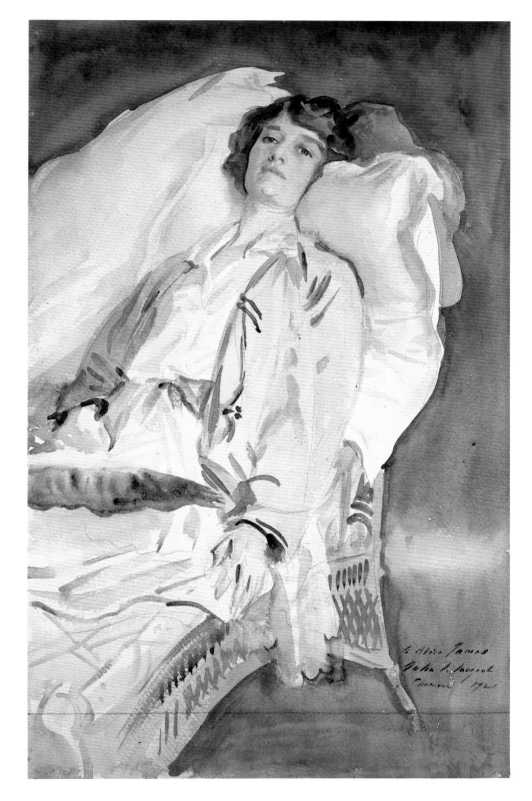

1. Richard Ormond, *John Singer Sargent: Paintings, Drawings, Watercolors* (New York, 1970), p. 68; Donelson Hoopes, *Sargent Watercolors* (New York, 1970), p. 17; Evan Charteris, *John Sargent* (New York, 1927), p. 178; Martin Hardie, *Water-colour Painting in Britain*, 3 vols. (London, 1966), III, p. 169.

2. Quoted in Charteris, *John Sargent*, p. 235.

3. The Fogg Art Museum, Harvard University, Cambridge, Massachusetts, owns a large collection of these sketchbooks.

4. Walter Launt Palmer, an American artist who met Sargent in Florence at this time, recorded in his diary, November 14, 1873: "He is but 17 & had done a most remarkable amount of work very little oil"; quoted in Maybelle Mann, *Walter Launt Palmer: Poetic Reality* (Exton, Pennsylvania, 1984), p. 12.

5. Charteris, *John Sargent*, p. 21. Whistler's tonal and moody watercolors, painted for the most part without gouache, bear little resemblance to Sargent's. Hardie, *Water-colour Painting in Britain*, p. 168, writes that for Whistler "watercolor was only an occasional dalliance," whereas for Sargent oil and watercolor were lifetime "companions."

6. Alain de Leiris in *From Delacroix to Cézanne: French Watercolor Landscapes of the Nineteenth Century*, exhibition catalogue (College Park, Maryland, University of Maryland Gallery, 1977), pp. 22 and 70 n. 5.

7. Henry Blackburn, "Pictures at the Paris Exhibition: The British School," *Magazine of Art*, 1 (1878), pp. 126–30.

8. Sargent's development in watercolor coincides both with the American departure from English watercolor conventions and heightened public appreciation of the medium. On his first trip to the United States in 1876, he visited the Centennial Exhibition in Philadelphia, where he could have seen a retrospective exhibition of the ten-year-old American Watercolor Society. Sargent's possible chance encounter would have exposed him to a significant group of watercolors by Winslow Homer, Thomas Eakins, Thomas Moran, and various Hudson River painters whose works, however luminescent, were for the most part tightly painted and opaque like their oils; see *Official Catalogue of the United States International Exhibition* (Philadelphia, 1876).

9. Details of the relationship between Duez and Sargent are found in Maureen O'Brien's entry on Sargent's *Portrait of Ernest-Ange Duez* in *The American Painting Collection of the Montclair Art Museum, Research Supplement I* (Montclair, New Jersey, 1979), pp. 11–16. Sargent owned a large watercolor by Duez.

10. See Richard Ormond, "Sargent's *El Jaleo*," in *Fenway Court: Isabella Stewart Gardner Museum, 1970* (Boston, 1971), p. 13.

11. Royal Cortissoz, *The Painter's Craft* (New York, 1930), p. 285. The numbers "1869" on *Figure in Costume* seem to have been added and are similar in hand and placement to numbers on a work in the collection of David Daniels. An unidentified clipping in the Sargent scrapbook at the Knoedler Gallery Art Reference Library, New York, mentions that Sargent's *Young Woman with Black Skirt* was thought to be by Boldini; *The New York Times*, January 22, 1926, p. 9, reported that a watercolor sketch of an *Italian Model with Cope* was withdrawn from the Sargent memorial exhibition at The Metropolitan Museum because it was thought to be by Boldini; it was, nevertheless, included in the catalogue. I am most grateful to Nancy Little for generously allowing me access to the Sargent material at Knoedler's.

12. Sargent probably met Giovanni Boldini and Antonio Mancini, or at least became aware of their work, in the mid-1870s. Sargent's collection also included works by such friends as Edwin Austin Abbey, Wilfrid von Glehn, Augustus John, Paul Helleu, Claude Monet, and P. Wilson Steer; see Christie's, London, July 24 and 27, 1925, *Catalogue of Pictures and Water Colour Drawings by J. S. Sargent and Works by Other Artists*. Martin Birnbaum, *John Singer Sargent: A Conversation Piece* (New York, 1941), p. 17, points out that Sargent also admired "some brilliant pyrotechnical water colours of the bull-ring by the Spaniard Roberto Domingo. . . ."

13. David McKibbin has suggested that the two Venetian watercolors exhibited at the Salon might be *Campo dei Frari, Venice* and *Canal Scene, Venice*; see Edward J. Nygren, *John Singer Sargent: Drawings from the Corcoran Gallery of Art*, exhibition catalogue

(Washington, D.C., Smithsonian Institution Traveling Exhibition Service and the Corcoran Gallery of Art, 1983), pp. 53–54.

14. Abbey, whom Sargent tutored in the use of oils, was Sargent's close friend and collaborator in the Boston Public Library mural project. He first exhibited with the American Watercolor Society in 1874 and was a member from 1877 to 1911; Frank Millet was a member from 1886 to 1912, and Parsons exhibited with that group at least once in 1871. Abbey was elected a member of The Royal Institute of Painters in Water Colour in 1883. For further information, see E. V. Lucas, *Edwin Austin Abbey, Royal Academician: The Record of His Life and Work*, 2 vols. (London and New York, 1921); and Kathleen A. Foster, "The Paintings," in *Edwin Austin Abbey*, exhibition catalogue (New Haven, Yale University Art Gallery, 1974).

15. The Tile Club was an informal group formed in 1877 and counted among its members such watercolorists as Winslow Homer and illustrators as Frank Millet and Alfred Parsons; see Mahonri Sharp Young, "The Tile Club Revisited," *The American Art Journal*, 2 (Fall 1970), pp. 81–91.

16. Carol A. Nathanson, "Hercules Brabazon and the Formation of the Watercolor Style of John Singer Sargent," unpublished paper, c. 1980, makes a case for a conjunction in style and technique as well as in subject. I am grateful to Patricia Hills for making this useful essay available to me, as well as for her advice and bonhomie. Charteris, *John Sargent*, pp. 224–25, notes that Sargent's watercolor production increased after he met Brabazon in 1886 or 1887, but he emphatically added that "for the most part he is entirely himself, deriving from no one." Three years later Martin Hardie, in *J. S. Sargent, R.A., R.W.F.* (New York and London, 1930), p. 4, reflected that "His actual method surely owes far more than has ever been stated to the influence of his friend Brabazon." Nevertheless he realized that Brabazon "never possessed Sargent's brilliant draughtsmanship and his power of manipulating a brush." Thirty years later Hardie, in his monumental *Water-colour Painting in Britain*, pp. 169–70, apparently reconsidered because he no longer mentions the connection. Hoopes, *Sargent Watercolors*, pp. 15 and 60, points out that Sargent never

commented on the influence Brabazon might have had on him, but that in certain loosely painted works like *Giudecca* (c. 1907; The Brooklyn Museum), there is a resemblance in technique and mood.

17. As reprinted in C. Lewis Hind, *Hercules Brabazon Brabazon 1821–1906: His Art and Life* (London, 1912), p. 86.

18. Although Brabazon greatly admired Sargent, and even painted adaptations of Sargent's works, it was Turner, not Sargent, who was his hero. Turner's color sense and complex watercolor technique appealed to Brabazon and probably to Sargent too, and his works were readily available in London museums; see Hilarie Faberman, *Hercules Brabazon Brabazon*, exhibition catalogue (New York, Godwin-Ternbach Museum, Queens College, 1985), p. 4. Charteris, *John Sargent*, p. 199, writes that Sargent preferred Turner's early works, with their contrasts of lights and darks, rather than his more misty later paintings.

19. William Starkweather, "John Singer Sargent: Master Portrait Painter," *The Mentor* (October 1924), p. 8; David McKibbin, *Sargent's Boston*, exhibition catalogue (Museum of Fine Arts, Boston, 1956), p. 20, said "encouraged by his mother and supported by his sister Emily."

20. Hardie, *J. S. Sargent*, p. 2.

21. Charteris, *John Sargent*, p. 95.

22. Adrian Stokes, "John Singer Sargent, R. A., R. W. S.," in Randall Davies, ed. *The Old Water-Colour Society's Club 1925–1926* (London, 1926), pp. 53–55.

23. Birnbaum, *John Singer Sargent*, p. 10.

24. Charteris, *John Sargent*, p. 95.

25. Quoted in Birnbaum, *John Singer Sargent*, p. 10. For Sargent's watercolor materials, see also Marjorie Cohn and Rachel Rosenfield in *Wash and Gouache*, exhibition catalogue (Cambridge, Massachusetts, Fogg Art Museum, 1977); Charteris, *John Sargent*, p. 95.

26. Hardie, *J. S. Sargent*, p. 3. Hardie's statement needs qualifying because some of Sargent's watercolors seem to have been painted on dry paper. Charteris, *John Sargent*, p. 224, was not strictly correct in claiming that Sargent never used "the opaque method."

27. In careful examination of the watercolors at The Brooklyn Museum, no watermarks were found, nor were any obvious on more

casual examination of the watercolors at The Metropolitan Museum of Art and the Museum of Fine Arts, Boston.

28. Birnbaum, *John Singer Sargent*, p. 9, says "the walls were given over to Sargent's own watercolours." Stanley Olson, conversation with the author, September 12, 1985, adds that Emily's flat was also decorated with Sargent's watercolors.

29. Charteris, *John Sargent*, p. 170.

30. Boston, Copley Hall, *Catalogue of Paintings and Sketches by John S. Sargent, R. A.*, exhibition catalogue (Boston, 1899).

31. Sargent sent no watercolors to the 1909 Society exhibition because eighty-six had gone to Knoedler's in New York for a joint exhibition with Edward D. Boit, another friend who painted in watercolor (see pp. 224–25, above). Sargent's friendship with Boit dates from the early eighties, when Boit commissioned Sargent to paint his daughters (Fig. 48). Boit submitted sixty-three watercolors to the show at Knoedler's.

32. Sargent also exhibited watercolors at the New English Art Club in 1907, according to Adrian Stokes, "John Singer Sargent," p. 59.

33. Ibid., pp. 61–63. Among those that remained with Sargent until 1909 were *La Riva* (Fig. 182) and some other Venetian scenes, *Portuguese Boats*, *All' Ave Maria*, *Aranjuez*, and *Spanish Soldiers* (Fig. 178).

34. From the moment The Brooklyn Museum received their cache in 1909, loan exhibitions took place, the first at Boston that very year. Brooklyn began their own Watercolor Biennials in 1921, often placing their Sargents (as well as their Homers) on display. In 1917 eighteen Sargent watercolors, many lent by the museums at Brooklyn and Worcester, were exhibited at the Cleveland Museum of Art and Carnegie Institute in Pittsburgh. In 1918 a watercolor exhibition toured Toledo, Detroit, Minneapolis, Milwaukee, St. Louis, and Rochester. In 1924 the Grand Central Art Galleries in New York held a retrospective exhibition that included ten watercolors from Worcester's collection, in which "Mr. Sargent . . . personally selected and approved all of the paintings . . . "; *Retrospective Exhibition of Important Works of John Singer Sargent*, exhibition catalogue (New York, 1924), p. 48.

35. According to Harold Bentley, "In the Galleries," *The International Studio*, 37 (April 1909), p. LV, Sargent had stipulated to Knoedler's that his "pictures must be bought *en bloc*, which caused dismay to the collectors, and he further insisted they must go to some public gallery." *The Bulletin of the Brooklyn Institute of Arts and Sciences*, March 3, 1909, p. 160, states that A. Augustus Healy, president of The Brooklyn Museum, saw the paintings on February 15, "recognized the value of these eighty-three paintings at once, and having been acquainted with Mr. Sargent for many years he cabled him in London." Within twenty-four hours a deal was struck — $20,000 for the lot. By February 19, just four days later, the Executive Committee approved the purchase and set about raising funds by public subscription. Healy donated a substantial sum as well. This was the "largest gathering of paintings" by Sargent in any collection at the time and the price paid was deemed very reasonable; if the group had been sold individually Sargent could have realized much more money.

Three of the eighty-six watercolors exhibited at Knoedler's in 1909 (nos. 67, 83, and 87 in Knoedler's printed exhibition checklist), were not bought by The Brooklyn Museum — a version of *Spanish Soldiers*, *Sketchers* (possibly the same one shown at the Carfax Gallery in 1904), and a *Portrait of Mrs. Wilfrid von Glehn* (all of which I have been unable to trace). There is no explanation as to why these three were excluded from the sale. It is possible they were privately owned, or previously promised and were lent only for exhibition. Legend has it that Sargent inadvertently included the watercolor inscribed to William Rathbone and had to give Rathbone another, perhaps one of the three returned. *Spanish Soldiers* in Brooklyn's collection is inscribed to Rathbone and another *Group of Spanish Convalescent Soldiers*, c. 1903, exists in the Rathbone family collection. I wish to thank Stanley Olson, who related this story to me based on his research, for sharing his ideas. I am most grateful to Odile Duff of the Coe Kerr Gallery, Inc. for spending much time searching the gallery files to help me, and to Donna Seldin and Warren Adelson for making material from the gallery's forthcoming catalogue raisonné of Sargent's oeuvre available to me.

213.
Mountain Fire, c. 1903–08
Watercolor on paper, 14 × 20 (35.6 × 50.8)
The Brooklyn Museum, New York; Purchased
by Special Subscription

In the pamphlet accompanying the joint exhibition of Sargent watercolors at The Brooklyn Museum and The Metropolitan Museum of Art (July 12–August 27, 1972), Sarah Faunce mistakenly says that eighty watercolors were purchased by The Brooklyn Museum; Hoopes, *Sargent Watercolors*, p. 19, and others perpetuate the error. The correct number of eighty-three is recorded in *The Bulletin of the Brooklyn Institute*, 1909, and in archival material in the Sargent files of Brooklyn's Department of Paintings and Sculpture. In January 1926, soon after Sargent's death, when the market for his watercolors was strong, twenty-nine of these works were returned to Knoedler's for sale and subsequently found their way to various public and private collections. Another letter in the departmental files, dated February 5, 1926, states that thirty-one were sold at that time. Brooklyn presently owns forty-three Sargent watercolors.

36. Charteris, *John Sargent*, p. 176, says that Sargent gave up portraiture in 1909, yet Charteris lists over fifty portraits done after that date.

37. *Museum of Fine Arts Bulletin*, 10 (April 1912), p. 19. Boston missed out because Brooklyn acted so quickly; see n. 35, above.

38. See William T. Fox, "John Singer Sargent and The Brooklyn Museum," *The Brooklyn Museum Quarterly* (July 1925), p. 112. Within Sargent's lifetime, The Brooklyn Museum acquired four of his oil paintings: *A Summer Idyll* (c. 1878–79) in 1914, *Dolce Far Niente* (c. 1908–09), placed on loan in 1911 and bequeathed by A. Augustus Healy, president of The Brooklyn Museum, upon his death in 1921, along with the portrait Sargent had painted of him. In 1920 Sargent's painting of *Paul Helleu Sketching with His Wife* (Fig. 89) came into the collection. According to letters on file in the Department of Paintings and Sculpture, this painting was purchased from Paul Helleu (probably acting as agent for the real owner). As early as 1900 Sargent instigated the purchase of more than four hundred gouache illustrations of New Testament scenes by James Jacques Joseph Tissot. On a visit to the States in 1907 he painted A. Augustus Healy, and two years later arranged for Healy to buy Boldini's 1897 portrait of *Whistler*, which Healey donated to the museum a year later.

39. These are not direct studies for the murals, commissioned in 1890, for which Sargent did some watercolor sketches. Tissot, and others before him, such as William Holman Hunt and John Frederick Lewis, were also attracted to this nomadic group of people, believing as Sargent probably did that they lived in virtually the same circumstances as in biblical times and were therefore

authentic models for an illustration of the history of Western religions.

40. Henry James, "John S. Sargent" (1887); reprinted in *Picture and Text* (New York, 1893), p. 104.

41. Sargent, probably aware of Chevreul's ideas through his relationship with Claude Monet, seems to have adapted and modified some of these tenets, as did the Impressionists themselves. He defined Impressionism as "the name given to a certain form of observation when Monet not content with using his eyes to see what things were . . . turned his attention to noting what took place *on his own retina* [emphasis original]"; see Charteris, *John Sargent*, p. 123, quoting a letter from Sargent to Frederick Jameson, March 20, 1911 or 1912.

42. Katrinka H. Leschey, Harvard University, wrote her senior thesis on Sargent's use of color. On a visit to The Brooklyn Museum, she showed me J. Scott Taylor's *Modern Water-colour Pigments*, published by Winsor and Newton Ltd. (London, 1887). I am indebted to her for bringing this book, which helps to identify the colors in Sargent's palette, to my attention and for sharing some of her ideas with me. Marjorie Cohn, in *Wash and Gouache*, pp. 65–66, lists some of the paints found in Sargent's palette and some of the brushes he used — ten assorted camel, sable, and badger brushes with metal ferrules and a scraper.

43. Hardie, *Water-colour Painting in Britain*, p. 169.

44. Fronia Wissman, "Sargent's Watercolor Views of Santa Maria della Salute," *Yale University Art Gallery Bulletin*, 37 (Summer 1979), p. 16.

45. The dates are those I attributed to these works in *The Brooklyn Museum: Watercolors, Pastels, Collages* (New York, 1984), pp. 64–68. All of these works have pencil foundations.

46. Other images of the church include: *The Salute, Venice* at the Yale University Art Gallery, a partial view of the top of the building seen from below; another in the Museum of Fine Arts, Boston, focuses on the steps leading up to the main door looking up; the one in the Fitzwilliam Museum, Cambridge, is seen from a similar vantage point, but further to one side. The watercolor at the Joslyn Art Museum, Omaha, and the oil at the Municipal Art Gallery, Johannesburg, focus on the steps leading to the main portal.

47. Wissman, "Sargent's Watercolor Views," pp. 14–19.

48. "The Water-Colors of Edward D. Boit and John S. Sargent," *Museum of Fine Arts Bulletin*, 10 (April 1912), p. 19. The museum also bought thirty-one tightly painted topographical watercolors by Boit from the second joint exhibition at Knoedler's, May 16–30, 1912.

49. Charteris, *John Sargent*, p. 178.

50. Another group was purchased in 1921 and the sketches for the museum's mural decorations were donated in Sargent's memory by his sisters.

51. Sargent seems to have begun using wax for masking as early as 1907; the technique served the purpose of masking the white of the paper or a wash of color from succeeding paint applications; Sargent probably scraped the wax off when the process was finished, for no raised surfaces are discernible. My thanks to Marjorie Cohn, conservator at the Fogg Art Museum and co-author of *Wash and Gouache*, for identifying the waxed areas for me. It was she and Andrea Kaliski, a Ph.D. candidate in the Department of Fine Arts at Harvard University, who first noted Sargent's use of wax.

52. I wish to thank Sherry Goodman for suggesting this connection and for her other invaluable suggestions and editorial comments. Cézanne's watercolors were first exhibited in Paris in 1905 but it is not known whether Sargent saw them.

53. Copies of the Sargent-Robinson correspondence are in The Metropolitan Museum of Art Archives. Sargent answered on December 31 that he had done few watercolors that year, that he had sold two or three but "kept back the two best for myself" and would be willing to sell one, of a fountain in Granada, to the Metropolitan. He also agreed "to reserve the best water colours that I shall do next year for the Museum." The price he requested was slightly higher than what he had charged Brooklyn. On January 20, 1913, Robinson acknowledged the approval of the purchase of *Spanish Fountain* and reminded Sargent that the museum also wanted a large oil in addition to the forthcoming watercolors.

54. Although Donelson Hoopes, *Sargent Watercolors*, p. 19, and Susan E. Strickler, "John Singer Sargent and Worcester," *Worcester Art Museum Journal*, 6 (1982–83), quoting Hoopes, p. 38 n. 50, say eleven, The Metropolitan Museum of Art Archives reveal that only ten were purchased in 1915.

55. The Metropolitan's *Spanish Fountain*, previously dated "after 1902" in Hoopes, *Sargent Watercolors*, p. 25 and pl. 2, was subsequently redated c. 1912 according to letters in the files of the American Arts department at The Metropolitan Museum. The Metropolitan's own brochure, which accompanied the Sargent watercolor exhibition in 1972, dates the work (listed as no. 14) 1902–03 or 1912. On the basis of Sargent's letters to Edward Robinson (see n. 53, above), it can now be definitely dated 1912. The photograph Sargent sent to Robinson verifies that *Granada Fountain* and *Spanish Fountain* are one and the same. The confirmation of the 1912 date for the Metropolitan's *Spanish Fountain* suggests a similar dating for the Fitzwilliam version (Fig. 177).

    According to the "Note" in the *Memorial Exhibition of the Work of John Singer Sargent* (New York, The Metropolitan Museum of Art, 1926), p. xi, Sargent's involvement with the museum, in "its growth and . . . its future," continued. He consented to sell *Madame X* to the museum the following year at one fifth the price he had offered it elsewhere; he also helped the Metropolitan purchase *Portrait of a Man* by El Greco in 1924 from a Spanish collection. Sargent forwarded letters and photographs to Robinson and upon Sargent's recommendation the painting was bought. I am grateful to Jeanie James, The Metropolitan Museum of Art Archives, for making these letters available to me.

56. Trevor J. Fairbrother, *Sargent Portrait Drawings: 42 Works by John Singer Sargent* (New York, 1983), n.p., records in his introduction that Sargent made over five hundred such drawings from 1910 until his death and only painted about thirty oil portraits in this same period.

57. Strickler, "John Singer Sargent and Worcester," pp. 31 and 39 n. 65. Sargent's connection with Worcester dated from the summer of 1890, when he visited that city to fulfill one of his many portrait commissions. By 1911 the Worcester Art Museum, established in 1898, had purchased Sargent's *Venetian Water Carriers* (Fig. 36); it acquired *Lady Warwick and Her Son* (1905) in 1913. For details of the problems surrounding the portrait purchase, see Strickler, pp. 27–30, 75. As with the Metropolitan and Brooklyn, Sargent's interest in the Worcester Art Museum went beyond that of securing a place for his own works. In 1921 he brought to the attention of the museum Ingres' *L'Odalisque à l'Esclave* (*La Petite Odalisque*) of 1842, but the director decided against the purchase.

58. Four of these watercolors were deaccessioned in 1948 and are in the McCormick family collection. Others in this series are found in the Ormond family collection and in various museums.

59. Quoted in Strickler, "John Singer Sargent and Worcester," p. 33.

60. Royal Cortissoz, *Exposition d'Art Américain: John Singer Sargent, Dodge Macnight, Winslow Homer and Paul Manship*, exhibition catalogue (Paris, L'Hôtel de la Chambre Synical de la Curiosité et des Beaux Arts, 1923), pp. 12, 16.

61. Ibid., p. 16.

62. Charteris, *John Sargent*, p. 98.

63. *Imperial War Museum: A Concise Catalogue of Paintings, Drawings and Sculpture of the First World War, 1914–1918* (London, 1963), p. 266. A similar number of war pictures is in the collection of The Metropolitan Museum of Art.

64. Sargent to Alfred Yockney, December 27, 1918, Archives of the Imperial War Museum. I am indebted to Stanley Olson for providing this material.

65. An oil painting *Pomegranates, Majorca* (illustration, p. 281) probably also painted around 1908, demonstrates the dialogue between technique and subject in some of Sargent's oils and watercolors. Both the earlier oil and watercolor are more solidly and heavily painted, with less varied brushwork and a more restricted palette than the war picture. Here and elsewhere when Sargent explored the same themes in both mediums, characteristics of each technique seem to permeate one another.

66. This emulation has served both to perpetuate Sargent's watercolor style and to debase it with inferior interpretations.

67. Charteris, *John Sargent*, p. 225.

A Portfolio of Drawings

PATRICIA HILLS

Sargent's childhood precocity in draftsmanship elicited the enthusiastic and lasting admiration of his family. Nor was it surprising that they encouraged his talents: his father, Dr. FitzWilliam Sargent, had illustrated the medical textbooks he had written, and his mother, Mary Newbold Singer, was herself an amateur water-colorist who took her young son on sketching expeditions.[1] These proud parents saved sketches done by Sargent from the age of four,[2] and they tucked samples of his skill with the pencil into their letters to distant relatives in America.[3] Young Sargent, according to family accounts, wrote of his own efforts in drawing when he was a mere eight years old; he penned a letter to his grandmother in which he mentioned a book noteworthy for its good models to copy.[4]

Those frequent letters home tell much about an education guaranteed to encourage Sargent's artistic eye and hand. FitzWilliam Sargent, for one, was intent on cultivating his son's visual memory:

I keep him well supplied with interesting books of natural history, of which he is very fond, containing well-drawn pictures of birds and animals, with a sufficient amount of text to interest him in their habits, etc. He is quite a close observer of animated nature, so much so that, by carefully comparing what he sees with what he reads in his books, he is enabled to distinguish the birds which he sees about where he happens to be. Thus, you see, I am enabled to cultivate his memory and his observing and discriminating faculties without his being bothered with the disagreeable notion that he is actually studying, which idea, to a child, must be a great nuisance.[5]

This kind of education, which valued the empirical apprehension of nature, determined the route that the budding artist would take. Individual drawings from his youth show a diversity of subjects, but always of things, views, and people that entered into his field of vision. As Evan Charteris observed, these drawings

were literal records of what was immediately before him. He drew whatever came to hand, never worrying to find special subjects, but just enjoying the sheer fun of translating on to paper the record of what he saw. He seems, as a boy, never to have drawn "out of his head." The usual fancies from history and mythology, which even the gravest artists in boyhood have turned to, do

214.
Kneeling Model, n.d.
Charcoal on paper, 24 × 18½ (61 × 47)
Harvard University Art Museums, Fogg Art
Museum, Cambridge, Massachusetts; Gift of
Mrs. Francis Ormond

215.
Engelsburg, 1872
Black chalk and pencil on paper, 10⅝ × 14¼
(27 × 36.2)
Trustees of the British Museum, London;
Presented by Mrs. Ormond

216.
Deer, c. 1872–74
Pencil on paper, 11⅜ × 15³⁄₁₆ (28.9 × 38.6)
Worcester Art Museum, Massachusetts

217.
Bartholomy Magagnosco, c. 1875
Pencil on paper, 10 × 7¾ (25.4 × 19.7)
Philadelphia Museum of Art; Gift of Miss
Emily Sargent and Mrs. Francis Ormond

218.
Gordon Greenough, 1880
Pencil on paper, 11 × 9 (27.9 × 22.9)
Mead Art Museum, Amherst College,
Amherst, Massachusetts

not appear to have engaged his attention. He was much more taken up with things there before his eyes, the shadow of an oleander on a wall, the attitude of a fellow-traveller in a railway carriage, the bronze figures round the tomb of Maximilian at Innsbruck, a country cart, a statue, or a corner of architecture — any detail, in fact, of the visible world.[6]

Throughout his life Sargent would continue to meet the challenge of transforming a corner of the three-dimensional, external world onto a flat surface. He would draw for "the sheer fun of translating onto paper the record of what he saw."

At the age of twelve, Sargent took lessons with the British artist Joseph Farquharson and the German-American landscape painter Carl Welsch,[7] and produced some competent if perhaps formulaic landscapes.[8] During the next few years, his efforts with the pencil reached new levels of skill as he learned how to handle perspective, model in light and dark, control outline, and differentiate textural nuances (Fig. 215). But his real professional training began in 1873 when he entered the life class of the Accademia delle Belle Arti in Florence.

However, Sargent soon outgrew the available resources at the Accademia. Encouraged by the glowing reports of the Parisian studios, he and his family moved to the French capital in 1874. Walter Launt Palmer was one young American artist who urged Sargent to enroll in the studio of Carolus-Duran.[9] When Sargent did take his portfolio to the fashionable portrait painter, the students were amazed both by the drawings and the oil studies he presented.

219.
Figure of a Child (study for *The Oyster Gatherers of Cancale*), c. 1877–78
Pencil on paper, 8⅛ × 5⅛ (20.6 × 13)
The Metropolitan Museum of Art, New York;
Gift of Mrs. Francis Ormond, 1950

Another American student, Will Low, recalled Sargent's marvelous drawings in his memoirs:

I can see the slim youth of seventeen, his arms entwined around a formidable roll of studies. . . . We crowded around our new comrade that was to be, as one by one he showed the master drawings innumerable, drawings from life, from the antique, and careful studies of Swiss scenery that, in their knowledge of the handling of the lead-pencil, recalled the lithographed work of Calame.[10]

220.

Dorothy Barnard (study for *Carnation, Lily, Lily, Rose*), 1885–86

Pencil on paper, 9¾ × 8¼ (24.8 × 21)

The Tate Gallery, London; Bequeathed by Miss Dorothy Barnard, 1949

221.

Polly Barnard (study for *Carnation, Lily, Lily, Rose*), 1885–86

Pencil on paper, 11 × 9¼ (27.9 × 23.5)

The Tate Gallery, London; Bequeathed by Miss Dorothy Barnard, 1949

222.
Study for *El Jaleo*, c. 1879–82
Pencil on paper, no. 20 in Venetian scrapbook,
11 × 9 (27.9 × 22.9)
Isabella Stewart Gardner Museum, Boston

223.
Study for *El Jaleo*, c. 1879–82
Pencil on paper, no. 18 in Venetian scrapbook,
11½ × 9 (29.2 × 22.9)
Isabella Stewart Gardner Museum, Boston

Low also mentioned the oil studies Sargent displayed that day, and concluded: "It might have been said of him . . . 'He had a splendid past behind him' and Sargent was barely seventeen."[11] Another American student, Julian Alden Weir, was equally impressed. He wrote home in October 1874 that he had just met "one of the most talented fellows I have ever come across; his drawings are like old masters, and his color is equally fine. . . ."[12]

For a beginning student, a mastery of draftsmanship would aid immensely in the competitive world of the art student in Paris. By September 1874 Sargent was preparing for the stiff two-week entrance examinations, the *concours des places*, in order to obtain a place in Adolphe Yvon's life-drawing class at the École des Beaux-Arts. He was admitted on October 27, 1874. As the result of his efforts at the École, in 1877 he received a Third Class Medal for ornament drawing.[13]

Although his days spent in Carolus-Duran's atelier were geared to studying and to painting in light and dark values, Sargent continued sketching outdoors on his holidays. When he, Emily, and his mother went to America in the summer of 1876, his cousins recalled "his continual sketching. . . ."[14] He filled sketchbooks with pencil drawings of people, artworks, and landscapes. They became notations to remind him of what he had seen and admired. In the late 1870s, when he painted outdoor subject pictures in his studio, he relied on such drawings (Fig. 219) as well as on oil sketches. Occasionally he drew careful portraits of a friend, presenting these exercises as gifts to the sitter (Fig. 218).

224.
Study for *El Jaleo*, c. 1879–82
Charcoal on paper, no. 8 in Venetian
scrapbook, 9⅜ × 13⅞ (23.8 × 35.2)
Isabella Stewart Gardner Museum, Boston

225.
Study for *El Jaleo*, 1882
Pencil on paper, 9½ × 7¼ (24.1 × 18.4)
Collection of Dr. and Mrs. William Hayden

226.
Two studies for *Madame X*
(*Madame Pierre Gautreau*), c. 1883
Pencil on paper, 9⅝ × 13⅜ (24.4 × 34)
Trustees of the British Museum, London;
Presented by Mrs. Ormond

227.
Study for *Madame X*
(*Madame Pierre Gautreau*), c. 1883
Pencil on paper, 11½ × 8¼ (29.2 × 21)
Collection of Mr. and Mrs. Jean-Marie
Eveillard

228.
Study for *Madame X*
(*Madame Pierre Gautreau*), c. 1883
Pencil on paper, 12¾ × 9⅜ (32.4 × 23.8)
Private collection

229.
Study for *Madame X*
(*Madame Pierre Gautreau*), c. 1883
Pencil on paper, 9¾ × 13³⁄₁₆ (24.8 × 33.5)
The Metropolitan Museum of Art, New York;
Purchase, Charles and Anita Blatt Fund, John
Wilmerding Gift, Rogers Fund, 1970

When Sargent was planning the composition of *El Jaleo* (Fig. 14) in the early 1880s, he did a variety of sketches in oil and pencil.[15] These indicate his interest in different approaches to his subject: the construction of a scene to conform with the rhythm of the music and the shouts of "olé! olé!" (Fig. 225), the tonal values of light against deep or blurred shadows (Fig. 224), and the movement of the dancer herself (Figs. 222, 223).

Sargent made pencil studies of his sitters before selecting the pose for the oil portrait on canvas. The most numerous studies (over a dozen) were done of Mme. Gautreau, whose beauty captivated Sargent in the early 1880s (Fig. 47).[16] None of the pencil studies focus on the light and dark values. They show, instead, Sargent's experiments with a variety of poses (Figs. 227, 229), and his attempt to capture the essence of her "unpaintable beauty and hopeless laziness"[17] through the salient lines of her body and dress — the bared, rounded shoulders, the indolent droop of the strap of her gown, and her emphatic nose (Figs. 226, 228).

Sargent's concern with the beauty of line and silhouette finds expression in the drawings *Dorothy Barnard* (Fig. 220) and *Polly Barnard* (Fig. 221), done as studies for *Carnation, Lily, Lily, Rose* (Fig. 72). There is a Botticellesque purity of line to the edges of their noses, the soft upturn of their top lips, and the fine arch of their eyebrows. In Broadway Sargent also drew the baby son of his friend Frank Millet

230.
Jack Millet as a Baby, 1888
Pencil on paper, 5½ × 9¼ (14 × 23.5)
Syndics of the Fitzwilliam Museum,
Cambridge, England

231.
Vernon Lee (Violet Paget), 1889
Pencil on paper, 13¼ × 9 (33.7 × 22.9)
Ashmolean Museum, Oxford

232.
Paul Helleu, 1889
Pastel on paper, 19½ × 17½ (49.5 × 44.8)
Harvard University Art Museums, Fogg Art
Museum, Cambridge, Massachusetts; Bequest
of Mrs. Annie Swan Coburn

233.
Paul Helleu Lying in a Field, c. 1889
Pastel on paper, 10¼ × 14⅞ (26 × 37.8)
Trustees of the British Museum, London;
Presented by Mrs. Ormond and Miss Sargent

(Fig. 230). The delicate touch of the tiny lashes snapped shut in sleep and the rendering of the slightly sagging lips and plump cheeks show an artist who has closely observed the nuances of infant physiognomy and expression. Sargent also tried his hand at pastels (Figs. 232, 233) during his summers spent in the English countryside around Broadway. But it was a medium he disliked and, therefore, did not fully exploit.[18] In these years, his experimentations with color were primarily confined to painting in oil.

When Sargent received the commission in 1890 to paint the ambitious cycle of murals for the Boston Public Library he again turned to drawing to work out the elaborate poses he was planning for those intricate figural compositions. Like Edwin Austin Abbey, who had also been commissioned to paint murals for the

235.
Studies of a Nude Youth, n.d.
Charcoal on paper, 18⅞ × 25 (47.9 × 63.5)
Harvard University Art Museums, Fogg Art
Museum, Cambridge, Massachusetts; Gift of
Mrs. Francis Ormond

236.
Torsos of Two Male Nudes, n.d.
Charcoal on paper, 48 × 63 (121.9 × 160)
Yale University Art Gallery, New Haven; Gift
of Miss Emily Sargent and Mrs. Francis
Ormond

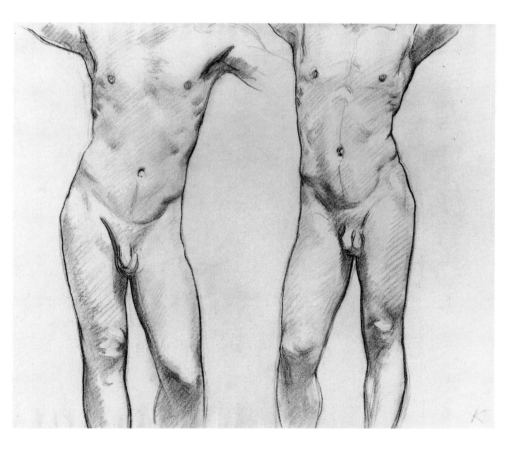

237.
Seated Model with Drapery, n.d.
Charcoal on paper, 24½ × 17⅛ (62.2 × 43.5)
Harvard University Art Museums, Fogg Art
Museum, Cambridge, Massachusetts; Gift of
Mrs. Francis Ormond

238.
Reclining Nude, n.d.
Charcoal on paper, 24½ × 18¾ (62.2 × 47.6)
Harvard University Art Museums, Fogg Art
Museum, Cambridge, Massachusetts; Gift of
Mrs. Francis Ormond

264

239.
Study of Ezekiel for *Frieze of the Prophets*,
c. 1891–92
Charcoal on paper, 24 × 18⅞ (61 × 47.9)
Corcoran Gallery of Art, Washington, D.C.

Library, Sargent enthusiastically embraced the project. Abbey, writing to Charles McKim, one of the architects for the building, reported visiting Sargent's New York studio:

I wonder . . . whether you have built [Sargent] a beautiful model [of the planned building] yet. I went into his studio a day or two before I sailed and saw stacks of sketches of nude people — saints, I dare say, most of them, although from my cursory observations of them they seemed a bit earthy. You will surely get a great thing from him. He can do anything, *and don't know himself what he can do. He is latent with all manner of possibilities, and the Boston people need not be afraid that he will be eccentric or impressionistic, or anything that is not perfectly serious and non-experimental when it comes to work of this kind.*[19]

The specific drawings to which Abbey referred are difficult to determine because Sargent did hundreds of drawings of the male nude from the time he began the layout of the Public Library murals through the early 1920s, when he was still working out the decorative scheme for the Rotunda of the Museum of Fine Arts. He began working from the male nude in earnest in 1891, after returning to England. Both he and Abbey set up studios in Morgan Hall, Fairford, the residence of Abbey and his family. In the early 1890s several Italian models came up from London to pose (Fig. 234), including Nicola d'Inverno, who was to become his valet as well as his model for the next two decades.[20]

Many of the drawings, now in the collections of the Museum of Fine Arts, Boston, the Boston Public Library, the Fogg Art Museum, and other places, are in the nature of "warm-up exercises" for Sargent's eye and hand. They document his concern to master the drawing of every imaginable and difficult pose: elbows up, knees bent, torsos twisted, backs reclined, feet flexed (Figs. 214, 235–238). At times he was preoccupied with the ripple of musculature beneath the skin; at other times, with a bit of contorted foreshortening. Sometimes he omits the figure and focuses only on the folds of clothing or fabric draped over the model (Fig. 239). Always we can visualize the rapid movement of Sargent's hand, pressing hard on the charcoal for a shadowed accent or lightly caressing a swelling contour.

A series of sketches in a portfolio at the Fogg Art Museum are among Sargent's most aesthetically self-contained drawings.[21] In these, the image is centered on the page and brought to a degree of finish, so that each drawing has the presence of an object — a "collectible" art object. However, from an artist's point of view, the more striking characteristic is the way the drawings reveal Sargent's artistic process. He turns the model in space, views it from multiple angles, and then captures in stilled images the three-dimensionality of the form (Figs. 240–242). Our recognition of the *process* of making art underlies the

243.
Man Screaming (study for *Hell*), c. 1895–1910
Charcoal and pencil on paper, 24⅜ × 18¾
(61.9 × 47.6)
Corcoran Gallery of Art, Washington, D.C.

244.
Male Nudes Wrestling, n.d.
Charcoal on paper, 20⅝ × 17⁷⁄₁₆ (52.4 × 44.3)
Collection of Carter Burden

245.
Mrs. Charles Hunter, c. 1902
Charcoal on paper, 23½ × 18½ (59.7 × 47)
Memorial Art Gallery of the University of
Rochester, New York; Gift of James O. Belden
in memory of Evelyn Berry Belden

246.
Ethel Smyth, 1901
Black chalk on paper, 23½ × 18⅛ (59.7 × 46)
National Portrait Gallery, London

247.
Mrs. George Swinton, 1906
Charcoal on paper, 24 × 18¾ (61 × 47.6)
Private collection

248.
Vaslav Nijinsky in Le Pavillon d'Armide, 1911
Charcoal on paper, 24 1/16 × 18 5/8 (61.1 × 47.3)
Bohemian Club, San Francisco

249.
William Butler Yeats, 1908
Charcoal on paper, 24 1/2 × 18 1/2 (62.2 × 47)
Private collection

sensuality of these nudes: the velvety appeal of the black charcoal and our empathetic response to Sargent's hand, which has moved with such grace over the surface of the paper.

As Sargent came closer to the actual designs of the murals, the drawings grew more specific. The poses became more complicated, he attempted multiple figure groups (Fig. 244) and, in many of the charcoal studies (Fig. 243), he focused on emotional expressions.

Sargent's production of charcoal portraits increased after the turn of the century, particularly once he cut down his output of portraits in oil. Soon the demand for these charcoal works grew among society hostesses, writers, and theater people: in 1908 he did about a dozen; in 1909, twenty; and in 1910, over forty. The charcoal portraits became a source of remuneration — done in the mornings, while he did his "serious" work on the murals in the afternoons.[22]

Among the best of these charcoal sketches were those done of his friends, such as *Mrs. Charles Hunter* (Fig. 245) and her sister, the composer and feminist *Ethel Smyth* (Fig. 246). Sargent also drew *Mrs. George Swinton* (Fig. 247) a few days before her singing debut at Aeolian Hall; the portrait captures her self-confident anticipation. He posed the dancer Vaslav Nijinsky (Fig. 248) in the costume he wore for *Le Pavillon d'Armide*. His drawing of *William Butler Yeats* (Fig. 249) seizes on the moody aspect of the poet; the drawing was used as a frontispiece for a book of Yeats' poetry.

For all their seeming spontaneity, the drawings, like the portraits in oil, were the products of a well-disciplined method. One of Sargent's students described a demonstration the master offered to a class at the Royal Academy Schools:

He then took up the charcoal, with arm extended to its full length, and head thrown well back; all the while intensely calculating, he slowly and deliberately mapped the proportions of the large masses of a head and shoulders, first the poise of the head upon the neck, its relation with the shoulders. Then rapidly indicate the mass of the hair, then spots locating the exact position of the features, at the same time noting their tone values and special character, finally adding any further accent or dark shadow which made up the head, the neck, the shoulders and head of the sternum.[23]

Sargent's sitters invariably remembered his performance of running pell-mell at the picture he was painting or drawing. But this was the result of his insistence on placing model and easel side by side so that both received identical lighting. He checked the match of the drawing (or painting) with the original model by frequently distancing himself from them both. He would then dash at the canvas to execute a stroke while his memory of any discrepancy in the match was still fresh. One such sitter was Mrs. Claude Bennington, who arranged for Sargent to draw a charcoal head of her in 1914. In her memoirs, she details the circumstances of the almost three-hour sitting: "he would dash on some lines with the charcoal, rub out with the French roll [a stump for removing charcoal from paper], occasionally retreat to the far end of the studio and then almost run at the portrait."[24] Sargent encouraged Mrs. Bennington to walk about the studio and even asked her to critique the portrait as it was progressing. All the time he kept up a steady flow of conversation and jokes.

Another sitter, Charles Knowles Bolton, librarian of the Boston Athenaeum, recorded a different experience when he went to the Pope Building in Boston, where Sargent was working on his Museum of Fine Arts murals in early 1918. Sargent first measured his face, and, in this case, would not permit the sitter to look at his portrait in progress. Bolton, too, noted a continuous flow of talk, including Sargent's judgment that men were easier to do than women. "'But,' he added, 'I lost my nerve for portraits long ago when harassed by mothers, critical wives and sisters.'"[25]

Sargent's methods and techniques yielded a variety of portraits — each suggesting the mood he wanted to capture. For *Mrs. Charles Hunter*, he covered the paper with light strokes that turned strong and deeply black in the shadow of her hat. The highlights, particularly along the ridge of her nose, have been cleaned away with the stump. Short, crisscrossing black strokes animate the surface, while suggesting the flutter of feathers and fur that were part of her costume. The contrast of accents against a uniform middle tone follows Sargent's dictum to his Royal Academy students: "Draw the things seen with the keenest point and let the things unseen fuse themselves into the adjoining tones."[26] *Mrs. George Swinton,*

250.

Oxen, 1911

Pencil on paper, 10 × 14 (25.4 × 35.6)

Philadelphia Museum of Art; Gift of Miss
Emily Sargent and Mrs. Francis Ormond

251.

Three Alligators, 1916

Pencil on paper, 7 × 10 (17.8 × 25.4)

Worcester Art Museum, Massachusetts; Gift
of Mrs. Francis Ormond and Miss Emily
Sargent

on the other hand, is a restrained and elegant image. Her head, neck, and shoulders are set off by long, soft diagonal strokes that create a middle range of value in the background.

For his portrait of Nijinsky, Sargent used hard, long vertical strokes to create a dark curtain on the left side of the face. The rich blacks form a contrast to the expanse of light paper on the right, where a single line along the contour of Nijinsky's columnar neck contains the modeled form. *William Butler Yeats* has no such background of strokes; contrasts between dark charcoal and white paper are contained within the face itself.

During those early years of the century, Sargent also traveled in the summers

252.
Henry Tonks, 1918
Pencil and ink on paper, 9¾ × 14⅝
(24.8 × 37.1)
Syndics of the Fitzwilliam Museum,
Cambridge, England

253.
Heads, Hands, and Figure (studies for *Gassed*),
1918
Charcoal on paper, 18⅝ × 24¼ (47.3 × 61.6)
Corcoran Gallery of Art, Washington, D.C.;
Gift of Miss Emily Sargent and Mrs. Violet
Sargent Ormond

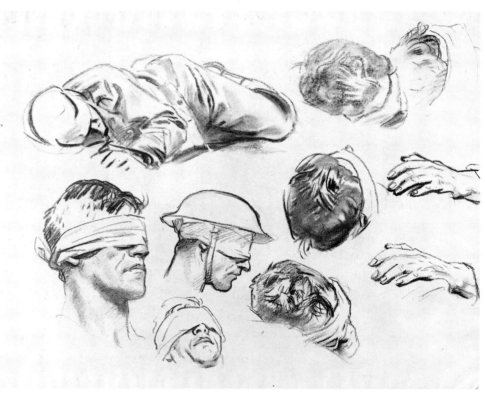

with his family and friends to Switzerland, Italy, Corfu and Spain, all countries he
had been frequenting since youth. Numerous drawings of animals figure in his
oeuvre, such as *Oxen* (Fig. 250), which was done when he made his trip to the
marble quarries at Carrara. In Florida in 1917, he attempted to catch with his
pencil the tough skin of the local alligators (Fig. 251).

In 1918, Sargent obtained permission from the British Ministry of
Information to travel to the French front with Henry Tonks, the Slade Professor of

272

254.
Two studies of soldiers for *Gassed*, 1918–19
Charcoal on paper, 18⅝ × 24⁷⁄₁₆ (47.3 × 62.1)
Corcoran Gallery of Art, Washington, D.C.;
Gift of Miss Emily Sargent and Mrs. Violet
Sargent Ormond

Fine Art at University College (Fig. 252), in order to observe and record the movement of American and British troops. Sargent brought back many watercolors (Figs. 206–210) as well as charcoal sketches of these soldiers (Figs. 253, 254), which he used as notes to produce one of his major commissions of those years, *Gassed* (Fig. 256), painted for the Imperial War Museum.[27] The drawings cover a variety of subjects: soldiers marching or at rest, motorcycles, covered trucks, cannons, and the foliage local to the bivouac areas. Perhaps the most moving of these sketches were those of the blindfolded soldiers who had fallen victim to mustard gas.

After Sargent's death, his assistant in Boston, Thomas A. Fox, catalogued the many sketches and portfolios of drawings the artist had done as studies for his murals. This material, along with other drawings, was distributed by his sisters Emily Sargent and Violet Ormond to American museums, particularly to The Metropolitan Museum of Art, New York, and the Museum of Fine Arts, Boston. A massive study of these works might yield new insights not only into Sargent's working methods, but into an artistic temperament that was deeply engaged in the process of seeing and matching reality with art.

255.
Study for *Hell*, c. 1903–09
Oil on canvas with applied cloth and gilding,
33¼ × 66¼ (84.5 × 168.3)
Smith College Museum of Art, Northampton,
Massachusetts; Gift of Mrs. Dwight W.
Morrow (Elizabeth Cutter '96), 1932

NOTES

1. Evan Charteris, *John Sargent* (New York, 1927), p. 2.

2. A drawing done by the four-year-old Sargent, depicting his father sitting at a writing desk, is now in the Sargent House Museum, Gloucester, Massachusetts; the museum has reproduced the drawing as a postcard.

3. Mary Newbold Patterson Hale, "The Sargent I Knew," *World Today*, 50 (November 1927), pp. 565–70; reprinted in Carter Ratcliff, *John Singer Sargent* (New York, 1982), pp. 235–36.

4. Ibid., p. 236. Much of the juvenalia is inscribed, perhaps in the hand of his mother, with the dates and places of its execution. For example, one drawing of a cock, hen, and chicks was inscribed "Johnny for Minnie, April 7, 1865." It was apparently a gift Sargent tendered his ailing sister Minnie, who died eleven days later; see Rachel Field, "John Sargent's Boyhood Sketches," *St. Nicholas*, 53 (June 1926), p. 777; reprod. p. 776.

5. Quoted in Charteris, *John Sargent*, pp. 4–5, from a letter written in 1863 or 1864.

6. Ibid., p. 13.

7. Edward J. Nygren, *John Singer Sargent: Drawings from the Corcoran Gallery of Art*, exhibition catalogue (Washington, D.C., Smithsonian Institution Traveling Exhibition Service and the Corcoran Gallery of Art, 1983), pp. 11–12.

8. See the discussion in Nygren, *John Singer Sargent: Drawings*, p. 12.

9. Maybelle Mann, *Walter Launt Palmer: Poetic Reality* (Exton, Pennsylvania, 1984), p. 13. Dr. Mann owns diaries written by Palmer that mention Sargent. One entry of May 20, 1874 notes: "Went chez Sargent and talked about the ateliers with him. . . . "

10. Will Low, *A Painter's Progress* (New York, 1910), pp. 89–90.

11. Ibid., p. 90. Sargent was in fact eighteen at the time.

12. Dorothy Weir Young, *The Life and Letters of J. Alden Weir* (New Haven, 1960), p. 50.

13. Regarding the training of American artists in Paris, see H. Barbara Weinberg, "Nineteenth-Century American Painters at the École des Beaux-Arts," *The American Art Journal*, 13 (Autumn 1981), pp. 66–84, and Weinberg, "The Lure of Paris: Late Nineteenth-Century American Painters and Their French Training," in *A New World: Masterpieces of American Painting, 1760–1910*, exhibition catalogue (Museum of Fine Arts, Boston, 1983).

14. Hale, "The Sargent I Knew," reprinted in Ratcliff, *John Singer Sargent*, p. 236. They

also remembered his extraordinary musical abilities.

15. See Richard Ormond, "Sargent's *El Jaleo*," in *Fenway Court: Isabella Stewart Gardner Museum, 1970* (Boston, 1971), pp. 2–18.

16. The various pencil sketches are listed in Doreen Bolger Burke, *American Paintings in the Metropolitan Museum of Art, III: A Catalogue of Works by Artists Born Between 1846 and 1864* (New York, 1980), pp. 229, 232.

17. Quoted in Charteris, *John Sargent*, p. 59.

18. His student Miss Heyneman reported that: "He disliked pastel, it seemed to him too artificial, or else it was made to look like oil or water colour, and in that case why not use oil or water colour"; quoted in Charteris, *John Sargent*, p. 185.

19. Quoted in E. V. Lucas, *Edwin Austin Abbey, Royal Academician: The Record of His Life and Work*, 2 vols. (London and New York, 1921), I, pp. 231–32.

20. See Charteris, *John Sargent*, p. 117.

21. This portfolio of drawings is discussed in Trevor J. Fairbrother, "A Private Album: John Singer Sargent's Drawings of Nude Male Models," *Arts Magazine*, 56 (December 1981), pp. 70–79.

22. James Lomax and Richard Ormond, *John Singer Sargent and the Edwardian Age*, exhibition catalogue (Leeds, England, Leeds Art Galleries; London, National Portrait Gallery; and The Detroit Institute of Arts, 1979), p. 71. Their discussion, pp. 71–91, is the most thorough regarding these late portrait drawings. See also Trevor J. Fairbrother, *Sargent Portrait Drawings: 42 Works by John Singer Sargent* (New York, 1983). I am grateful to Dr. Fairbrother for assisting me in locating *Vaslav Nijinsky in Le Pavillon d'Armide* (Fig. 248).

23. From Mr. Haley's account of Sargent's teaching at the Royal Academy Schools, 1897–1900, quoted in Charteris, *John Sargent*, p. 186.

24. Mrs. Claude Bennington, *All That I Have Met* (London, 1929), p. 154. Mrs. Bennington was intimidated at first by Sargent: "For years before I met Sargent I had heard alarming legends of his forbidding and fierce manner with the ladies: they said he was a confirmed misogynist; that he was rude to his fair sitters; that at times he even — like Georgie Porgie in the nursery-rhyme — made them cry, and so forth"; ibid., p. 153. I am grateful to Herb Adler for bringing Mrs. Bennington's autobiography to my attention.

25. News clipping of an article by Charles Bolton, affixed to the verso of the framed portrait of Bolton in the Boston Athenaeum.

26. Quoted in Charteris, *John Sargent*, p. 187.

27. For an interesting interpretation of *Gassed*, see Jon Bird, "Representing the Great War," *Block*, no. 3 (1980), pp. 41–52.

256.

Gassed, 1918–19

Oil on canvas, 90½ × 240 (229.9 × 609.6)

The Trustees of the Imperial War Museum, London

Chronology

STANLEY OLSON

Gertrude Vanderbilt Whitney, 1914
Charcoal and pencil on paper, 26 × 20 (66 × 50.8)
Collection of Flora Whitney Miller

The following chronology is a much abbreviated version of that which will appear in the catalogue raisonné of Sargent's works being prepared by the Coe Kerr Gallery, Inc., New York.

1856
January 12, born in Florence to Dr. FitzWilliam Sargent (1820–1889) and Mary Newbold Singer Sargent (1826–1906), who had left Philadelphia for Europe in the autumn of 1854. Summer, Geneva; winter, Rome.

1857
January 29, Emily Sargent born in Rome. Dr. Sargent submits his resignation as attending surgeon, Wills Hospital, Philadelphia. Spring and summer, Vienna.

1858–59
Rome. Maternal grandmother dies in Rome on November 12, 1859. Summer, Switzerland.

1860–61
Nice. December 1860, first drawing — a portrait of Dr. Sargent writing a letter (see p. 274 n. 2). February 1, 1861, Mary Winthrop Sargent born. Spring and summer, Switzerland; September, Nice.

1862
Nice; June, London; July, Switzerland; October, Nice.

1863
June–October, Switzerland; November, Nice.

1864
March–September, Swtizerland; November, Nice.

1865
April 18, sister Mary Winthrop dies in Pau, France. May, Biarritz. Dr. Sargent sails to America; rest of family in Switzerland. September, family rejoins Dr. Sargent in London; October, Paris; November, Nice.

1866
Nice; meets Violet Paget (Vernon Lee). Summer, Lake Como and the Engadine; autumn, Nice; Sargent given own room in Maison Virello.

1867
March 7, FitzWilliam Winthrop Sargent born in Nice. Summer, Paris, the Rhine, Munich, the Tyrol, Salzburg, Milan, Genoa; October, Nice.

1868
March, Spain; May, Biarritz; October, Nice. November, Rome; "studies" with German-American landscape painter Carl Welsch — copies watercolors and fetches beer for the studio.

1869
Rome; May, Naples, Sorrento, Padua to Botzen; June 28, brother FitzWilliam Winthrop dies at Kissingen. July, St.-Moritz; October, Florence. Does copy work in the Bargello.

1870
February 9, Violet Sargent born in Florence. Sargent attends M. Domengé's day school and dancing class in Florence. May, Venice and Lake Maggiore; June–October, Switzerland; October, Florence.

1871
Summer, the Tyrol; October, Munich; November, Dresden, to prepare for entry into the Gymnasium zum Heilige Kreuz. Tutored in Latin, German, chemistry, history, and geography; does copy work in the Albertinum.

1872
January, Emily dangerously ill. Early spring, tutorials abandoned, family travels to Berlin, Leipzig, Carlsbad, Munich, Auchensee. Summer, the Tyrol; September, Florence.

1873
May–July, Venice, while Dr. Sargent is in America. July, rejoins father in Pontresina, Switzerland; they travel in the Alps. September, Bologna; October, Florence, where he enrolls in the Accademia delle Belle Arti, which closes in December. Meets American artists Walter Launt Palmer, Edwin White, and Frank Fowler, and English artists Edward Clifford and Heath Wilson.

1874
March, Accademia reopens. May 16, in Paris to investigate teaching studios; about May 21, enters atelier of Carolus-Duran at 81, Boulevard Montparnasse. July 3, studio closes for the summer; Caen, Rouen, with family. September, returns to Paris to prepare for the *concours des places* at the École des Beaux-Arts (September 26–October 16). October 19, atelier Carolus-Duran reopens; October 26, *concours* results posted; matriculates at the École; lives with family. Among fellow students are James Carroll Beckwith, Will Low, C. M. Newton, John Tracey, Stephen Parker Hills, Paul Batifaud-Vaur, Robert C. Hinckley. Meets Julian Alden Weir.

1875
January, to Nice with Stephen Parker Hills, Robert Hinckley, and Carolus-Duran; February, *concours*. June, joins family in St.-Enogat, Brittany; August, *concours*; takes studio in Paris with Beckwith. September, St.-Enogat; October, settles in Mme. Darode's boardinghouse in the Rue de l'Odéon; at atelier Carolus-Duran and the École. Christmas with Beckwith at St.-Enogat. Sometime during the year, meets Paul-César Helleu.

1876
April, meets and dines with Monet (and Helleu). May 13, sails for America from Liverpool with mother and Emily. Visits Centennial Exhibition in Philadelphia; meets his Newbold and Sargent cousins; Newport, guests of Admiral Case; visits Weirs at West Point; Montreal; Niagara Falls; September, Chicago. October 4, sails for Liverpool; November, returns to the École and atelier Carolus-Duran; lives with family.

1877
February, places second in the *concours*; March, completes *Frances Sherburne Ridley Watts* (Fig. 1), which is selected for the Salon; May, receives Third Class Medal for ornament drawing. June–August, at Cancale in Britanny; September, joins family in Bex, Switzerland; October, Paris. At atelier Carolus-Duran and the École, works with Carolus-Duran and Beckwith on the ceiling decorations for the Palais du Luxembourg. Selected as one of the jurymen for the new Association of American Artists (founded in June and later called the Society of American Artists); meets Augustus Saint-Gaudens and Stanford White.

1878
May, *En Route pour la Pêche* (*The Oyster Gatherers of Cancale*; Fig. 9) at the Salon; *Fishing for Oysters at Cancale* (*The Oyster Gatherers of Cancale*; Fig. 7) at the first Society of American Artists exhibition in New York; Carolus-Duran's ceiling mural for the Palais du Luxembourg at the Salon. June, Carolus-Duran sits for Sargent's portrait of him. July, Sargent stops at Aix-les-Bains en route to Naples; August, Capri; paints numerous studies of Rosina Ferrara. September, Paris; October–November, Nice. November, paints *Rehearsal of the Pas de Loup Orchestra at the Cirque d'Hiver* (Fig. 16); ceases to attend atelier Carolus-Duran with much frequency.

1879
May, portrait of *Carolus-Duran* (Fig. 4) receives Honorable Mention at the Salon. Capri and Neapolitan pictures at the Society of American Artists and National Academy of Design exhibitions in New York. August, Ronjoux, paints portraits of Pailleron family, including *Madame Edouard Pailleron* (Fig. 3). Visits family in Aix-les-Bains; October, goes to Spain; rides through Ronda to Gibraltar, stopping in Seville (where he meets Henry and Clover Adams), Granada, and Madrid in December; copies works by Velázquez at the Prado. End of December, crosses to Morocco.

1880
January, Tangier, Tunis; end of February, Paris. Paints *Fumée d'Ambre Gris* (Fig. 50). May, *Madame Edouard Pailleron* and *Fumée d'Ambre Gris* at the Salon; June, Venice for a week (?). August 15, to Holland with the American artists Ralph Curtis and Francis Brooks Chadwick; copies Frans Hals paintings in Haarlem; does portrait of *Ralph Curtis on the Beach at Scheveningen* (Fig. 11). Mid-September, meets his family at Aix-les-Bains and travels with them to Venice; sets up studios in the Palazzo Rezzonico and off the Piazza San Marco.

1881
Winter, Venice; meets Whistler. March, visits family in Nice. May, *Madame Ramón Subercaseaux* awarded a Second Class Medal at the Salon. Goes to England to see his mother and Emily off to America. Paints *Vernon Lee* (Fig. 19) in London; meets Burne-Jones. July, goes to northern France; August, Paris; works on *Dr. Pozzi at Home* (Fig. 55). October, begins picture of Spanish dancers, *El Jaleo* (Fig. 14).

1882
February, *El Jaleo* finished; March, begins *The Daughters of Edward D. Boit* (Fig. 48); May, *El Jaleo* and *Charlotte Louise Burckhardt*, later known as *Lady with the Rose* (Fig. 98) at the Salon; *Dr. Pozzi at Home* at the Royal Academy; Venetian scenes at the Grosvenor Gallery. July, goes to Haarlem with Helleu and Albert de Belleroche; Aix-les-Bains and Champery to visit parents. August, Venice, stays with his cousins the Curtises at the Palazzo Barbaro; October, Rome, Siena; *El Jaleo* shown at the Schwab Gallery, New York, and later in Boston. November, Paris.

1883
February, begins *Madame X* (*Madame Pierre Gautreau*) and *Mrs. Henry White* (Figs. 47, 64). April, *Lady with the Rose* at the Society of American Artists exhibition. May, *The Daughters of Edward D. Boit* at the Salon. July, *The Pailleron Children* (Fig. 6) at the Fine Art Gallery, London; Oscar Wilde decries it. August, at Paramé to paint *Madame X*; October, Florence, Siena, and Rome(?).

Attributed to Sargent, *Caricature*
(*Self-Portrait: Painting Carnation, Lily, Lily, Rose*),
c. 1885–86
Ink on paper, 3¼ × 3⅜ (8.6 × 8.8)
Archives of American Art, Smithsonian Institution,
Washington, D.C.; Francis Davis Millet Papers

1884
January–February, Nice; meets Henry
James. March, London; visits Reynolds
exhibition at the Royal Academy; James
plays attentive host. April, Paris; works
on *Mrs. Kate A. Moore* (Fig. 101); Albert
Vickers commissions portrait of his
daughters, *The Misses Vickers* (Fig. 61).
May, *Madame X* at the Salon; *Mrs. Henry
White* at the Royal Academy; *Mrs. Thomas
Wodehouse Legh* at the Grosvenor Gallery.
June, goes to England for the Vickers
commission; London, Sheffield, Petworth;
paints *Edith, Lady Playfair* (Fig. 65).
November, Bournemouth; paints *Robert
Louis Stevenson*; end of December, Paris.

1885
January–February, finishes portraits of
Madame Paul Poirson (Fig. 100),
Mademoiselle Poirson, *Mrs. Alice Sumner
Mason*, and the double portrait *Louise and
Mrs. Edward Burckhardt*. March, annual

visit to family in Nice. May, *The Misses
Vickers* shown at the Salon; *Edith, Lady
Playfair* at the Royal Academy; *Mrs. Alice
Sumner Mason* at the Grosvenor Gallery;
exhibits *Dr. Pozzi at Home* with works by
Monet, among others, at the Galerie
Georges Petit, Paris, and the Exposition
Internationale, Brussels ("Les XX"). July,
London; takes studio in Lowndes Square;
August, boating tour on the Thames with
Edwin Austin Abbey. Swimming accident
at Pangbourne Weir; Abbey takes him to
stay with the F. D. Millets at Farnham
House in Broadway, Worcestershire.
Paints in the garden of Farnham House;
starts *Carnation, Lily, Lily, Rose* (Fig. 72).
September, influx of London visitors:
Edmund Gosse, Frederick Barnard, Alfred
Parsons, Alma-Tadema, Henry James.
November, Bournemouth; December,
tours southern England with Abbey;
Christmas at Farnham House.

1886
January, London; works in various studios
in Kensington and lives at Bailey's Hotel.
April–May, Paris and Nice; packs up
Paris studio and moves to London; shows
at the New English Art Club (of which he
is a founding member), the Grosvenor
Gallery, the Royal Academy. End of June,
takes up residence at Russell House,
Broadway, with the Millets and Abbey.
July, in Paris briefly, and then goes to
Gossensass, Switzerland, with his family;
mid-July, Cheltenham and southern
England with Abbey; August, Bayreuth.
September, Broadway; in addition to
residents of the previous year, finds
Edwin Blashfield, J. Comyns Carr
(director of the Grosvenor Gallery), and
Dora Wheeler Keith from New York.
Works on *Carnation, Lily, Lily, Rose*; takes
Whistler's old studio in Tite Street,
London. October, Ralph Curtis
introduces him to Mrs. Isabella Stewart
Gardner; back and forth between London
and Broadway.

1887
May, *Carnation, Lily, Lily, Rose* at the
Royal Academy and *Robert Louis Stevenson
and His Wife* (Fig. 70) at the New English
Art Club; June, signs three-year lease for
his studio in Tite Street. Summer,

Giverny(?), painting with Monet;
Shiplake, visits Alfred Parsons and stays
with Mr. and Mrs. Robert Harrison; sets
up floating studio on Thames in Henley;
receives commission (on Alma-Tadema's
recommendation) to paint a portrait of
Mrs. Henry Marquand of Newport,
Rhode Island. September 17, sails to
Boston; stays in Newport with Admiral
Goodrich; paints *Elizabeth Allen Marquand
(Mrs. Henry G. Marquand)* (Fig. 102); sees
Stanford White again. Late October, New
York; with Beckwith's help finds a studio
in Washington Square. December,
Boston; stays with the Boits and takes a
studio in Exeter Street; completes *General
Lucius Fairchild, Dennis Miller Bunker, Mrs.
Edward D. Boit* (Fig. 103), among others;
begins *Isabella Stewart Gardner* (Fig. 59).

1888
January, New York, Boston, New York;
portrait commissions. January 28–
February 11, exhibition of paintings at the
St. Botolph Club, Boston, including
*Isabella Stewart Gardner, Mrs. Edward D.
Boit, El Jaleo, The Sulphur Match*, and
Venetian Bead Stringers (Figs. 14, 21, 23).
Elizabeth Allen Marquand and *Mrs. Edward
D. Boit* sent to England for the Royal
Academy. May 19, sails to Liverpool;
uncertain about plans for the summer
because of his father's declining health.
June, moves with his family to Calcot
Mill, near Reading in Berkshire; visited
by Dennis Bunker, Flora Priestley, the
Helleus, Vernon Lee and, possibly,
Monet; *plein-air* experiments.

1889
January; sees Ellen Terry's debut as Lady
Macbeth, wearing costumes by Alice
Comyns Carr; paints *Ellen Terry as Lady
Macbeth* (Fig. 67). March–April, serves on
the jury of the Salon; visits Monet at
Giverny; contributes 1,000 francs to
purchase Manet's *Olympia* for the Louvre;
has six paintings in the American section
of the Exposition Universelle in Paris and
paints Javanese dancers; made Chevalier
of the Legion of Honor; April 25,
Dr. FitzWilliam Sargent dies in
Bournemouth. May, portraits at the
Royal Academy and Impressionist studies
at the New English Art Club; *Ellen Terry*

A Game of Bowls, Ightham Mote, Kent, 1889
Oil on canvas, 56¼ × 90¼ (142.9 × 229.2)
Whitney Museum of American Art,
New York; Gift of Mr. and Mrs. Lester
Avnet 67.41

as *Lady Macbeth* at the New Gallery.
June–July, moves to Fladbury Rectory,
Pershore, with his mother and sisters for
the summer; residents the same as the
previous year at Calcot, minus Bunker,
plus Abbey. September, teaches Abbey
how to paint in oil. August, Ightham Mote
in Kent; paints *Miss Elsie Palmer*
(Fig. 105). December 4, sails with
younger sister Violet to New York; Violet
goes to Boston to stay with the Fairchilds.

1890
January, the St. Botolph Club winter
exhibition, which includes *George Henschel*
and *A Morning Walk* (Figs. 71, 80).
February, New York; sees Carmencita
dance; Union League exhibition includes
Paul Helleu Sketching with His Wife (Fig. 89)
and *A Morning Walk*. March, begins *La
Carmencita* (Fig. 106) in New York studio;
Carmencita also dances and poses for
J. Carroll Beckwith and William Merritt
Chase. May, *A Game of Bowls, Ightham Mote*
(illustration above) shown at New
Gallery; seven paintings at the Society of
American Artists exhibition, *La Carmencita*
among them; preliminary negotiations
with Charles Follen McKim and Augustus
Saint-Gaudens about the mural
decorations for the Boston Public Library.
June, Worcester, Massachusetts; August,
Nahant, Manchester, Worcester; *Mrs.
Edward L. Davis and Her Son Livingston*
(Fig. 97). September–October, visits

Dennis Miller Bunker and attends his
wedding; October, trustees of the Boston
Public Library confirm commission.
November 5, sails for Liverpool with
Violet; December, Egypt with mother
and sisters.

1891
January, Cairo, then Upper Egypt;
March, Cairo; April, Greece,
Constantinople; tours Turkey. June,
Paris; July, Violet Sargent marries Louis
Francis Ormond in Paris. At some point in
early 1891 changes subject of Boston
Public Library mural from medieval
Spanish imagery to what later evolves as
The History of Religion. August,
Switzerland; September, London.
November, shares Morgan Hall, Fairford,
with the Abbeys and works in the vast
iron studio at the bottom of the garden on
his Boston murals; elected Associate of
the National Academy of Design.

1892
January–June, London and Fairford,
portraits and murals; first mural sketches
appear; April, *Mrs. Hugh Hammersley*
(Fig. 127); meetings in Fairford with
McKim and Abbey about the murals.
August, Spain, to join his mother and
sister and see his newborn niece;
September, Amsterdam. December, Paris;
introduces Whistler to McKim and
Abbey; discussions about Whistler's
possible contribution to the Boston project.

1893
January 18, signs first of three contracts
for the Boston murals; models come to
Fairford from London to pose for Abbey
and then for Sargent's *Frieze of the Prophets*,
among them Colarossi and the d'Inverno
brothers. Refuses to make any decorative
contribution to the World's Columbian
Exposition; sneers at the entire enterprise
but sends several paintings for exhibition,
including *Madame X* (Fig. 47). May,
portraits at the New Gallery, New
English Art Club and Royal Academy,
among them *Lady Agnew of Lochnaw*
(Fig. 110). November, completes lunette
of *The Children of Israel Beneath the Yoke of
Their Oppressors*, except for bas-relief
additions.

1894
January, elected Associate of the Royal Academy; vaulting with *Pagan Deities* for Boston project completed; starts painting *Frieze of the Prophets*. April–May, sittings for *W. Graham Robertson* portrait (Fig. 69). May, shows Boston vaulting and lunette, complete with bas-reliefs, at the Royal Academy; Paris, briefly; sees Whistler's portrait of *Comte de Montesquiou*; consults Frederick MacMonnies about sculpture for murals. June, Fairford. July, dismantles decorations at Royal Academy, crates and ships them to America. September, paints *Coventry Patmore*.

1895
January, portrait commissions postponed while he makes final corrections on *Frieze of the Prophets*, reworking the figure of Moses as a bas-relief. April 6, sails to Boston; superintends installation of murals at the north end of the Special Libraries Hall; Abbey busy on the floor below with his *Holy Grail* sequence. April 25, McKim holds reception for Abbey and Sargent at Boston Public Library to unveil the murals; subscription taken to pay for the next section of murals ($15,000), and Sargent is formally asked to continue. May, *Coventry Patmore* and *W. Graham Robertson* portraits at the Royal Academy; goes to Asheville, North Carolina, to George Vanderbilt's new mansion, "Biltmore"; executes portraits of Vanderbilt, the architect Richard Morris Hunt, and Frederick Law Olmstead, the landscape designer. June, sails for Spain to join mother and Emily. July, Gibraltar while mother recovers from peritonitis. End of August, London; portrait work; gives up his share in Morgan Hall, Fairford; takes twenty-one-year lease on two studios in Fulham Road. October, Visitor at the Royal Academy Schools. December, second Boston Public Library contract signed.

1896
January, lends Fulham Road studios to Paul Helleu, then Whistler; February, receives commission to paint *Henry G. Marquand* for The Metropolitan Museum of Art. May, Paris; *Miss Priestley* at the Royal Academy. Summer, in London for portrait work. October, begins *Mrs. Carl Meyer and Her Children* (Fig. 114). December, Visitor, Royal Academy Schools.

1897
January–February, Sicily, Rome, and Florence for mural research. March, London; learns of election to the National Academy of Design and submits a portrait of Monet as a diploma picture; also learns of election to the Royal Academy and lodges *Johannes Woolf* as diploma picture; shows *Dr. Pozzi at Home* in Venice. May, *Mrs. Carl Meyer and Her Children*, *The Hon. Laura Lister* at the Royal Academy; *Mrs. George Swinton* (Fig. 118) at the New Gallery. June, sittings for *Mr. and Mrs. I. N. Phelps Stokes* (Fig. 115). August, sittings for *Henry G. Marquand*. October, Visitor, Royal Academy Schools; begins Christian section of Boston Public Library murals.

1898
January–February, *Asher Wertheimer* (Fig. 116), *Mrs. Charles Hunter* sittings. May, Wertheimer portrait at the Royal Academy; goes to Venice, staying at the Palazzo Barbaro; begins painting *An Interior in Venice* (Fig. 44); Bologna, Milan, Bergamo, Ravenna. June, London; portrait sittings; increases fee to 1,000 guineas. October–December, executes *The Dogma of Redemption*, with crucifix, for Boston project.

1899
February, sittings for *The Wyndham Sisters* (Fig. 112); February 20–March 13, first one-man show, for the Boston Art Student's Association, Copley Hall. March, Mrs. Daniel Curtis refuses gift of *An Interior in Venice* as an unsatisfactory portrait of her family. April, serves on Hanging Committee of the Royal Academy; Paris, to consult with Saint-Gaudens about casting crucifix in *Dogma of Redemption*. July, Whistler remarks on Sargent's "dullness" after meeting on a train. August, mural work; September, meets Edith Wharton. November, Henry James complains that Sargent is getting very fat; on the council of the Royal Academy. December, Visitor, Royal Academy Schools; submits *An Interior in Venice* as official diploma picture.

1900
February, gives *Autumn on the River* (Fig. 85) to the South African Relief Fund for sale. March, sittings for *The Sitwell Family*. End of April, Paris; sees Monet, Boldini, Saint-Gaudens. May, *The Wyndham Sisters*, *The Duke of Portland*, and *An Interior in Venice* at the Royal Academy; *The Hon. Victoria Stanley* at the New Gallery; *Miss Carey Thomas* at the Exposition Universelle, Paris; *Asher Wertheimer* (Fig. 116) at the Salon. August, enlarges London studio; September, Switzerland, Italy. October, Visitor, Royal Academy Schools.

1901
January, Fairford. May, refuses commission to paint the coronation of Edward VII. Crucifix from *The Dogma of Redemption* at the Royal Academy; *Mrs. Garrett Anderson* at the New Gallery; nine pictures at the Pan-American Exposition in Buffalo. August–September, Norway; paints *On His Holidays*. October, Sicily, Palermo, Rome. December, Visitor, Royal Academy Schools.

1902
January, Welbeck Abbey; struggles with portrait of *The Duchess of Portland*. May, *The Misses Hunter*, *The Duchess of Portland*, *Alfred Wertheimer* at the Royal Academy; *On His Holidays* and portraits of the younger members of the Wertheimer family at the New Gallery. September–October, Venice; October, paints *William Merritt Chase*. November, Naples, Rome; informs trustees of the Boston Public Library that the Christian lunette, *The Dogma of Redemption*, is nearing completion; Visitor, Royal Academy Schools; James admires his Venice watercolors.

1903
January, Boston; installs first portion of the Christian end of the Library project: the lunette, frieze, and crucifix; arranges special viewing for Stanford White, Daniel Chester French, Saint-Gaudens, Mrs. Gardner, the Robinsons; wants to change the color of the background in *Frieze of the Prophets*. February, the White House, for *Theodore Roosevelt* sittings; Philadelphia.

Pomegranates, Majorca, c. 1908
Oil on canvas, 28¼ × 22¼ (71.8 × 56.5)
The Warner Collection of Gulf States Paper
Corporation, Tuscaloosa, Alabama

Turkey, n.d.
Bronze, 18¾ × 19⅛ × 18¼ (47.6 × 48.6 × 46.4)
Corcoran Gallery of Art, Washington, D.C.;
Museum Purchase

March–April, Boston; works in the
Gothic room at Fenway Court; portrait
commissions. May–June, honorary degree,
University of Pennsylvania; one-man
show at Carfax Gallery, London; portrait
exhibition, Museum of Fine Arts, Boston.
June, sails to Spain; August, to Venice;
September–October, Venice. December,
paints *Millicent, Duchess of Sutherland*
(Fig. 123). Publication of Alice Meynell's
Sargent monograph with reproductions,
which he sends to friends as Christmas
presents.

1904
Winter, *Charles Stewart, Sixth Marquess of
Londonderry* sittings (Fig. 124). June,
honorary degree from Oxford University.
August–September, Purtud, Switzerland.
September–October, Venice, at the
Palazzo Barbaro; paints *Lady Helen
Vincent*; meets mother and sister en route
to Egypt. November, Visitor, Royal
Academy Schools; Roger Fry starts his
campaign against Sargent with a review of
his pictures at the winter New English
Art Club show.

1905
February, begins to rail against the chore
of producing portraits on commission.
May, *The Marlborough Family* (Fig. 120) at
the Royal Academy; *Sir Frank Swettenham*
(Fig. 122), *Mrs. Adolph Hirsch*, *Mrs. E. G.
Raphael* at the New Gallery; Venetian and
Spanish interiors at the New English Art
Club; forty-seven watercolors at the
Carfax Gallery, London; elected to the
National Academy of Arts and Letters in
New York. August–September, Purtud
with the Harrisons. November, Syria and
Palestine.

1906
January 21, mother dies in London.
February 2, returns to London; funeral
and memorial service. April, serves on
Hanging Committee of the Royal
Academy; contributes $100 to the San
Francisco Earthquake Relief organized by
the National Academy of Design; May,
The Four Doctors (Fig. 121) at the Royal
Academy; *Padre Sebastiano* at the New
Gallery, landscape and *Behind the Curtain*
at the New English Art Club. August–

September, Purtud, Val d'Aosta, Turin,
Bologna, Venice with Emily; again meets
Eliza Wedgwood, a close friend of Emily's.
October, Rome; meets Mrs. Charles
Hunter, a celebrated hostess, who
becomes a good friend; rejoins Eliza
Wedgwood. November, Visitor, Royal
Academy Schools.

1907
February–March, organizes a series of
musical evenings for Gabriel Fauré. *Lady
Sassoon* at the Royal Academy; *Mrs. Harold
Harmsworth* at the New Gallery; Italian
and Palestinian scenes at the New English
Art Club. May, vows to give up
portraiture. June, Edward VII
recommends a knighthood for both
Sargent and Abbey; neither can accept
because of his American citizenship.
August, Purtud; September–October,
Venice at the Palazzo Barbaro; travels
with Eliza Wedgwood and Emily to
Perugia, Narni, Frascati, Rome, where
they meet Jane and Wilfrid von Glehn;
Paris. November, Visitor, Royal Academy
Schools.

1908
March (Easter), at Cliveden; May, *The Rt.
Hon. A. J. Balfour, HRH the Duke of
Connaught* at the Royal Academy; *The
Misses Vickers* (Fig. 61) and *Lady Lewis* at
the New Gallery; Italian subjects at the
New English Art Club; *Miss Helen Brice*
and *Joseph Pulitzer* at the National
Academy of Design, New York. June,
watercolors at the Carfax Gallery,
London; Majorca, briefly; July, London.
September, with Emily to Avignon to
meet Eliza Wedgwood, then Barcelona,
Majorca. October, Majorca; watercolor
and oil portraits of Eliza Wedgwood and
Emily. November, Visitor, Royal
Academy Schools.

1909
February, eighty-six watercolors
exhibited in joint show with Edward D.
Boit at Knoedler's, New York (eighty-
three bought by The Brooklyn Museum).
March, works on vaultings and lunettes
for Boston Public Library; May, *The
Cashmere Shawl, Mrs. Astor, The Earl of
Wemyss* at the Royal Academy; *The Black*

Brook, Dolce Far Niente, and others at the New English Art Club. August, Val d'Aosta with Emily. September, meets the von Glehns, Eliza Wedgwood in Venice; all go to Corfu; October–November, Corfu; portraits of them all. November–December, Visitor, Royal Academy Schools. Awarded Order of Merit from France, Order of Leopold from Belgium.

1910

January, influenza; February, goes to Holland to recover; withdraws from active social life in London. May, landscapes and figures with landscapes at the Royal Academy and the New English Art Club. June–November, Italy and Switzerland. November–December, Visitor, Royal Academy Schools; argues with Roger Fry because Fry listed Sargent's name among the supporters of the exhibition of Post-Impressionist painting. Working on east and west wall lunettes for Boston project (*Gog and Magog, Hell*); finishes *Gog and Magog*.

1911

January, row with Fry continues in *The Nation*; goes to Rouen to study the Cathedral. May, to Paris for the Ingres exhibition; landscapes at the New English Art Club. June, to Munich with the Adrian Stokes; called back to London to help Abbey finish murals for State Capitol rotunda, Harrisburg, Pennsylvania. July, returns to Simplon Pass with Emily. August 1, death of Abbey. September, Venice, at the Palazzo Barbaro. October, Carrara; selects 322 works for Abbey's memorial exhibition at the Royal Academy; Visitor, Royal Academy Schools.

1912

March 16–30, second watercolor exhibition (with Edward D. Boit) at Knoedler's, New York; Sargent's forty-five pictures bought by the Museum of Fine Arts, Boston; friends of Henry James arrange to have Sargent paint a portrait of the writer on the occasion of his seventieth birthday. April 15, death of Millet. June, to Alps; Broadway. September–November, Spain with Emily and the von Glehns.

1913

May–June *Henry James* sittings (Fig. 133); honorary degree from Cambridge University. August, briefly in Paris for wedding of his niece Rose-Marie Ormond. Venice; meets the von Glehns. September, the Dolomites; San Vigilio, Lake Garda with Emily, the von Glehns, Eliza Wedgwood, and others; takes up photography.

1914

March–April, serves on Selection Committee, Royal Academy; May, *Lady Rocksavage* at the Royal Academy; *Henry James* portrait slashed by suffragette. July, Gold Medal awarded by the American Academy of Arts and Sciences; joins the Stokes in the Austrian Tyrol. When war breaks out in August, he is unable to leave Austria because the Stokes, as British subjects, are now enemy aliens. November, goes to Vienna for a passport. December, Visitor, Royal Academy Schools; appointed chairman of the London Committee of the Panama-Pacific Exposition.

1915

Sends thirteen pictures to the Panama-Pacific Exposition, among them *Madame X*. July, is astonished and impressed when Henry James becomes a British subject. October, negotiations about architectural changes to the Special Libraries Hall of the Boston Public Library. Has discussions with the British War Office at the request of the American painter Abbott Thayer, whose theories and experiments in camouflage suggested a military application.

1916

January, murals rolled up for shipment to America; offers *Madame X* to The Metropolitan Museum of Art for purchase. February, death of Henry James; designs Red Cross notepaper. March 20, sails to Boston. May, begins third Library installation; experiments with lighting. June, Worcester; honorary degrees from Yale and Harvard; travels to Glacier National Park, Montana. August–September, British Columbia; paints *Yoho Falls* and *Lake O'Hara*

(Figs. 155, 156). October, Boston; Library trustees anxious for him to complete installation. November, installation completed; agrees to decorate Rotunda of the Museum of Fine Arts, Boston; model of the dome moved into his Columbus Avenue studio.

1917

February, goes to Ormond Beach, Florida, to paint the elderly John D. Rockefeller. March, stays with Charles Deering at Brickell Point, Miami; visits the unfinished mansion, "Villa Vizcaya," then being built by Charles' brother James Deering. April, fishing expedition off Miami; the United States declares war on Germany. May, Philadelphia; Boston; New York, Pocantico Hills for sittings for a second portrait of Rockefeller; shares Beckwith's studio. October, Washington D.C., paints President Wilson's portrait for Red Cross charity. November, death of Beckwith; retouches paintings for Beckwith's studio sale. December, resigns from the Royal Academy of Art, Berlin.

1918

April 3, learns of niece Rose-Marie Ormond's death during German bombardment in Paris on March 29. April 20, draws up will; Nicola d'Inverno, his valet for over twenty years, decides to leave Sargent's employ and stay in America. May, sails to England. June, works on second Red Cross charity portrait, *Mrs. Percival Duxbury and Daughter*; negotiations with Lord Beaverbrook and the Ministry of Information about becoming a war artist; encouraged to run for president of the Royal Academy. July 2, leaves for France; spends four months at the front, along with Henry Tonks. September, witnesses the scene on the road to Arras which becomes *Gassed* (Fig. 256). December, categorically refuses to become president of the Royal Academy.

1919

January, reluctantly accepts commission for a large group portrait of war officers. February, rumors circulate that he will marry Mrs. Hunter. May, sails to Boston with Emily and niece Reine Ormond; works on bas-reliefs for Museum of Fine

Arts Rotunda; takes second and larger studio; *Gassed* at the Royal Academy (named Picture of the Year). October, controversy arises regarding the religious symbolism of his addition to the Special Libraries Hall (renamed Sargent Hall) — *The Synagogue* and *The Church*.

1920
Helps Mrs. Hunter to sell her pictures to Isabella Stewart Gardner; April, makes donations of family memorabilia and dining room wallpaper to the Sargent House Museum in Gloucester, Massachusetts. May, Emily returns to England with Reine. June, Museum of Fine Arts Rotunda installation. July, sails to Liverpool, after fourteen months in Boston. September, begins *Some General Officers of the Great War*.

1921
January, sails to New York; sees Paul Helleu; Boston, resumes work on museum decorations, bas-reliefs, and oval panels. June, Montreal for work on *Some General Officers*. August, sisters and niece Reine arrive in America. September–October, complicated Boston museum Rotunda installation; agrees to decorate staircase of the museum as well. October 15, sails to Liverpool with sisters and niece. November, agrees to paint huge staircase

panels for the Widener Memorial Library, Harvard University.

1922
February, death of Ralph Curtis. March 29, sails for Boston. Summer, two large panels painted and installed in the Widener Memorial Library, on the subject of American soldiers in victory and defeat. September, Isabella Stewart Gardner agrees to sit for watercolor portrait. October, Museum of Fine Arts decorations delivered. December 9, sails for Liverpool; Christmas in London.

1923
January, the group of Wertheimer portraits installed in the National Gallery, London; works on Boston museum staircase panels at Fulham Road studio; laments that they are taking too long and are too large to execute in his Boston studio. March–April, contributes to American Art section of an exhibition in aid of the French Red Cross. July 16, bicentennial of Reynolds' birth, wreath laying at St. Paul's in the afternoon and celebration at the Royal Academy in the evening; nervously delivers speech on Reynolds. August, U.S. Ambassador commissions charcoal portrait of Duke of York (later George VI) as wedding present; October 25, sails with Emily for

Boston. November, begins negotiations with Grand Central Art Galleries, New York, for retrospective exhibition; November 23, attends public opening day of Fenway Court; improvises verses with President Lowell of Harvard for memorial panels in Widener Library.

1924
February 23–March 22, Grand Central Art Galleries retrospective (sixty oils, twelve watercolors); does not attend. July 14, sails with Emily from Boston for Liverpool; July 17, death of Isabella Stewart Gardner; in Fulham Road studio, continues work, which he calls "occupational therapy."

1925
March, Boston decorations completed. April, books passage for Boston to supervise final installation; April 14, dines with Emily and several friends at Carlyle Mansions; April 15, dies in his sleep at age sixty-nine. April 18, body taken by special train from Paddington Station to Brookwood Cemetery, Woking, for private burial; April 24, memorial service, Westminster Abbey.

1926
Studio sale, Christie's; retrospective exhibition at the Royal Academy and The Metropolitan Museum of Art.

Classical and Romantic Art, 1916–21
Oil on canvas
Rotunda, Museum of Fine Arts, Boston; Francis
Bartlett Donation of 1912

Selected Bibliography

Adelson, Warren. *John Singer Sargent: His Own Work* (exhibition catalogue). New York, Coe Kerr Gallery, Inc., 1980.

Bacon, Henry. *Parisian Art and Artists*. Boston, 1883.

Baldry, A. Lys. "The Art of J. S. Sargent, R.A.: Part I." *International Studio*, 10 (March 1900), pp. 3–21.

——. "The Art of John S. Sargent, R.A.: Part II." *International Studio*, 10 (April 1900), pp. 107–19.

Baxter, Sylvester. "Sargent's 'Redemption' in the Boston Public Library." *The Century Magazine*, 66 (May 1903), pp. 129–34.

Bell, Quentin. "John Sargent and Roger Fry." *The Burlington Magazine*, 99 (November 1957), pp. 380–82.

Belleroche, Albert de. "The Lithographs of Sargent." *Print Collector's Quarterly*, 13 (February 1926), pp. 31–45.

Bienenstock, Jennifer A. Martin. "The Formation and Early Years of the Society of American Artists: 1877–1884." Ph.D. dissertation, The City University of New York, 1983.

Bird, Jon. "Representing the Great War." *Block*, no. 3 (1980), pp. 41–52.

Birnbaum, Martin. *John Singer Sargent: A Conversation Piece*. New York, 1941.

Boston, Museum of Fine Arts. *A Catalogue of the Memorial Exhibition of the Works of the Late John Singer Sargent* (exhibition catalogue). Boston, 1925.

Boston Public Library. "Sargent Hall." In *A New Handbook of the Boston Public Library and Its Mural Decorations*. Boston, 1916, pp. 37–58.

Brinton, Christian. "Sargent and His Art." *Munsey's Magazine*, 36 (December 1906), pp. 265–84.

Burke, Doreen Bolger. "*Astarte*: Sargent's Study for *The Pagan Gods* Mural in the Boston Public Library." In *Fenway Court: Isabella Stewart Gardner Museum,* *1976*. Boston, 1977, pp. 8–19.

——. *American Paintings in the Metropolitan Museum of Art, III: A Catalogue of Works by Artists Born Between 1846 and 1864*. New York, 1980.

Caffin, Charles A. *American Masters of Painting: Being Brief Appreciations of Some American Painters*. New York, 1902.

——. "John S. Sargent: The Greatest Contemporary Portrait Painter." *World's Work*, 7 (November 1903), pp. 4099–4116.

——. "Drawings by John Sargent." *Metropolitan Magazine*, 30 (July 1909), pp. 412–18.

Charteris, Evan. *John Sargent*. New York, 1927.

Coburn, Frederick W. "The Sargent Decorations in the Boston Public Library." *The American Magazine of Art*, 8 (February 1917), pp. 129–36.

Coffin, William A. "Sargent and His Painting: With Special Reference to His Decorations in the Boston Public Library." *The Century Magazine*, 52 (June 1896), pp. 163–78.

Cortissoz, Royal. "John S. Sargent." *Scribner's Magazine*, 34 (November 1903), pp. 515–32.

——. "The Field of Art: Illustrations from Paintings by Sargent and Others." *Scribner's Magazine*, 75 (March 1924), pp. 345–52.

Downes, William Howe. *John S. Sargent: His Life and Work*. Boston, 1925.

Fairbrother, Trevor J. "The Shock of John Singer Sargent's 'Madame Gautreau.'" *Arts Magazine*, 55 (January 1981), pp. 90–97.

——. "A Private Album: John Singer Sargent's Drawings of Nude Male Models." *Arts Magazine*, 56 (December 1981), pp. 70–79.

——. "Notes on John Singer Sargent in New York, 1888–1890." *Archives of American Art Journal*, 22, no. 4 (1982), pp. 27–32.

——. *Sargent Portrait Drawings: 42 Works by John Singer Sargent*. New York, 1983.

——. *The Bostonians: Painters of an Elegant Age, 1870–1930*. Boston, 1986.

——. *John Singer Sargent and America*. New York, 1986.

Field, Rachel. "John Sargent's Boyhood Sketches." *St. Nicholas*, 53 (June 1926), pp. 774–77.

Fowler, Frank. "The Field of Art: Sargent's New Wall Paintings." *Scribner's Magazine*, 34 (September 1903), pp. 767–68.

Gammell, R. H. Ives. "The Enigma of John Sargent's Art." *Classical America*, 1977, pp. 153–61.

Gerdts, William H. *American Impressionism*. New York, 1984.

Hale, Mary Newbold Patterson. "The Sargent I Knew." *World Today*, 50 (November 1927), pp. 565–70. Reprinted in Ratcliff, *John Singer Sargent*, pp. 235–38.

Hoopes, Donelson F. *The Private World of John Singer Sargent* (exhibition catalogue). Washington, D.C., Corcoran Gallery of Art, 1964.

——. "John S. Sargent: The Worcestershire Interlude, 1885–89." *The Brooklyn Museum Annual*, 7 (1965–66), pp. 74–89.

——. *Sargent Watercolors*. New York, 1970.

James, Henry. "John S. Sargent." *Harper's New Monthly Magazine*, 75 (October 1887). Reprinted in *Picture and Text*. New York, 1893, pp. 92–115.

Karo, Rebecca W. "Ah Wilderness! Sargent in the Rockies, 1916." In *Fenway Court: Isabella Stewart Gardner Museum, 1976*. Boston, 1977, pp. 21–29.

Kingsbury, Martha. "John Singer Sargent: Aspects of His Works." Ph.D. dissertation, Harvard University, Cambridge, Massachusetts, 1969.

———. "Sargent's Murals in the Boston Public Library." *Winterthur Portfolio*, 11 (1976), pp. 153–72.

La Farge, John. "Sargent the Artist." *Independent*, 51 (April 27, 1899), pp. 1140–42.

Lee, Vernon. "Imagination in Modern Art. Random Notes on Whistler, Sargent, and Besnard." *The Fortnightly Review*, 62 (October 1, 1897), pp. 513–21.

———. "J. S. S. *In Memoriam*" (1925). In Charteris, *John Sargent*, pp. 235–55.

Leeper, John Palmer. "John Singer Sargent: A Revaluation." *Magazine of Art*, 44 (January 1951), pp. 11–15.

Lomax, James, and Richard Ormond. *John Singer Sargent and the Edwardian Age* (exhibition catalogue). Leeds, England, Leeds Art Galleries; London, National Portrait Gallery; and The Detroit Institute of Arts, 1979.

London, Royal Academy. *The Sargent Exhibition: 1926* (exhibition catalogue). London, 1926.

Lovell, Margaretta M. "A Visitable Past: Views of Venice by American Artists, 1860–1915." Ph.D. dissertation, Yale University, New Haven, 1980.

———. *Venice: The American View, 1860–1920* (exhibition catalogue). The Fine Arts Museums of San Francisco, 1984.

Low, Will H. "Carolus-Duran: An Appreciation." *Scribner's Magazine*, 61 (June 1917), pp. 771–74.

Lucas, E. V. *Edwin Austin Abbey, Royal Academician: The Record of His Life and Work*. 2 vols. London and New York, 1921.

Mather, Frank Jewett, Jr. "The Enigma of Sargent." In *Estimates in Art*. New York, 1916, pp. 235–67.

Mechlin, Leila. "The Sargent Exhibition: Grand Central Galleries, New York." *The American Magazine of Art*, 15 (April 1924), pp. 168–90.

McKibbin, David. *Sargent's Boston* (exhibition catalogue). Museum of Fine Arts, Boston, 1956.

Meynell, Alice Christina. *The Work of John S. Sargent, R.A.* London and New York, 1903.

Mount, Charles Merrill. *John Singer Sargent: A Biography*. New York, 1955.

———. "John Singer Sargent and Judith Gautier." *The Art Quarterly*, 18 (Summer 1955), pp. 136–45.

———. "New Discoveries Illumine Sargent's Paris Career." *The Art Quarterly*, 20 (Autumn 1957), pp. 304–16.

———. "Carolus-Duran and the Development of Sargent." *The Art Quarterly*, 26 (Winter 1963), pp. 385–417.

———. "The English Sketches of J. S. Sargent." *Country Life*, 135 (April 16, 1964), pp. 931–34.

New York, Coe Kerr Gallery, Inc. *Sargent at Broadway: The Impressionist Years* (exhibition catalogue). New York, 1986. Essays by Warren Adelson, Richard Ormond, and Stanley Olson.

New York, Grand Central Art Galleries. *Retrospective Exhibition of Important Works of John Singer Sargent* (exhibition catalogue). New York, 1924.

Nygren, Edward J. *John Singer Sargent: Drawings from the Corcoran Gallery of Art* (exhibition catalogue). Washington, D.C., Smithsonian Institution Traveling Exhibition Service and the Corcoran Gallery of Art, 1983.

O'Brien, Maureen C. "Sargent, John Singer 1856–1925. A Boating Party." In *Museum of Art, Rhode Island School of Design, Selection VII: American Paintings from the Museum's Collection, c. 1800–1930*. Providence, 1977, pp. 179–82.

Olson, Stanley. *John Singer Sargent: His Portrait*. New York, 1986.

Ormond, Richard. *John Singer Sargent: Paintings, Drawings, Watercolors*. New York, 1970.

———. "Sargent's *El Jaleo*." In *Fenway Court: Isabella Stewart Gardner Museum, 1970*. Boston, 1971, pp. 2–18.

———. "The Letters of Dr. FitzWilliam Sargent: The Youth of John Singer Sargent." *Archives of American Art Journal*, 14, no. 1 (1974), pp. 16–18.

Ratcliff, Carter. *John Singer Sargent*. New York, 1982.

Robertson, Meg. "John Singer Sargent: His Early Success in America, 1878–1879." *Archives of American Art Journal*, 22, no. 4 (1982), pp. 20–26.

San Francisco, California Palace of the Legion of Honor. *Sargent and Boldini* (exhibition catalogue). San Francisco, 1959.

Schulze, Franz. "J. S. Sargent, Partly Great." *Art in America*, 68 (February 1980), pp. 90–96.

Seldin, Donna. *Americans in Venice: 1879–1913* (exhibition catalogue). New York, Coe Kerr Gallery, Inc., 1983.

Sickert, Walter. "Sargentolatry." *The New Age*, 7 (May 19, 1910), pp. 56–57. Reprinted in Ratcliff, *John Singer Sargent*, pp. 233–34.

Smith, Preserved. "The Field of Art: Sargent's New Mural Decorations." *Scribner's Magazine*, 71 (March 1922), pp. 379–84.

Stevenson, Robert A. M. "J. S. Sargent." *The Art Journal*, 50 (March 1888), pp. 64–69.

Strickler, Susan E. "John Singer Sargent and Worcester." *Worcester Art Museum Journal*, 6 (1982–83), pp. 19–39.

Sturgis, Russell. "Sargent's New Wall Painting." *Scribner's Magazine*, 34 (September 1903), pp. 765–67.

Sutton, Denys. "The Yankee Brio of John Singer Sargent." *Portfolio*, 1 (October/November 1979), pp. 46–53.

Sweet, Frederick A. *Sargent, Whistler and Mary Cassatt* (exhibition catalogue). The Art Institute of Chicago, 1954.

Van Dyke, John C. "Sargent the Portrait Painter." *The Outlook*, 74 (May 2, 1902), pp. 31–39.

Van Rensselaer, Mariana Griswold. "Mr. Sargent's Portrait of La Carmencita." *Harper's Weekly*, 34 (June 14, 1890), pp. 457, 467.

———. "American Artists Series: John S. Sargent." *The Century Magazine*, 43 (March 1892), p. 798.

Weinberg, H. Barbara. "John Singer Sargent: Reputation Redivivus." *Arts Magazine*, 54 (March 1980), pp. 104–09.

———. "Nineteenth-Century American Painters at the École des Beaux-Arts." *The American Art Journal*, 13 (Autumn 1981), pp. 66–84.

——— "The Lure of Paris: Late Nineteenth-Century American Painters and Their French Training." In Stebbins, Theodore E., Jr., Carol Troyen, and Trevor J. Fairbrother. *A New World: Masterpieces of American Painting, 1760–1910* (exhibition catalogue). Museum of Fine Arts, Boston, 1983.

Works in the Exhibition

Dimensions are in inches, followed by centimeters; height precedes width. An asterisk (*) indicates that a work will be shown only at the Whitney Museum of American Art, a dagger (†) that it will be shown only at The Art Institute of Chicago.

PAINTINGS

Frances Sherburne Ridley Watts, 1877
Oil on canvas, 41⅝ × 32⅞ (105.7 × 83.5)
Philadelphia Museum of Art; The Mr. and Mrs. Wharton Sinkler Collection

Capri, 1878
Oil on canvas, 20 × 25 (50.8 × 63.5)
The Warner Collection of Gulf States Paper Corporation, Tuscaloosa, Alabama

The Oyster Gatherers of Cancale, 1878
Oil on canvas, 31 × 48 (78.7 × 121.9)
Corcoran Gallery of Art, Washington, D.C.; Museum Purchase

Rehearsal of the Pas de Loup Orchestra at the Cirque d'Hiver, 1878
Oil on canvas, 36⅝ × 28¾ (92.1 × 71.9)
Private collection; on loan to The Art Institute of Chicago

Young Man in Reverie, 1878 (inscribed 1876)
Oil on canvas, 30 × 24 (76.2 × 61)
Private collection

Carolus-Duran, 1879
Oil on canvas, 46 × 37¹³⁄₁₆ (116.8 × 96)
Sterling and Francine Clark Art Institute, Williamstown, Massachusetts

Edouard Pailleron, 1879
Oil on canvas, 50 × 37 (127 × 94)
Musée National du Château de Versailles

In the Luxembourg Gardens, 1879
Oil on canvas, 25½ × 36 (64.8 × 91.4)
John G. Johnson Collection at the Philadelphia Museum of Art

Madame Edouard Pailleron, 1879
Oil on canvas, 82 × 39 (208.3 × 99.1)
Corcoran Gallery of Art, Washington, D.C.; Purchase and Gift of Katharine McCook Knox, John A. Nevius, and Mr. and Mrs. Lansdell K. Christie

Mrs. Charles Gifford Dyer, 1880
Oil on canvas, 24 × 17 (61 × 43.2)
The Art Institute of Chicago; Friends of American Art Collections

Ralph Curtis on the Beach at Scheveningen, 1880
Oil on board, 11 × 14 (27.9 × 35.6)
The High Museum of Art, Atlanta; Gift of the Walter Clay Hill Family Foundation, 1973

Eugene Carriers, c. 1880
Oil on canvas, 22 × 18½ (55.9 × 47)
Nebraska Art Association, Nelle Cochrane Woods Collection at the Sheldon Memorial Art Gallery, University of Nebraska, Lincoln

Venetian Glass Workers, 1880 or 1882
Oil on canvas, 22 × 33 (55.9 × 83.8)
The Art Institute of Chicago; Mr. and Mrs. Martin A. Ryerson Collection

Venetian Bead Stringers, 1880–82
Oil on canvas, 26¾ × 30¾ (68 × 78.1)
Albright-Knox Art Gallery, Buffalo, New York; Friends of the Albright Art Gallery Fund, 1916

†*Venetian Interior*, 1880–82
Oil on canvas, 27 × 34 (68.6 × 86.4)
Museum of Art, Carnegie Institute, Pittsburgh; Museum Purchase, 1920

A Venetian Interior, 1880–82
Oil on canvas, 19¹⁄₁₆ × 23¹⁵⁄₁₆ (48.4 × 60.8)
Sterling and Francine Clark Art Institute, Williamstown, Massachusetts

*Venetian Street, 1880–82
Oil on canvas, 29 × 23¾ (73.7 × 60.3)
Collection of Rita and Daniel Fraad

Dr. Pozzi at Home, 1881
Oil on canvas, 80½ × 43⅞ (204.5 × 111.4)
The Armand Hammer Collection, Los Angeles

The Pailleron Children (Edouard and Marie-Louise), 1881
Oil on canvas, 60 × 69 (152.4 × 175.3)
Des Moines Art Center; Edith M. Usry Bequest Fund in memory of her parents, Mr. and Mrs. George Franklin Usry, and additional funds from Dr. and Mrs. Peder T. Madsen and the Anna K. Meredith Endowment Fund, 1976

Vernon Lee, 1881
Oil on canvas, 21⅛ × 17 (53.7 × 43.2)
The Tate Gallery, London; Bequeathed by Miss Vernon Lee through Miss Cooper Willis, 1935

Italian Girl with Fan, 1882
Oil on canvas, 93¾ × 52½ (238.1 × 133.4)
Cincinnati Art Museum; The Edwin and Virginia Irwin Memorial

Mr. and Mrs. John W. Field, 1882
Oil on canvas, 44 × 33 (111.8 × 83.8)
Pennsylvania Academy of the Fine Arts, Philadelphia; Presented by Mrs. John W. Field, 1891

The Sulphur Match, 1882
Oil on canvas, 23 × 16 (58.4 × 40.6)
Collection of Jo Ann and Julian Ganz, Jr.

Venetian Water Carriers, c. 1882
Oil on canvas, 25⅜ × 27¾ (64.5 × 70.5)
Worcester Art Museum, Massachusetts

François Flameng and Paul Helleu, c. 1882–85
Oil on canvas, 21 × 17 (53.3 × 43.2)
Private collection

A Dinner Table at Night, 1884
Oil on canvas, 20¼ × 26¼ (51.4 × 66.7)
The Fine Arts Museums of San Francisco;
Gift of the Atholl McBean Foundation

Garden Study of the Vickers Children, 1884
Oil on canvas, 54³⁄₁₆ × 35⅞ (137.6 × 91.1)
Flint Institute of Arts, Flint, Michigan;
Gift of the Viola E. Bray Charitable Trust

Madame X (Madame Pierre Gautreau), 1884
Oil on canvas, 82⅛ × 43¼ (208.6 × 109.9)
The Metropolitan Museum of Art, New
York; A. H. Hearn Fund, 1916

The Misses Vickers, 1884
Oil on canvas, 54 × 72 (137.2 × 182.9)
Sheffield City Art Galleries, England

Mrs. Kate A. Moore, 1884
Oil on canvas, 71⅝ × 45¾ (181.9 × 116.2)
Hirshhorn Museum and Sculpture Garden,
Smithsonian Institution, Washington, D.C.

Fête Familiale: The Birthday Party, 1885
Oil on canvas, 24 × 29 (61 × 73.7) The
Minneapolis Institute of Arts; The
Ethel Morrison and John R. Van Derlip Funds

*The Old Chair, 1885
Oil on canvas, 26 × 22 (66 × 55.9)
Collection of the Ormond Family

*Robert Louis Stevenson and His Wife, 1885
Oil on canvas, 20½ × 24½ (52.1 × 62.2)
Collection of Mrs. John Hay Whitney

Teresa Gosse, 1885
Oil on canvas, 25 × 19 (63.5 × 48.3)
Collection of Dr. and Mrs. John J.
McDonough

Millet's Garden, 1886
Oil on canvas, 27 × 34 (68.6 × 86.4)
Collection of Mrs. John William Griffith

Self-Portrait, 1886
Oil on canvas, 14 × 10 (35.6 × 25.4)
Aberdeen Art Gallery and Museums, Scotland

A Backwater, Calcot Mill near Reading, 1888
Oil on canvas, 20³⁄₁₆ × 27 (51.3 × 68.6)
The Baltimore Museum of Art; Gift of
J. Gilman D'Arcy Paul

Dennis Miller Bunker Painting at Calcot, 1888
Oil on canvas, 26¾ × 25 (67.9 × 63.5)
Terra Museum of American Art, Chicago;
Daniel J. Terra Collection

Mrs. Adrian Iselin, 1888
Oil on canvas, 60½ × 36⅝ (153.7 × 93)
National Gallery of Art, Washington,
D.C.; Gift of Ernest Iselin

St. Martin's Summer, 1888
Oil on canvas, 36 × 27 (91.4 × 68.6)
Collection of Mr. and Mrs. Peter Jay Solomon

**Autumn on the River (Miss Violet Sargent)*,
1889
Oil on canvas, 30 × 20 (76.2 × 50.8)
Private collection

Paul Helleu Sketching with His Wife, 1889
Oil on canvas, 26⅛ × 32⅛ (66.4 × 81.6)
The Brooklyn Museum, New York;
Museum Collection Fund

Two Girls with Parasols at Fladbury, 1889
Oil on canvas, 29½ × 25 (74.9 × 63.5)
The Metropolitan Museum of Art, New
York; Gift of Mrs. Francis Ormond, 1950

*Violet Fishing, 1889
Oil on canvas, 28 × 21 (71.1 × 53.3)
Collection of the Ormond Family

A Boating Party, c. 1889
Oil on canvas, 34 × 36 (86.4 × 91.4)
Museum of Art, Rhode Island School of
Design, Providence; Gift of Mrs.
Houghton P. Metcalf in memory of her
husband Houghton P. Metcalf

Charles Stuart Forbes, c. 1889
Oil on canvas, 29 × 24 (73.7 × 61)
Henry E. Huntington Library and Art
Gallery, San Marino, California

Miss Elsie Palmer, 1889–90
Oil on canvas, 75 × 45 (190.5 × 114.3)
Colorado Springs Fine Arts Center

Mrs. Edward L. Davis and Her Son Livingston, 1890
Oil on canvas, 86 × 48 (218.4 × 121.9)
Los Angeles County Museum of Art;
Frances and Armand Hammer Foundation
Purchase Fund

Egyptians Raising Water from the Nile, 1890–91
Oil on canvas, 25 × 21 (63.5 × 53.3)
The Metropolitan Museum of Art, New
York; Gift of Mrs. Francis Ormond, 1950

Study from Life, 1891
Oil on canvas, 73 × 23 (185.4 × 58.4)
Private collection; on loan to The Art
Institute of Chicago

A Bedouin Arab, c. 1891
Oil on canvas, 26 × 20¼ (66 × 51.4)
Private collection

Miss Helen Dunham, 1892
Oil on canvas, 48 × 32 (121.9 × 81.3)
Private collection

Lady Agnew of Lochnaw, c. 1892–93
Oil on canvas, 49 × 39¼ (124.5 × 99.7)
The National Galleries of Scotland,
Edinburgh

Mrs. Carl Meyer and Her Children, 1896
Oil on canvas, 79 × 53 (200.7 × 134.6)
Private collection

Catherine Vlasto, 1897
Oil on canvas, 58½ × 33⅝ (148.6 × 85.4)
Hirshhorn Museum and Sculpture
Garden, Smithsonian Institution,
Washington, D.C.

Mr. and Mrs. I. N. Phelps Stokes, 1897
Oil on canvas, 84¼ × 39¾ (214 × 101)
The Metropolitan Museum of Art, New
York; Bequest of Edith Phelps Stokes,
1938

Mrs. George Swinton, 1897
Oil on canvas, 90 × 49 (228.6 × 124.5)
The Art Institute of Chicago; Wirt D.
Walker Collection

Mrs. Charles Thursby, c. 1897–98
Oil on canvas, 78 × 39¾ (198.1 × 101)
The Newark Museum, New Jersey

Asher Wertheimer, 1898
Oil on canvas, 58 × 38½ (147.3 × 97.8)
The Tate Gallery, London

The Pavement, 1898
Oil on canvas, 21 × 28½ (53.3 × 72.4)
Collection of Mr. and Mrs. Steven J. Ross

An Interior in Venice, 1899
Oil on canvas, 25 × 31 (63.5 × 78.7)
Royal Academy of Arts, London

A Hotel Room, after 1900
Oil on canvas, 24 × 17½ (61 × 44.5)
Collection of the Ormond Family

Ena and Betty, Daughters of Mr. and Mrs. Asher Wertheimer, 1901
Oil on canvas, 73 × 51½ (185.4 × 130.8)
The Tate Gallery, London

Study for *Hell*, c. 1903–09
Oil on canvas with applied cloth and gilding, 33¼ × 66¼ (84.5 × 168.3)
Smith College Museum of Art, Northampton, Massachusetts; Gift of Mrs. Dwight W. Morrow (Elizabeth Cutter '96), 1932

†*Charles Stewart, Sixth Marquess of Londonderry, Carrying the Great Sword of State at the Coronation of King Edward VII, August, 1902, and Mr. W. C. Beaumont, His Page on That Occasion*, 1904
Oil on canvas, 113 × 77 (287 × 195.6)
Collection of Henry R. Kravis

Millicent, Duchess of Sutherland, 1904
Oil on canvas, 100 × 57½ (254 × 146.1)
Thyssen-Bornemisza Collection, Lugano, Switzerland

Near the Mount of Olives, 1905–06
Oil on canvas, 25½ × 38 (64.8 × 96.5)
Syndics of the Fitzwilliam Museum, Cambridge, England

Alberto Falchetti, c. 1905–08
Oil on canvas, 29½ × 21½ (74.9 × 54.6)
Collection of Mr. and Mrs. Richard M. Thune

The Brook, 1907
Oil on canvas, 21 × 27½ (53.3 × 69.9)
Collection of the Ormond Family

The Fountain, Villa Torlonia, Frascati, Italy, 1907
Oil on canvas, 28½ × 22 (72.4 × 55.9)
The Art Institute of Chicago; Friends of American Art Gift

Oxen Resting, 1907
Oil on canvas, 22 × 28 (55.9 × 71.1)
Private collection

Self-Portrait, 1907
Oil on canvas, 30 × 25 (76.2 × 63.5)
Galleria degli Uffizi, Florence

The Chess Game, c. 1907
Oil on canvas, 28 × 21¾ (71.1 × 55.2)
The Harvard Club of New York City

Pomegranates, Majorca, c. 1908
Oil on canvas, 28¼ × 22¼ (71.8 × 56.5)
The Warner Collection of Gulf States Paper Corporation, Tuscaloosa, Alabama

*Group with Parasols (*A Siesta*), c. 1908–11
Oil on canvas, 21¾ × 27⅞ (55.2 × 70.8)
Collection of Rita and Daniel Fraad

Albanian Olive Gatherers, 1909
Oil on canvas, 37 × 44 (94 × 111.8)
Manchester City Art Galleries, England

Alpine Pool, 1909
Oil on canvas, 27½ × 38 (69.9 × 96.5)
The Metropolitan Museum of Art, New York; Gift of Mrs. Francis Ormond, 1950

Jane de Glehn in Corfu (In the Garden, Corfu), 1909
Oil on canvas, 36 × 28⅛ (91.4 × 71.4)
Terra Museum of American Art, Chicago; Daniel J. Terra Collection

Olive Trees at Corfu, 1909
Oil on canvas, 28⅛ × 36¼ (71.4 × 92.1)
Collection of Mr. and Mrs. Marshall Field

Simplon Pass, 1910
Oil on canvas, 28 × 36 (71.1 × 91.4)
Corcoran Gallery of Art, Washington, D.C.; Bequest of James Parmelee

Muleteria, c. 1910
Oil on canvas, 22 × 28 (55.9 × 71.1)
The Warner Collection of Gulf States Paper Corporation, Tuscaloosa, Alabama

†*Val d'Aosta: A Man Fishing*, c. 1910
Oil on canvas, 22 × 28 (55.9 × 71.1)
Addison Gallery of American Art, Phillips Academy, Andover, Massachusetts

†*Bringing Down Marble from the Quarries to Carrara*, 1911
Oil on canvas, 28⅛ × 36⅛ (71.4 × 91.8)
The Metropolitan Museum of Art, New York; Harris Brisbane Dick Fund, 1917

A Marble Fountain at Aranjuez, Spain, 1912
Oil on canvas, 22 × 28 (55.9 × 71.1)
Collection of Mr. and Mrs. Isaac Arnold, Jr.

Church of St. Stäe, Venice, 1913
Oil on canvas, 28 × 22 (71.1 × 55.9)
Private collection

Henry James, 1913
Oil on canvas, 33 × 26 (83.8 × 66)
National Portrait Gallery, London

†*Moorish Courtyard*, 1913
Oil on canvas, 28 × 36 (71.7 × 91.5)
The Forbes Magazine Collection, New York

Palazzo Labia and San Geremia, Venice, 1913
Oil on canvas, 21½ × 27½ (54.6 × 69.9)
Private collection

Gypsy Encampment, c. 1913
Oil on canvas, 28⅛ × 36⅛ (71.4 × 91.8)
Addison Gallery of American Art, Phillips Academy, Andover, Massachusetts

Carl Maldoner, 1914
Oil on canvas, 25¼ × 20 (64.1 × 50.8)
Collection of Mr. and Mrs. William F. Reighley

The Sketchers, 1914
Oil on canvas, 22 × 28 (55.9 × 71.1)
Virginia Museum of Fine Arts, Richmond; The Arthur and Margaret Glasgow Endowment Fund

Tyrolese Crucifix, 1914
Oil on canvas, 36 × 28 (91.4 × 71.1)
Private collection

Lake O'Hara, 1916
Oil on canvas, 37¼ × 44 (94.6 × 111.8)
Harvard University Art Museums, Fogg Art Museum, Cambridge, Massachusetts; Louise G. Bettens Fund

The Artist Sketching, 1922
Oil on canvas, 22 × 28 (55.9 × 71.1)
Private collection; on loan to the Museum of Art, Rhode Island School of Design, Providence

WORKS ON PAPER

Engelsburg, 1872
Black chalk and pencil on paper,
10⅝ × 14¼ (27 × 36.2)
Trustees of the British Museum, London;
Presented by Mrs. Ormond

Deer, c. 1872–74
Pencil on paper, 11⅜ × 15³⁄₁₆ (28.9 × 38.6)
Worcester Art Museum, Massachusetts

Bartholomy Magagnosco, c. 1875
Pencil on paper, 10 × 7¾ (25.4 × 19.7)
Philadelphia Museum of Art; Gift of Miss
Emily Sargent and Mrs. Francis Ormond

Figure in Costume, c. 1875–76
(inscribed 1869)
Watercolor on paper, 14 × 19⅞
(35.6 × 50.5)
The Metropolitan Museum of Art, New
York; Gift of Mrs. Francis Ormond, 1950

The Model, c. 1876
Watercolor and pencil on paper,
11¹¹⁄₁₆ × 9¹⁄₁₆ (29.7 × 23)
Museum of Fine Arts, Houston; Gift of
Miss Ima Hogg

†*Young Woman with Black Skirt*, c. 1876–82
Watercolor on paper, 14 × 9⅞ (35.6 × 25.1)
The Metropolitan Museum of Art, New
York; Gift of Mrs. Francis Ormond, 1950

Study for *El Jaleo*, c. 1879–82
Charcoal on paper, no. 6 in Venetian
scrapbook, 9½ × 13 (24.1 × 33)
Isabella Stewart Gardner Museum, Boston

Study for *El Jaleo*, c. 1879–82
Charcoal on paper, no. 8 in Venetian
scrapbook, 9⅜ × 13⅞ (23.8 × 35.2)
Isabella Stewart Gardner Museum, Boston

Study for *El Jaleo*, c. 1879–82
Charcoal on paper, no. 12 in Venetian
scrapbook, 13½ × 9¼ (34.3 × 23.5)
Isabella Stewart Gardner Museum, Boston

Study for *El Jaleo*, c. 1879–82
Charcoal on paper, no. 13 in Venetian
scrapbook, 9½ × 13 (24.1 × 33)
Isabella Stewart Gardner Museum, Boston

Campo dei Frari, Venice, c. 1880
Watercolor and pencil with gouache on
paper, 9⅞ × 14 (25.1 × 35.6)
Corcoran Gallery of Art, Washington,
D.C.; Bequest of Mrs. Mabel Stevens Smithers

A Moorish Patio, c. 1880
Watercolor and pencil on paper,
9¾ × 13½ (24.8 × 34.3)
Trustees of the British Museum, London;
Presented by Mrs. Ormond

Bedroom, c. 1880–82
Watercolor on paper, 11⅛ × 8 (28.3 × 20.3)
Private collection

†*Venice*, c. 1880–82
Watercolor on paper, 9⅞ × 13¹³⁄₁₆
(25.1 × 35.1)
The Metropolitan Museum of Art, New
York; Gift of Mrs. Francis Ormond, 1950

Study for *El Jaleo*, 1882
Watercolor on paper, 11¾ × 7⅞ (29.8 × 20)
Dallas Museum of Fine Arts; Foundation
for the Arts Collection, Gift of Mr. and
Mrs. George V. Chariton in memory of
Eugene McDermott

†Study for *El Jaleo*, 1882
Pencil on paper, 9½ × 7¼ (24.1 × 18.4)
Collection of Dr. and Mrs. William
Hayden

Study for *Madame X (Madame Pierre
Gautreau)*, c. 1883
Pencil on paper, 12¾ × 9⅜ (32.4 × 23.8)
Private collection; lent through the
courtesy of Hirschl & Adler Galleries,
New York

Study for *Madame X (Madame Pierre
Gautreau)*, c. 1883
Pencil on paper, 11½ × 8¼ (29.2 × 21)
Collection of Mr. and Mrs. Jean-Marie
Eveillard

Study for *Madame X (Madame Pierre
Gautreau)*, c. 1883
Pencil on paper, 9¾ × 13³⁄₁₆ (24.8 × 33.5)
The Metropolitan Museum of Art, New
York; Purchase, Charles and Anita Blatt
Fund, John Wilmerding Gift, Rogers
Fund, 1970

*Two studies for *Madame X (Madame Pierre
Gautreau)*, c. 1883
Pencil on paper, 9⅝ × 13⅜ (24.4 × 34)
Trustees of the British Museum, London;
Presented by Mrs. Ormond

Dorothy Barnard (study for *Carnation, Lily,
Lily, Rose*), 1885–86
Pencil on paper, 9¾ × 8¼ (24.8 × 21)
The Tate Gallery, London; Bequeathed
by Miss Dorothy Barnard, 1949

Polly Barnard (study for *Carnation, Lily,
Lily, Rose*), 1885–86
Pencil on paper, 11 × 9¼ (27.9 × 23.5)
The Tate Gallery, London; Bequeathed
by Miss Dorothy Barnard, 1949

Jack Millet as a Baby, 1888
Pencil on paper, 5½ × 9¼ (14 × 23.5)
Syndics of the Fitzwilliam Museum,
Cambridge, England

Vernon Lee (Violet Paget), 1889
Pencil on paper, 13¼ × 9 (33.7 × 22.9)
Ashmolean Museum, Oxford

Paul Helleu Lying in a Field, c. 1889
Pastel on paper, 10¼ × 14⅞ (26 × 37.8)
Trustees of the British Museum, London;
Presented by Mrs. Ormond and Miss
Sargent

Preliminary drapery study for *Frieze of the
Prophets*, c. 1891–92
Charcoal heightened with white chalk on
paper, 24⅜ × 18¹¹⁄₁₆ (61.9 × 47.5)
Corcoran Gallery of Art, Washington,
D.C.

Man Screaming (study for *Hell*),
c. 1895–1910
Charcoal and pencil on paper, 24⅜ × 18¾
(61.9 × 47.6)
Corcoran Gallery of Art, Washington,
D.C.

A Tramp, after 1900
Watercolor on paper, 19¹¹⁄₁₆ × 13³⁄₁₆
(50 × 33.5)
The Brooklyn Museum, New York;
Purchased by Special Subscription

*View from a Window at Genoa, after 1900
Pencil, watercolor, and oil on paper,
15¾ × 20¾ (40 × 52.7)
Trustees of the British Museum, London;
Presented by Mrs. Ormond

Mrs. Charles Hunter, c. 1902
Charcoal on paper, 23½ × 18½ (59.7 × 47)
Memorial Art Gallery of the University of
Rochester, New York; Gift of James O.
Belden in memory of Evelyn Berry Belden

†Spanish Soldiers, c. 1902–03
Watercolor and pencil on paper,
12 × 18 (30.5 × 45.7)
The Brooklyn Museum, New York;
Purchased by Special Subscription

*Spanish Soldiers, c. 1902–03
Watercolor on paper, 18¹⁄₁₆ × 12¹⁄₁₆
(45.9 × 30.6)
The Brooklyn Museum, New York;
Purchased by Special Subscription

*Mountain Fire, c. 1903–08
Watercolor on paper, 14 × 20 (35.6 × 50.8)
The Brooklyn Museum, New York;
Purchased by Special Subscription

*Santa Maria della Salute, 1904
Watercolor and pencil heightened with
white on paper, 18⅛ × 23 (46 × 58.4)
The Brooklyn Museum, New York;
Purchased by Special Subscription

Sketching on the Giudecca, Venice, c. 1904
Watercolor and gouache on paper,
14 × 20¾ (35.6 × 52.7)
Private collection

†Bedouin Mother, 1905
Watercolor on paper, 18¹⁄₁₆ × 12
(45.9 × 30.5)
The Brooklyn Museum, New York;
Purchased by Special Subscription

*Arab Gypsies in a Tent, c. 1905–06
Watercolor heightened with white on
paper, 12 × 18 (30.5 × 45.7)
The Brooklyn Museum, New York;
Purchased by Special Subscription

†Bedouin Women, c. 1905–06
Watercolor heightened with white on
paper, 12 × 18¹⁄₁₆ (30.5 × 45.9)
The Brooklyn Museum, New York;
Purchased by Special Subscription

*Bedouins, c. 1905–06
Watercolor on paper, 18 × 12 (45.7 × 30.5)
The Brooklyn Museum, New York;
Purchased by Special Subscription

†In a Levantine Port, c. 1905–06
Watercolor and pencil on paper,
12¹⁄₁₆ × 18⅛ (30.6 × 46)
The Brooklyn Museum, New York;
Purchased by Special Subscription

†Bridge of Sighs, c. 1905–08
Watercolor heightened with white on
paper, 10 × 14 (25.4 × 35.6)
The Brooklyn Museum, New York;
Purchased by Special Subscription

†From the Gondola, c. 1905–08
Watercolor and pencil on paper, 10 × 14
(25.4 × 35.6)
The Brooklyn Museum, New York;
Purchased by Special Subscription

†Gourds, c. 1905–08
Watercolor on paper, 14 × 20 (35.6 × 50.8)
The Brooklyn Museum, New York;
Purchased by Special Subscription

Mrs. George Swinton, 1906
Charcoal on paper, 24 × 18¾ (61 × 47.6)
Private collection

Doorway of a Venetian Palace, c. 1906–10
Watercolor on paper, 23 × 18 (58.4 × 45.7)
Westmoreland Museum of Art,
Greensburg, Pennsylvania

The Library in Venice, c. 1906–10
Watercolor and pencil with gouache on
paper, 22⅛ × 17¾ (56.2 × 45.1)
National Gallery of Art, Washington,
D.C.; Ailsa Mellon Bruce Collection

Piazza Navona, Rome, 1907
Watercolor and sepia ink on paper,
20¾ × 16½ (52.7 × 41.9)
Collection of Erving and Joyce Wolf

A Turkish Woman by a Stream, c. 1907
Watercolor and gouache on paper,
14⅛ × 20 (35.9 × 50.8)
Victoria and Albert Museum, London

*Pomegranates, 1908
Watercolor and pencil on paper,
21³⁄₁₆ × 14⁷⁄₁₆ (53.8 × 36.7)
The Brooklyn Museum, New York;
Purchased by Special Subscription

William Butler Yeats, 1908
Charcoal on paper, 24½ × 18½ (62.2 × 47)
Private collection

Oxen in Repose, c. 1908
Watercolor on paper, 13½ × 20 (34.3 × 50.8)
Collection of the Ormond Family

Villa di Marlia, Lucca, c. 1910
Watercolor on paper, 15¾ × 20¾ (40 × 52.7)
Museum of Fine Arts, Boston; The
Hayden Collection

Oxen, 1911
Pencil on paper, 10 × 14 (25.4 × 35.6)
Philadelphia Museum of Art; Gift of Miss
Emily Sargent and Mrs. Francis Ormond

Reading, 1911
Watercolor and gouache on paper, 20 × 14
(50.8 × 35.6)
Museum of Fine Arts, Boston; The
Hayden Collection

Simplon Pass: Avalanche Track, 1911
Watercolor on paper, 13 × 20½ (33 × 52.1)
Museum of Fine Arts, Boston; The
Hayden Collection

Simplon Pass: The Lesson, 1911
Watercolor on paper, 15 × 18¼ (38.1 × 46.4)
Museum of Fine Arts, Boston; The
Hayden Collection

Simplon Pass: The Tease, 1911
Watercolor on paper, 15¾ × 20¾ (40 × 52.7)
Museum of Fine Arts, Boston; The
Hayden Collection

Vaslav Nijinsky in Le Pavillon d'Armide, 1911
Charcoal on paper, 24¹⁄₁₆ × 18⅝
(61.1 × 47.3)
Bohemian Club, San Francisco

Carrara: Lizzatori I, c. 1911
Watercolor on paper, $20\frac{7}{8} \times 15\frac{13}{16}$
(53×40.2)
Museum of Fine Arts, Boston; The
Hayden Collection

Carrara: Trajan's Quarry, c. 1911
Watercolor on paper, $15\frac{13}{16} \times 20\frac{15}{16}$
(40.2×53.2)
Museum of Fine Arts, Boston; The
Hayden Collection

Simplon Pass: Mountain Brook, c. 1911
Watercolor on paper, $14 \times 19\frac{7}{8}$
(35.6×50.5)
Museum of Fine Arts, Boston; The
Hayden Collection

†*Workmen at Carrara*, c. 1911
Watercolor and pencil on paper,
$15\frac{1}{2} \times 20\frac{1}{2}$ (39.4×52.1)
The Art Institute of Chicago; Olivia
Shaler Swan Collection

Young Girl Wearing a Bonnet, c. 1911
Watercolor on paper, $6 \times 4\frac{1}{2}$ (15.2×11.4)
Private collection

Blind Musicians, 1912
Watercolor on paper, $15\frac{1}{2} \times 21$
(39.4×53.3)
Aberdeen Art Gallery and Museums,
Scotland

†*Spanish Fountain*, 1912
Watercolor and gouache on paper,
$21 \times 13\frac{3}{4}$ (53.3×34.9)
Syndics of the Fitzwilliam Museum,
Cambridge, England

Gertrude Vanderbilt Whitney, 1914
Charcoal and pencil on paper,
26×20 (66×50.8)
Collection of Flora Whitney Miller

Camping at Lake O'Hara, 1916
Watercolor on paper, $15\frac{3}{4} \times 20\frac{7}{8}$ (40×53)
The Newark Museum, New Jersey

Three Alligators, 1916
Pencil on paper, 7×10 (17.8×25.4)
Worcester Art Museum, Massachusetts;
Gift of Mrs. Francis Ormond and Miss
Emily Sargent

Two Alligators, 1916
Pencil on paper, 7×10 (17.8×25.4)
Worcester Art Museum, Massachusetts;
Gift of Mrs. Francis Ormond and Miss
Emily Sargent

Palmettos, 1917
Watercolor on paper, $13\frac{1}{2} \times 18$
(34.3×45.7)
Collection of the Ormond Family

Camouflaged Tanks, Berles-au-Bois, 1918
Watercolor on paper, $13\frac{3}{8} \times 20\frac{9}{16}$
(34×52.3)
The Trustees of the Imperial War
Museum, London

Heads, Hands, and Figure (studies for
Gassed), 1918
Charcoal on paper, $18\frac{5}{8} \times 24\frac{1}{4}$
(47.3×61.6)
Corcoran Gallery of Art, Washington,
D.C.; Gift of Miss Emily Sargent and Mrs.
Violet Sargent Ormond

Henry Tonks, 1918
Pencil and ink on paper, $9\frac{3}{4} \times 14\frac{5}{8}$
(24.8×37.1)
Syndics of the Fitzwilliam Museum,
Cambridge, England

†*Highlanders Resting at the Front*, 1918
Watercolor and pencil on paper,
$13\frac{1}{2} \times 21\frac{1}{4}$ (34.3×54)
Syndics of the Fitzwilliam Museum,
Cambridge, England

The Interior of a Hospital Tent, 1918
Watercolor on paper, $15\frac{3}{16} \times 20\frac{7}{16}$
(38.5×51.9)
The Trustees of the Imperial War
Museum, London

A Street in Arras, 1918
Watercolor on paper, $15\frac{3}{16} \times 20\frac{11}{16}$
(38.5×52.5)
The Trustees of the Imperial War
Museum, London

Thou Shalt Not Steal, 1918
Watercolor on paper, $20\frac{3}{4} \times 13\frac{1}{4}$
(52.7×33.6)
The Trustees of the Imperial War
Museum, London

Alice Runnels James (Mrs. William James), 1921
Watercolor on paper, $21\frac{1}{8} \times 13\frac{1}{2}$ (53.7×34.3)
Museum of Fine Arts, Boston; Gift of
William James, 1977

Crescenzo Fusciardi, n.d.
Charcoal on paper, $24 \times 18\frac{1}{4}$ (61×46.4)
Harvard University Art Museums, Fogg
Art Museum, Cambridge, Massachusetts;
Gift of Mrs. Francis Ormond

*Figure with Red Drapery, n.d.
Watercolor on paper, $14\frac{1}{2} \times 21\frac{13}{16}$ (36.8×55.4)
The Metropolitan Museum of Art, New
York; Gift of Mrs. Francis Ormond, 1950

†*Italian Model*, n.d.
Watercolor on paper, $14\frac{1}{2} \times 22$ (36.8×55.9)
The Metropolitan Museum of Art, New
York; Gift of Mrs. Francis Ormond, 1950

Kneeling Model, n.d.
Charcoal on paper, $24 \times 18\frac{1}{2}$ (61×47)
Harvard University Art Museums, Fogg
Art Museum, Cambridge, Massachusetts;
Gift of Mrs. Francis Ormond

Male Nude Seen from Behind, n.d.
Charcoal on paper, $24\frac{1}{2} \times 18\frac{3}{4}$ (62.2×47.6)
Harvard University Art Museums, Fogg
Art Museum, Cambridge, Massachusetts;
Gift of Mrs. Francis Ormond

Reclining Nude, n.d.
Charcoal on paper, $24\frac{1}{2} \times 18\frac{3}{4}$ (62.2×47.6)
Harvard University Art Museums, Fogg
Art Museum, Cambridge, Massachusetts;
Gift of Mrs. Francis Ormond

Seated Model with Drapery, n.d.
Charcoal on paper, $24\frac{1}{2} \times 17\frac{1}{8}$ (62.2×43.5)
Harvard University Art Museums, Fogg
Art Museum, Cambridge, Massachusetts;
Gift of Mrs. Francis Ormond

Studies of a Nude Youth, n.d.
Charcoal on paper, $18\frac{7}{8} \times 25$ (47.9×63.5)
Harvard University Art Museums, Fogg
Art Museum, Cambridge, Massachusetts;
Gift of Mrs. Francis Ormond

Torsos of Two Male Nudes, n.d.
Charcoal on paper, 48×63 (121.9×160)
Yale University Art Gallery, New Haven; Gift of
Miss Emily Sargent and Mrs. Francis Ormond

Index

Abbey, Edwin Austin, 21–22, 112, 113, 182, 216, 244 n. 12, 262, 265–66
Ada Rehan, 148, 154
Albanian Olive Gatherers, Fig. 150
Alberto Falchetti, 178; Fig. 130
Alice Runnels James (Mrs. William James), 215; Fig. 212
All'Ave Maria, 228, 246 n. 33
Alpine Pool, 191; Fig. 145
Arab Gypsies in a Tent, 225; Fig. 181
Aranjuez, 246 n. 33
Arnold, Matthew, 33–35
The Artist Sketching, 203; Fig. 165
Asher Wertheimer, 148, 174; Fig. 116
Astarte, see Pagan Deities: Astarte and Neith
Aurier, Albert, 36
Autumn on the River (Miss Violet Sargent), Fig. 85
Avegno, Anatole Placide, 88
Avegno, Marie Virginie de Ternant, 88

Bacher, Otto, 54, 72 n. 22
A Backwater, Calcot Mill near Reading, 122; Fig. 78
Baignères, Arthur, 150
Balfour, Alfred, 97
Barnard, Dorothy, 113, 116, 183, 186, 195; Fig. 220
Barnard, Polly, 113, 116, 183, 186, 195, 221, 224; Fig. 221
Bartholomy Magagnosco, Fig. 217
Bathers, 234; Fig. 201
The Bead Stringers of Venice, 55, 70; Fig. 31
Beatrice Goelet, 148, 151, 159
Beaux, Cecilia, 177
Bechstein, Friedrich, 69–70
Beckwith, J. Carroll, 25 nn. 13, 14; 29, 70
A Bedouin Arab, 182; Fig. 137
Bedouins, 225; Fig. 180
Bedroom, 225; Fig. 172
Bell, Clive, 177
Bell, Malcolm, 151
Belleroche, Albert de, 182
Bennington, Mrs. Claude, 270
Blaas, Eugène de, 64
Blaney, Dwight, 203; Fig. 165
Blashfield, Edwin, 115, 117, 118

Blind Musicians, Fig. 196
Blond Model, 28; Fig. 2
Blum, Robert, 50, 64; Fig. 22
A Boating Party, 128–29; Fig. 88
Boats, 232
Boit, Edward D., 248 n. 48
Boldini, Giovanni, 58, 176, 177, 213–14, 247 n. 38; Fig. 111
Bolton, Charles Knowles, 270
Bourget, Paul, 76, 93, 95
Boys on the Beach (Innocents Abroad), Fig. 8
Brabazon, Hercules, 216–17, 219
Bramley, Frank, 118, 137; Fig. 91
Breakfast in the Loggia, Fig. 142
Brimmer, Martin, 67
Bringing Down Marble from the Quarries to Carrara, 198; Fig. 151
Brinton, Christian, 147, 148, 151, 170
The Brook, 186, 224; Fig. 144
Brown, Gerard Baldwin, 36
Bunker, Dennis Miller, 123–24, 131, 134; Fig. 81
Burne-Jones, Edward, 76, 104, 170
By the River, 122

Caffin, Charles H., 43, 148, 150, 174, 176, 177, 207 n. 27
Camouflaged Tanks, Berles-au-Bois, 273; Fig. 210
Camping at Lake O'Hara, 199, 232; Fig. 205
Campo Behind the Scuola di San Rocco, Venice, 63; Fig. 42
Campo dei Frari, Venice, 214; Fig. 174
Capri, Boston, 29, 31; Fig. 10; Warner Collection, 31–32; Fig. 12
Carl Maldoner, Fig. 131
La Carmencita, 144 n. 49, 159; Fig. 106
Carnation, Lily, Lily, Rose, 81, 100, 112–17, 118–19, 131, 137, 138, 186, 224; Figs. 72, 220, 221
Carolus-Duran, Émile Auguste, 17, 18, 20, 27, 28, 64, 81–83, 108 n. 35, 111, 147, 148, 150, 210, 253, 256; Figs. 4, 51
Carolus-Duran, 27, 82–83, 149; Figs. 4, 51
Carrara, Lizzatori I, Fig. 194
Carrara: Trajan's Quarry, 231; Fig. 193
Catherine Vlasto, 174; Fig. 113
Cazin, Jean, 70, 72 n. 12

Chaplin, Charles, 107 n. 35; Fig. 57
Charles Stuart Forbes, 178; Fig. 129
Charles Stewart, Sixth Marquess of Londonderry, 174; Fig. 124
Charlotte Louise Burckhardt, see Lady with the Rose
Chase, William Merritt, 134, 176
The Chess Game, 186, 224; Fig. 143
Church of St. Stäe, Venice, 198–99; Fig. 157
Classical and Romantic Art, 283
Claude Monet Painting at the Edge of a Wood, 119–21, 124; Fig. 77
Coffin, William A., 42–43
Comyns Carr, Alice, 76, 104
Comyns Carr, J., 76, 104
Coquelin, Benoît-Constant, 69
Cortissoz, Royal, 69, 138, 234, 236
Courtois, Gustave, 163
Cox, Kenyon, 207 n. 18
Crescenzo Fusciardi, 266; Fig. 234
Currier, J. Frank, 71 n. 8
Curtis, Daniel Sargent, 49
Curtis, Mrs. Daniel Sargent, 73 n. 54; Fig. 40
Curtis, Ralph, 29, 56, 71 n. 8; Fig. 11
Curzon, George Nathaniel, 97
Cushman, Charlotte, 16

The Daughters of Edward D. Boit, 63, 79, 112, 149; Fig. 48
Deer, Fig. 216
Deering, Charles, 233
Dennis Miller Bunker Painting at Calcot, 123–24, 131; Fig. 81
Dewing, Thomas, 138
A Dinner Table at Night, Fig. 62
Dolce Far Niente, 186, 247 n. 38
Doorway of a Venetian Palace, Fig. 184
Dorothy Barnard, 259; Fig. 220
Dr. FitzWilliam Sargent, 16
Dr. Pozzi at Home, 85–86, 148, 150; Fig. 55
Duez, Ernest-Ange, 212
Duveneck, Frank, 64, 72 n. 24

Edith, Lady Playfair, 98, 102, 150; Fig. 65
Edmund Gosse, Fig. 20
Edouard Pailleron, 83; Figs. 5, 52
Edward VII (Prince of Wales), 97, 104
Egyptian Woman with Earrings, 182

Egyptians Raising Water from the Nile, 181;
  Fig. 138
El Greco, 249 n. 55
El Jaleo, 39–40, 51, 79, 181, 194, 212, 259;
  Figs. 14, 15, 175, 222–225
Elcho, Lord and Lady, 97
*Elizabeth Allen Marquand (Mrs. Henry G.
  Marquand)*, 22, 23, 102, 152; Fig. 102
Ellen Terry as Lady Macbeth, 102; Fig. 67
Emily Sargent, 17
*Ena and Betty, Daughters of Mr. and Mrs.
  Wertheimer*, 174; Fig. 117
Engelsburg, 253; Fig. 215
The Escutcheon of Charles V, 232
Ethel Smyth, 269; Fig. 246
Eugene Carriers, Fig. 70

Falguière, Alexandre, 108 n. 35; Fig. 56
Farquharson, Joseph, 253
Favretto, Giacomo, 64
Ferrara, Rosina, 29, 31
Fête Familiale: The Birthday Party, Fig. 63
Figure in Costume, 212; Fig. 169
Figure of a Child, 256; Fig. 219
Figure with Red Drapery, Fig. 211
Fildes, Luke, 64, 71 n. 5, 177
Flaubert, Gustave, 95
Forbes, Edward W., 199
Forbes-Robertson, John, 40
Fortuny, Mariano, 64
The Fountain, Villa Torlonia, Frascati, Italy,
  191–93; Fig. 149
Fourcaud, Louis de, 89–92
The Four Doctors, 174, 183; Fig. 121
Fox, Thomas A., 273
Frances Sherburne Ridley Watts, 27, 149; Fig. 1
François Flameng and Paul Helleu, Fig. 128
Frieseke, Frederick, 138
From the Gondola, 228; Fig. 183
Fry, Roger, 36, 137, 177
Fumée d'Ambre Gris, 50, 63, 79, 84–85, 86;
  Figs. 50, 68

Gainsborough, Thomas, 174; Fig. 126
A Game of Bowls, Ightham Mote, Kent, 279
Garden Sketch, 132
Garden Study of the Vickers Children, 112, 224;
  Fig. 74
Gardner, Isabella Stewart, 141 n. 39, 199;
  Fig. 59
Gassed, 240, 273; Figs. 253, 254, 256
Gautier, Judith, Fig. 176
Gautreau, Virginie, 79, 86, 88–93, 96;
  Figs. 47, 58, 226–229

George Henschel, Fig. 71
Gertrude Vanderbilt Whitney, 276
Gigia Viani, Fig. 38
Giudecca, 232, 245 n. 16
Glehn, Jane Emmet von, 137, 182, 183–84,
  186, 191, 195, 197, 232; Fig. 148
Glehn, Wilfrid von, 137, 182, 184, 186, 191,
  195, 244 n. 12
Gordon Fairchild, 159
Gordon Greenough, 256; Fig. 218
Gosse, Edmund, 39, 76, 97, 100, 114, 116;
  Fig. 20
Gourds, Fig. 192
Group of Spanish Convalescent Soldiers, 246 n. 35
Group with Parasols (A Siesta), 203; Fig. 162
Gypsy Encampment, Fig. 153

Hale, Mary Newbold Patterson, 195, 202
Hale, Philip Leslie, 138
Hals, Frans, 28, 73 n. 34, 149
Harrison, Peter, 141 n. 33, 195
Harrison, Mr. and Mrs. Robert, 122
Hassam, Childe, 138; Fig. 93
Healy, A. Augustus, 246 n. 35, 247 n. 38
Hell, 269; Figs. 243, 255
Helleu, Alice Louise Guérin, 128–31; Fig. 89
Helleu, Paul-César, 29, 128–31, 134, 176,
  244 n. 12, 247 n. 38; Figs. 89, 232, 233
Henry James, Fig. 133
Henry Tonks, 272–73; Fig. 252
Henschel, George, 104, 121; Fig. 71
The Hermit (Il Solitario), 193–95; Fig. 146
Highlanders Resting at the Front, 273; Fig. 209
Hinckley, Robert C., 17, 25 n. 14
Home Fields, 117, 139 n. 17; Fig. 75
Homer, Winslow, 233–34; Fig. 202
Hoschedé, Suzanne, 120, 121, 123, 136;
  Fig. 87
Hoschedé-Monet, Blanche, 136; Fig. 87
Hosmer, Harriet, 16
A Hotel Room, Fig. 134
Huysmans, Joris-Karl, 77, 85

Idle Sails, 232
In a Levantine Port, 226, 228; Fig. 189
Incensing the Veil, 85, 86
An Interior in Venice, 70; Fig. 44
The Interior of a Hospital Tent, 240, 273;
  Fig. 207
In the Generalife, 232
In the Luxembourg Gardens, 31–32, 117; Fig. 17
Ingres, Jean-Auguste-Dominique, 249 n. 47
Inverno, Nicola d', 42, 195, 199, 266
Irving, Henry, 104

Isabella Stewart Gardner (1888), 93, 95, 152;
  Fig. 59; (1922), 215
Isham, Samuel, 66, 68
Italian Girl with Fan, 59, 62, 63, 72 n. 24;
  Fig. 39
Italian Model with Cope, 244 n. 11

Jack Millet as a Baby, 259, 262; Fig. 230
James, Henry, 16, 22, 23, 33, 50, 64, 73 n. 39,
  75, 76–77, 79–81, 84, 85, 97, 105,
  108 n. 35, 112, 141 n. 36, 151, 152, 162,
  226; Fig. 133
Jane de Glehn in Corfu (In the Garden, Corfu),
  193; Fig. 148
John, Augustus, 244 n. 12
Judith Gautier, 215, 224; Fig. 176

Khnopff, Fernand, 170
Kneeling Model, 266; Fig. 214

Lady Agnew of Lochnaw, 154, 162; Fig. 110
Lady and Boy Asleep in a Punt under a Willow,
  121
Lady Fishing—Mrs. Ormond, 127; Fig. 83
Lady Warwick and Her Son, 249 n. 57
Lady with the Rose (Charlotte Louise Burckhardt),
  63, 148, 149, 151, 159; Fig. 98
Lake O'Hara, 202; Fig. 156
Langtry, Lillie, 88, 97, 104
Latimer, Ralph, 72 n. 31
Lavery, John, 177
Lawless, Valentine, 70
Laszlo, Philip de, 177
Lee, Vernon, 33, 35, 76, 79, 88, 95, 122, 151,
  209; Figs. 19, 231
Lewis, George Henry, 104
Lewis, Mrs. George Henry, 104, 182
The Library in Venice, Fig. 185
Logsdail, William, 64
Lord Ribblesdale, 104; Fig. 66
Low, Will, 20, 25 n. 14, 254, 256

Madame Edouard Pailleron, 27, 54–55, 63,
  83–84, 112, 148, 149; Fig. 3
Madame Paul Poirson, 150; Fig. 100
Madame Pierre Gautreau, see *Madame X*
Madame Ramón Subercaseaux, 63
Madame X (Madame Pierre Gautreau), 75, 86,
  88–93, 96, 112, 147, 149, 151, 154, 163,
  215, 249 n. 55, 259; Figs. 47, 58,
  226–229
Male Nude Seen from Behind, 266; Fig. 240
Male Nudes Wrestling, 269; Fig. 244
Mancini, Antonio, 213–14

A Marble Fountain at Aranjuez, Spain, Fig. 158
The Marlborough Family, 102, 104, 174;
    Fig. 120
Mazzinghi, Joseph, 116
McKim, Charles, 265
Millet, Frank, 21–22, 113–14, 117, 118, 216,
    245 n. 14, 259
Millet, Kate, 113
Millet, Lucia, 116, 118, 139 n. 15
Millet's Garden, 117; Fig. 76
Millicent, Duchess of Sutherland, 174; Fig. 123
Miss Elsie Palmer, 162; Fig. 105
Miss Helen Dunham, 174; Fig. 109
The Misses Vickers, 98, 150, 159; Fig. 61
The Model, 212; Fig. 170
Monet, Claude, 40, 81, 111, 118, 119–21, 123,
    126, 128, 134, 135–36, 145 n. 50,
    244 n. 12, 248 n. 41; Figs. 77, 86, 87
Montesquiou, Robert de, 33, 75–77, 85, 86,
    96, 105
A Moorish Patio, Fig. 173
A Morning Walk, 123, 126, 127, 134,
    141 n. 28; Fig. 80
Mountain Fire, 288; Fig. 213
The Mountains of Moab, 183
Mountain Stream, 232
Mr. and Mrs. I. N. Phelps Stokes, 174; Fig. 115
Mr. and Mrs. John W. Field, 159; Fig. 107
Mrs. Adrian Iselin, 154; Fig. 104
Mrs. Carl Meyer and Her Children, 167, 170,
    174, 177; Fig. 114
Mrs. Charles Gifford Dyer, 63; Fig. 41
Mrs. Charles Hunter, 269, 270; Fig. 245
Mrs. Charles Inches, 68
Mrs. Charles Thursby, 154, 170, 174; Fig. 119
Mrs. Daniel Sargent Curtis, 63; Fig. 40
Mrs. Edward D. Boit, 152, 174, 177; Fig. 103
Mrs. Edward L. Davis and Her Son Livingston,
    159; Fig. 97
Mrs. Elliott Fitch Shepard, 155
*Mrs. FitzWilliam Sargent (Mary Newbold
    Singer)*, 16
Mrs. George Swinton, 167, 269, 270–71;
    Figs. 118, 247
Mrs. Henry G. Marquand, see Elizabeth Allen
    Marquand
Mrs. Henry White, 97, 98, 148, 150; Fig. 64
Mrs. Hugh Hammersley, 177; Fig. 127
Mrs. Kate A. Moore, 174; Fig. 101
Mrs. Robert Harrison, 98, 151
Mrs. Thomas Wodehouse Legh, 98
Mrs. Wilfrid von Glehn, 246 n. 35
Mrs. William James, see Alice Runnels James

Muddy Alligators, Fig. 204
Muleteria, Fig. 147

Nadar, Charles, Fig. 54
Naya, Carlo, 66; Fig. 46
Near the Mount of Olives, 183; Fig. 139
Nittis, Giuseppe de, 32; Fig. 18

The Old Chair, Fig. 96
Olive Trees at Corfu, Fig. 152
Ormond, Rose-Marie, 186
Ormond, Violet Sargent, 14, 15, 122, 123,
    127–29, 135, 138, 158, 181, 183, 184,
    273; Figs. 83–85
Osborne, Walter, 137; Fig. 90
An Out-of-Doors Study, see Paul Helleu Sketching
    with His Wife
Oxen, 272; Fig. 250
Oxen in Repose, Fig. 190
Oxen Resting, Fig. 154
The Oyster Gatherers of Cancale, Boston, 28;
    Fig. 7; Washington, 27, 28–29; Fig. 9

Pagan Deities: Astarte and Neith, 95; Fig. 60
Paget, Violet, see Lee, Vernon
*The Pailleron Children (Edouard and
    Marie-Louise)*, 149; Fig. 6
Pailleron, Edouard, 83, 108 n. 35; Figs. 5, 52
Pailleron, Mme. Edouard, 83–84; Fig. 3
Palazzo Labia and San Geremia, Venice, 199;
    Fig. 159
Palmer, Walter Launt, 25 n. 12, 244 n. 4, 253
Palmettos, 236; Fig. 203
Parsons, Alfred, 118, 122, 216, 245 n. 14
Pater, Walter, 97
Paul Helleu, 262; Fig. 232
Paul Helleu Lying in a Field, 262; Fig. 233
Paul Helleu Sketching with His Wife, 81, 130–32,
    134, 138, 143 n. 46, 247 n. 38; Fig. 89
The Pavement, 64; Fig. 43
Pennington, Harper, 177
Perdican, 93, 107 nn. 23, 31, 35, 108 nn. 37–39
Piazza Navona, Rome, Fig. 188
The Plains of Esdraelon, 183; Fig. 136
Playfair, William, 104
Polly Barnard, 259; Fig. 221
Pomegranates, 240; Fig. 191
Pomegranates, Majorca, 249 n. 65, 281
*Portrait of a Boy (Homer Saint-Gaudens and His
    Mother)*, 144 n. 50, 159; Fig. 108
Portuguese Boats, 246 n. 33
Pozzi, Samuel Jean, 75, 85–86; Figs. 54, 55
Pratt, Frederick S., 233

Prendergast, Maurice, 72 n. 24
Priestley, Flora, 122, 141 n. 35

Quilter, Harry, 118

Ralph Curtis on the Beach at Scheveningen,
    Fig. 11
Reading, 202; Fig. 199
Reclining Nude, 266; Fig. 238
*Rehearsal of the Pas de Loup Orchestra at the
    Cirque d'Hiver*, 31; Fig. 16
Rennell Rodd, James, 76
Reubell, Henrietta, 76
Ribblesdale, Lord, 97, 104; Fig. 66
La Riva, 229, 246 n. 33; Fig. 182
Robert Louis Stevenson and His Wife, Fig. 49
Robertson, W. Graham, 76, 104; Fig. 69
Robinson, Edward, 194, 231–32
Robinson, Theodore, 134, 138
Rockefeller, John D., 233
Roger-Jourdain, Joseph, 212
Rogers, Randolph, 16
Ruskin, John, 35, 38–39, 69
Russell, John, 150

St. Martin's Summer, 122–23, 126; Fig. 79
Sally Fairchild, 132; Fig. 95
The Salute, Venice, 248 n. 46
Santa Maria della Salute, 229; Fig. 186
Sargent, Emily, 14, 17, 19, 49, 181, 183, 219,
    232, 256, 273
Sargent, FitzWilliam, 13–17, 19, 20, 21, 24,
    81, 126, 251
Sargent, Mary Newbold Singer, 13–17, 19,
    81, 181, 183, 209, 251, 256
Sargent, Violet, see Ormond, Violet Sargent
Sassoon, Aline, 97
Seated Model with Drapery, 266; Fig. 237
Self-Portrait, Aberdeen, frontispiece;
    Florence, Fig. 132
Sickert, Walter, 138, 162
Simplon Pass, Fig. 163
Simplon Pass: At the Top, 203; Fig. 160
Simplon Pass: Mountain Brook, 202–03; Fig. 164
Simplon Pass: The Lesson, Fig. 200
Simplon Pass: The Tease, Fig. 198
Sir Frank Swettenham, 174; Fig. 122
Sirmione, 232
Sitwell, George, 105
Sitwell, Osbert, 102
The Sketchers, Richmond, 137, 203; Fig. 161;
    whereabouts unknown, 246 n. 35
Sketching on the Giudecca, Venice, Fig. 187

Sortie de l'Église, 63, 67

Spanish Fountain, Cambridge, 232; Fig. 177; New York, 232

Spanish Madonna, 85; Fig. 53

Spanish Soldiers, Brooklyn, 225, 246 nn. 33, 35; Fig. 178; whereabouts unknown, 246 n. 35

Spitzer, Baron, 108 n. 37

Standing Nude, 266; Figs. 241, 242

Steer, Philip Wilson, 137, 244 n. 12

Stevenson, Robert Louis, 23; Fig. 49

Stokes, Adrian, 219

Story, William Wetmore, 16

A Street in Arras, 273; Fig. 208

Street in Venice, Ormond Family, 58; Fig. 37; Washington, 56, 63, 67–69; Fig. 35; Williamstown, 56, 58, 68–70; Fig. 33

Strettell, Alma, 76, 141 n. 33

Studies of a Nude Youth, 266; Fig. 235

Study from Life, 182; Fig. 135

Study of Ezekiel for *Frieze of the Prophets*, 266; Fig. 239

Subercaseaux, Ramón, 71 n. 4

The Sulphur Match, 55, 59, 64, 72 n. 24; Fig. 21

A Summer Idyll, 247 n. 38

Summer Morning, see A Morning Walk

Taine, Hippolyte, 47 n. 24

Tarbell, Edmund, 138; Fig. 94

Tennant, Margot, 97, 104

Teresa Gosse, Fig. 73

Terry, Ellen, 97, 104; Fig. 67

Thou Shalt Not Steal, 240, 273; Fig. 206

Three Alligators, 272; Fig. 251

Tissot, James Jacques Joseph, 247 n. 38; Fig. 99

Tonks, Henry, 195, 272–73; Fig. 252

Torsos of Two Male Nudes, 266; Fig. 236

A Tramp, Fig. 179

Tree, Herbert Beerbohm, 97

Turkey, 281

A Turkish Woman by a Stream, 221, 224; Fig. 141

Twain, Mark, 67

Two Girls with Parasols at Fladbury, 127; Fig. 82

Tyrolese Crucifix, Brooklyn, 232; private collection, Fig. 166

Tyrolese Interior, 232

Under the Willows, 121

Val d'Aosta: A Man Fishing, 186; Fig. 140

Van Dyck, Anthony, 174; Fig. 125

Van Dyke, John C., 148, 162

Van Gorder, Luther, 138; Fig. 92

Van Haanen, Cecil, 55, 64

Van Rensselaer, Mariana Griswold, 149, 151, 162

Vaslav Nijinsky in Le Pavillon d'Armide, 269, 271; Fig. 248

Velázquez, Diego, 28, 54, 55, 149, 174; Fig. 26

Venetian Bead Stringers, 50–52, 55, 68, 70, 214; Fig. 23

Venetian Canal, 232

Venetian Courtyard, 55–56, 64, 73 n. 52; Fig. 34

Venetian Glass Workers, 55, 64, 69–70; Fig. 30

Venetian Interior, Ormond Family, 214; Pittsburgh, 50, 52–54, 55, 59, 62; Fig. 25; Williamstown, 50, 52, 53, 70; Fig. 24

Venetian Street, 56, 58, 69; Fig. 32

Venetian Water Carriers, 56, 69–70, 72 n. 24, 249 n. 57; Fig. 36

Venise par Temps Gris, 54

Vernon Lee, Fig. 19

Vernon Lee (Violet Paget), Fig. 231

Viani, Gigia, 50, 53–54, 56, 59, 62, 71 n. 8, 72 n. 26; Fig. 38

Vickers, Mr. and Mrs. Albert, 112, 113; Fig. 62

View from a Window at Genoa, Fig. 167

Villa di Marlia, Lucca, Fig. 168

Vinton, Frederick Porter, 158

Violet Fishing, 127, 138; Fig. 84

W. Graham Robertson, Fig. 69

Wargrave, Backwater, 141 n. 34

Watts, Frances Sherburne Ridley, 27; Fig. 1

Watts, George Frederic, 170

Wedgwood, Eliza, 183, 195

Weir, John F., 37, 47 n. 24

Weir, Julian Alden, 20, 37, 256

Welsch, Carl, 210, 253

Wendel, Theodore, 134

Wertheimer, Asher, 105; Fig. 116

Wharton, Edith, 23

Whistler, James Abbott McNeill, 24, 37–38, 54, 64, 72 n. 14, 148, 176, 210, 244 n. 5, 247 n. 38; Figs. 27–29

White, Margaret Stuyvesant, 97; Fig. 64

Wilde, Oscar, 33, 75–80, 89, 97, 102, 104, 107 n. 29, 109 nn. 49, 58

Wiles, Irving, 177

William Butler Yeats, 269–70, 271; Fig. 249

Woods, Henry, 64

Workmen at Carrara, 231; Fig. 195

The Wyndham Sisters: Lady Elcho, Mrs. Adeane, and Mrs. Tennant, 97, 170, 174; Fig. 112

Yeats, William Butler, 42; Fig. 249

Yockney, Alfred, 249 n. 64

Yoho Falls, 202; Fig. 155

Young Girl Wearing a Bonnet, Fig. 197

Young Man in Reverie, 31; Fig. 13

Young Woman with Black Skirt, 64, 212, 244 n. 11; Fig. 171

Yvon, Adolphe, 256

Zorn, Anders, 177

Zuleika, 224

PHOTOGRAPH CREDITS

Photographs of the works of art reproduced have been supplied, in the majority of cases, by the owners or custodians of the works, as cited in the captions. The following list applies to photographs for which an additional acknowledgment is due:

Alinari/Art Resource, New York:
  Figs. 45, 59
Linda Ayres: Fig. 46
E. Irving Blomstrann: Fig. 255
Trustees of the Boston Public Library:
  Fig. 60
Brenwasser: Fig. 28
The Brooklyn Museum, New York:
  Fig. 127
Jerome Brown: Fig. 11
The Alan Mason Chesney Medical
  Archives of the Johns Hopkins Medical
  Institutions: Fig. 121
Geoffrey Clements: Fig. 197
Davis and Langdale Co., Inc., New York:
  Fig. 244
Greg Heins: Fig. 249
Helga Photo Studio: Figs. 42, 70, 130, 175,
  225, 227, 228
Hirschl & Adler Galleries, New York:
  Figs. 42, 225, 226
Bill Jacobson: Figs. 81, 143
Los Angeles County Museum of Art:
  Fig. 56
Richard Margolis: Fig. 245
Otto E. Nelson: Fig. 159
Phillips Studio: Fig. 107
Eric Pollitzer: Fig. 49
John D. Schiff: Fig. 34
Tom Scott: Fig. 247
Lee Stalsworth: Fig. 113
Richard A. Stoner: Fig. 184
Studio/Nine, Inc.: Fig. 244
John Webb: Fig. 19
Sarah Wells: Fig. 137
Jeremy Whitaker: Fig. 120
Derrick Witty: Fig. 187